Opera on the Couch

In this widely ranging collection of essays, a group of contemporary psychoanalyst/authors turn their finely honed listening skills and clinical experience to plumb the depths and illuminate themes of character, drama, myth, culture, and psychobiography in some of the world's most beloved operas.

The richly diverse chapters are unified by a psychoanalytic approach to the nuances of unconscious mental life and emotional experience as they unfold synergistically in opera's music, words, and drama. Opera creates a unique bridge between thought and feeling, mind and body, and conscious and unconscious that offers fertile ground for psychological exploration of profound human truths.

Each piece is written in a colorful and non-technical manner that will appeal to mental health professionals, musicians, academics, and general readers wishing better to understand and appreciate opera as an art form.

Steven H. Goldberg, M.D., is a Training and Supervising Analyst at the San Francisco Center for Psychoanalysis, and a Personal and Supervising Analyst at the Psychoanalytic Institute of Northern California. In addition to many publications, he has co-chaired *Opera on the Couch* in collaboration with the San Francisco Opera.

Lee Rather, Ph.D., is a Personal and Supervising Analyst at the Psychoanalytic Institute of Northern California and a faculty at the San Francisco Center for Psychoanalysis. As a teacher, presenter, and writer he has a long-time interest in the unconscious aspects of creativity in music, literature, and the arts.

Opera on the Couch

Music, Emotional Life, and Unconscious Aspects of Mind

Edited by Steven H. Goldberg and Lee Rather

Routledge
Taylor & Francis Group

LONDON AND NEW YORK

First published 2022
by Routledge
4 Park Square, Milton Park, Abingdon, Oxon OX14 4RN

and by Routledge
605 Third Avenue, New York, NY 10158

Routledge is an imprint of the Taylor & Francis Group, an informa business

© 2022 selection and editorial matter, Steven H. Goldberg and Lee Rather; individual chapters, the contributors

The right of Steven H. Goldberg and Lee Rather to be identified as the authors of the editorial material, and of the authors for their individual chapters, has been asserted in accordance with sections 77 and 78 of the Copyright, Designs and Patents Act 1988.

British Library Cataloguing-in-Publication Data
A catalogue record for this book is available from the British Library

Library of Congress Cataloging-in-Publication Data
A catalog record has been requested for this book

ISBN: 9781032210766 (hbk)
ISBN: 9781032210773 (pbk)
ISBN: 9781032271408 (ebk)

DOI: 10.4324/9781032271408

Typeset in Bembo
by Apex CoVantage, LLC

Contents

Contributors

Anna Balas, M.D., is Associate Professor of Psychiatry at the New York Presbyterian Hospital, Payne Whitney Division and Training and Supervising Analyst at the New York Psychoanalytic Society & Institute. Dr. Balas is in private practice working with adults, adolescents and children on the Upper East Side of Manhattan. She teaches on Psychic Trauma and on Normal and Pathological Narcissism. Dr. Balas has written and presented on applied psychoanalysis and she is an avid opera lover.

Ralph H. Beaumont, M.D., is a psychiatrist and psychoanalyst, located in Portland, Oregon. He is a co-founder and recent director of the Oregon Psychoanalytic Institute. He has worked extensively there with the Portland Opera in presenting psychoanalytically informed discussions of operas, and has co-chaired a discussion group on psychoanalytic perspectives on opera at the meetings of the American Psychoanalytic Association since 2007. He has also presented on operas for the Seattle Opera, and the Psychoanalytic Institute of New England, East.

Steven H. Goldberg, M.D., is a Training and Supervising Analyst at the San Francisco Center for Psychoanalysis, and a Personal and Supervising Analyst at the Psychoanalytic Institute of Northern California. For many years, he has co-chaired, with Milton Schaefer, *Opera on the Couch*, a collaboration between the San Francisco Center for Psychoanalysis and the San Francisco Opera. His papers on psychoanalysis and opera have appeared in *Fort/Da*, and in *The Psychoanalytic Quarterly*, where he is currently an associate editor.

Jeanne C. Harasemovitch, L.C.S.W., is a psychoanalyst and Founding Committee Member of the Berkeley Psychoanalytic Society. A faculty member of the San Francisco Center for Psychoanalysis, the Psychoanalytic Institute of Northern California, and the Oregon Center for Psychoanalysis, she writes essays and film and book reviews on psychoanalysis and its intimate relations with the arts and humanities. She is a discussant for *Opera on the Couch*, a collaboration between the San Francisco Opera and the San Francisco Center for Psychoanalysis.

Debbie Hindle is a consultant child and adolescent psychotherapist, who trained at the Tavistock Clinic. For 10 years, she was Head of the Clinical Training in Child Psychotherapy at the Scottish Institute of Human Relations in Edinburgh and worked clinically in a specialist fostering and adoption Child and Adolescent Mental Health Service in Glasgow. Now retired from the NHS, she continues as an external tutor on the Scottish Child Psychotherapy Clinical Training.

L. Eileen Keller, Ph.D., is a psychologist/psychoanalyst in private practice of psychoanalysis and psychotherapy with adults and children in Oakland. She is on the faculty of the San Francisco Center for Psychoanalysis and has taught for NCSPP, Access Institute, The Wright Institute and the Ann Martin Center. Her love of psychoanalysis and her love of opera merge in participation in Opera on the Couch. For her publications, on topics ranging from addiction to mourning and to applied psychoanalysis, see her website: www.kellerphd.com

Catherine Mallouh, M.D., is on the faculty of the San Francisco Center for Psychoanalysis and the University of California, San Francisco, School of Medicine. She has spoken on a number of operas from a psychoanalytic perspective, and has also taught and written on film and psychoanalysis. She has an interest in women's development and psychology, and specializes in working with pregnant and postpartum women. She is in private practice in San Francisco.

John J. H. Muller IV is Professor of Music History at The Juilliard School, where he teaches a wide variety of courses for undergraduate and graduate students, as well as for adult laymen. Since 2010, he has been the English language lecturer at the internationally renowned Wagner festival in Bayreuth. He is also a noted lecturer for the Metropolitan Opera Guild and other organizations, including the Wagner Society of New York. He has been a presenter at numerous meetings of the American Psychoanalytic Association. His essay on *Parsifal* appeared in the book *Wagner Outside the Ring*.

Julie Jaffee Nagel, Ph.D., is a graduate of The Juilliard School, The University of Michigan, and The Michigan Psychoanalytic Institute. She blends her dual education and experience in her work on stage fright and music as a nonverbal entry into emotion. She is author of the books "Melodies of the Mind" (Routledge, 2013) and "Managing Stage Fright: A Guide for Musicians and Music Teachers" (Oxford University Press, 2017). She has a private practice in Ann Arbor, Michigan.

Lee Rather, Ph.D., is on the faculties of the San Francisco Center for Psychoanalysis and the Psychoanalytic Institute of Northern California, where he is also a Personal and Supervising Analyst. He has published and presented on a wide range of topics including the integration of psychoanalytic theories, the existential dynamics of desire, mourning and acceptance, and the unconscious aspects of creativity in drama, literature, and music. He is in private practice in San Francisco.

Richard Rusbridger is a Training Analyst and a Child Analyst with the British Psychoanalytical Society, in private practice in London. He read Music and English at Cambridge. He trained as a child psychotherapist at the Tavistock Clinic before training at the Institute of Psychoanalysis in London. He is Honorary Reader at University College, London, and Hon Sec of the Melanie Klein Trust. He has written papers on psychoanalytic theory, and on psychoanalysis and music, and has edited the collected papers of Elizabeth Spillius and Edna O'Shaughnessy.

Milton Schaefer, Ph.D., is a psychologist and psychoanalyst in private practice in San Francisco and is on the faculty of the San Francisco Center of Psychoanalysis. He has presented and published on children's adjustment in high conflict divorcing families, ethical issues, and the interface of psychoanalysis and the arts. He is a co-chair with Steven H. Goldberg of Opera on the Couch, a joint program of the San Francisco Opera. He is a co-editor with Shelley Nathans of Couples on the Couch: Psychoanalytic Couple Therapy and the Tavistock Model (Routledge, 2017).

Adele Tutter, M.D., Ph.D., is Assistant Professor of Psychiatry, Columbia University Vagelos School of Medicine; faculty, Center for Psychoanalytic Training and Research; and Co-director, the Graduate School of Arts and Sciences Psychoanalytic Studies Program. She is also on the faculty at the New York Psychoanalytic Institute. Dr. Tutter is the author of *Dream House: An Intimate Portrait of the Philip Johnson Glass House* (2016), co-editor of *Grief and its Transcendence: Memory, Identity, and Creativity* (2015) and the editor of *The Muse: Psychoanalytic Explorations of Creative Inspiration* (2016). Her scholarship has earned her the Menninger, Hartmann, Liebert, and Ticho prizes. She sits on the editorial boards of *The International Journal of Psychoanalysis*, *Psychoanalytic Quarterly*, and *American Imago* and maintains a private practice in Manhattan.

Amy Tyson, M.D., is an adult and child psychiatrist and psychoanalyst in private practice in San Francisco. She is an Associate Clinical Professor in the Department of Psychiatry at the University of California, San Francisco, and faculty at the San Francisco Center for Psychoanalysis. She has taught classes on a number of topics, including psychodynamic theories of child development, the history of psychoanalysis, and trans-generational transmission of trauma. She has spoken on several operas from a psychoanalytic perspective.

Acknowledgments

Steven H. Goldberg

First, I want to thank Lee Rather, my co-editor, co-author, colleague, and friend for collaborating with me on this book project. Working with Lee has been a pleasure throughout the various phases of envisioning, collecting, and editing the contributions in this volume. I also want very much to thank my colleague and friend, Dr. Milton Schaefer, who has co-chaired "Opera on the Couch" with me over the ten plus years of our collaboration with the San Francisco Opera. That program has consisted of post-performance, psychoanalytically oriented talks for a general audience of opera-goers after selected matinee performances. Without Dr. Schaefer's collaboration, the program would not have been nearly as enjoyable and successful as it has been. And it was originally in discussions with Dr. Schaefer that the idea for this book project emerged.

There are a number of others I want to thank for their roles in the success of our collaboration with San Francisco Opera, most of all the analysts who have served as discussants of the opera productions over the years, a number of whom are represented as authors in this collection. "Opera on the Couch" was originally conceived by my psychoanalyst colleague, the late Dr. Linda Lagemann, who had already created a similar collaboration between the San Francisco Center for Psychoanaysis and the American Conservatory Theatre in San Francisco. Dr. Lagemann was fortunate enough to have found an able and enthusiastic collaborator at the San Francisco Opera, Genevieve Neumuth, who was in essence a co-creator of the program. Thanks also go to those who followed Genevieve at the Opera and have lent their energies and creativity to our collaboration.

Thanks go as well to the contributors to this volume, who have written from their passion and expertise in both psychoanalysis and opera. They have good-naturedly collaborated with our numerous requests throughout the various phases of the editing process.

Finally I want very much to thank my wife Sandee Blechman, for her unerring support, patience, encouragement, and helpful suggestions, without which I could not have completed, or perhaps even contemplated, this endeavor.

We come to our love of opera in myriad ways. For me, it began with listening as a young child to my mother at the piano, singing and accompanying herself in various Broadway show tunes. A lover of music, opera, and other performing arts, and a talented amateur artist herself, her passion for music and theatre has inspired my own.

Lee Rather

I want to thank Steven H. Goldberg, M.D., for inviting me to be part of this project. It was during a fortuitous meeting at the San Francisco Museum of Modern Art (SFMOMA) in 2009 that we realized our shared passion for opera, and he suggested that I become part of the "Opera on the Couch" speaker series. Becoming a regular presenter provided an opportunity to venture beyond clinical writing, to integrate my long-standing pursuits in music and psychoanalysis, and eventually to co-editing this volume. In addition, I also want thank all of our contributors for the passionate work they put into the manuscripts included in this volume, and for the consistent responsiveness with which they met our editing suggestions.

There is an ever-evolving aesthetic loop between one's earliest experiences of certain works of art, literature, and music, and one's deepening appreciation of these works as time passes. I am pleased to contribute a chapter on Mozart's *The Magic Flute*, which is one such work for me, one which represents the confluence of many currents. To begin with, it was my first opera, experienced in 1963 in the renown Marionetten Theater in Munich, in the company of my father, an opera enthusiast and intellectual historian. Many years later, in the aforementioned meeting with Steve at SFMOMA, it turned out we were each there on repeat visits to an exhibition that featured drawings, stage sets, and video images for William Kentridge's production of *The Magic Flute*. And finally, in an uncanny coincidence, I was to discover that *The Magic Flute* had long been one of my wife's favorite operas. In fact, as a sixteen-year-old, she and her friends had spent a year building their own marionettes, stage sets, and a small puppet theater to perform and videotape their own neighborhood production of the opera.

Writing and editing are creative processes pursued in relative seclusion, but I have always felt in communion with a host of persons past and present including my colleagues, patients, and the many literary, musical, and cultural heroes that have inspired me. But above all, I want to express my deepest gratitude to Stefanie Nickel-Rather. Her absolutely unwavering love, support, humor, and capacity for deep and sustained critical thinking have enriched my life in ways words could never express.

Permissions acknowledgments

Every effort has been made to contact copyright holders for their permissions to reprint selections and quotations in this book where applicable. The publishes would be grateful to hear from any copyright holder who is not here rightfully acknowledged and will undertake to rectify any errors or omissions in future editions of this book.

Chapter 2 was first published as "The Internal world of *Don Giovanni*" by Richard Rusbridger in The International Journal of Psychoanalysis, 2008, 89:181–194.

We would like to thank the editors of *International Journal of Psychoanalysis* for permission to use this material.

Chapter 4 has been extensively rewritten from "Psychoanalytic and Musical Perspectives on Shame in Donizetti's *Lucia di Lammermoor* by Julie Jaffee Nagel in the *Journal of the American Psychoanalytic Association*, 2008, 56 (2): 551–63, and "Shame and Rage – The Breakdown of Lucia in *Lucia di Lammermoor*" by Julie Jaffe Nagel in *Melodies of the Mind: Connections Between Psychoanalysis and Music*, 2013, pp. 89–99, published by Routledge. We would like to thank Sage Publishing for permission to use this material.

Chapter 5 has been extensively rewritten from "Inside the Mind of Senta: A Psychoanalyst's View " by L. Eileen Keller in *Leitmotiv: Journal of the Wagner Society of Northern California*, Winter 2013–2014, pp 24–27. We would like to thank *Leitmotiv* for permission to use this material.

Chapter 9 was first published as "Sliding Walls and Glimpses of the Other in Puccini's *Madama Butterfly*" by Steven H. Goldberg in the *Psychoanalytic Quarterly*, 2018, 87(3), pp. 479–495. We would like to thank the Taylor & Francis for permission to use this material.

Chapter 10: We would like to thank Sarah Baxter of the Society of Authors for permission to quote Virginia Woolf.

Chapter 13 was extensively rewritten form "Text as Muse, Muse as Text: Janáček, Kamila, and the Role of Fantasy in Musical Creativity" by Adele Tutter in *American Imago*, 2015, 72(4):407–450. We would like to thank Johns Hopkins Press for permissions to use this material.

We would like to thank Jim Friedman, the literary executor for John Tyrell for permission to quote from *Intimate letters: Leoš Janáček to Kamila Stösslová*. J. Tyrell (Ed. & Trans.). 1994, Princeton: Princeton University Press.

For Chapter 13 we would like to thank Bernd Uhlig for his permission to use two photographs (Figure 13.1 and Figure 13.2).

Chapter 15 was rewritten from "Sendak and Knussen's *Where the Wild Things Are:* A Developmental Journey" by Debbie Hindle, 2017, *Infant Observation: International Journal of Infant Observations and Its Applications*, pp. 1–16. We would like to thank Taylor & Francis for permissions to use this material.

The only true voyage of discovery, the only really rejuvenating experience, would be not to visit strange lands but to possess other eyes, to see the universe through the eyes of another, of a hundred others, to see the hundred universes that each of them beholds, that each of them is. . .

Marcel Proust, *Remembrance of Things Past*, 1923

1 Psychoanalysis and Opera

A Felicitous Match

Steven H. Goldberg and Lee Rather

Opera as an Art Form

As an art form, opera is particularly well-suited as subject matter for psycho-analytic investigation. The great operas tell stories, in words and in music, that unfold timeless and universal themes of love, death, war, power, rivalry, class, and religious faith. With opera's unique integration of music, lyrics, stagecraft, and acting, these themes are brought to life in drama and in character. A par-ticular strength of opera is its potential to convey emotional complexity and conflict on multiple levels and in multiple registers simultaneously. The music may support, reflect, and add nuance to the emotions and lyrics evident on stage, or may suggest unconscious emotions underlying, and even contrast-ing with, what the audience witnesses. The synergistic power of opera affords a penetrating and complex view of character and motivation, emotion and meaning, to which both opera and psychoanalysis aspire.

It is a premise of this collection that psychoanalysis and opera have much to offer each other. While the same could be said about psychoanalysis and music in general, opera's unique synthesis of music, text, dramatic realization, and the communication of meanings at multiple levels offers particular opportunities for the psychoanalytic understanding and deepening appreciation of the art form. Conversely, we attempt to demonstrate that opera can open new areas of understanding for the theory and practice of psychoanalysis.

Psychoanalysis and opera both explore the depths of human emotional and psychological experience at conscious and unconscious levels, enlarging our awareness and setting change in motion. Both seek to uncover realms of human experience that are difficult, if not impossible, to access, either because they are experiences not yet formulated and represented in words, or because they are emotionally intolerable and rendered inaccessible by defensive operations. Both involve moments of heightened emotional intensity that we sometimes seek to experience, and at other times seek to avoid. Both have prominent corporeal aspects – opera through the intimate bodily expression of emotion in the acts of singing and acting, and psychoanalysis in its emphasis on embodied aspects of emotion and psychosexuality. And both call for complex and heightened forms of attentiveness, in which one listens, observes, and resonates at multiple

DOI: 10.4324/9781032271408-1

levels to the words, the music of the words, the unique quality of the voice, and bodily presence and movement. While such multifaceted attentiveness occurs to some degree in response to all forms of art and even normal conversational speech, it is especially heightened in opera and psychoanalysis.

As different approaches to understanding the meanings and challenges of being alive, opera and psychoanalysis each expand and enhance the potential of the other. While on one side of the curtain operatic artists look to psychology to render their performances as powerful and transformative as possible, on the other side of the curtain, psychoanalysis gives opera aficionados the opportunity to deepen their experience and understanding not only of opera but also of themselves.

Applied Psychoanalysis

It is not surprising that the application of psychoanalytic thinking to the arts and music begins with Freud and his early circle of adherents. Freud arrived at his intellectual maturity in *fin de siècle* Vienna, a city of two million people characterized by a surge of creative activity in the arts, music, sciences, and humanities. The cultural milieu of museums, concert halls, and myriad salons and coffee houses set the stage for an unusual cross-fertilization among disciplines (Gay, 1988; Kandel, 2012; Schorske, 1980). For Freud and his early followers, clinical discoveries illuminated artistic and cultural realms, while the artistic and cultural realms contributed invaluably to clinical thinking. Topics such as group phenomena, culture, and the arts were considered to be integral aspects of psychoanalytic study. Prominent within the 24-volume Standard Edition of Freud's work are a number of essential papers and monographs on topics that would only later be labeled "applied psychoanalysis" (e.g. Freud, 1910, 1911, 1914, 1928). While the term may have had the effect of marginalizing this area of psychoanalytic research, it is clear that psychoanalysis from Freud to the present time offers not only a comprehensive basis for the exploration and treatment of mental life in the clinic, but also a body of hypotheses and observations that can be used to investigate a variety of non-clinical fields of inquiry.

While according to his biographer, Peter Gay (1988, pp. 316–317), Freud's relationship to artists was complex and ambivalent, his famous remark to the Minister of Culture of pre-Nazi Germany in 1928 is nonetheless emblematic: when the Minister said, "I have come to greet the great discoverer of the unconscious," Freud replied, "The poets and the philosophers discovered the unconscious long before I did; I merely discovered its laws and the method to study it scientifically" (quoted from Lehrman, 1954, p. 264).

Freud had recognized early on that an investigation of dreams was a "royal road to a knowledge of the unconscious activities of the mind" (1900, p. 608). From there, it was a natural step to consider the possibility that the unconscious might also be revealed in more intentional creative acts and cultural practices. In the fertile ground of *fin de siècle* Vienna, Freud's exceptionally broad vision detected reflections of his clinical discoveries in the great myths and other artistic creations, and Freud even noted the similarity of his case studies to the development of character by novelists. Respect for this vein of inquiry sent many subsequent analysts and psychoanalytically informed academics on a journey of applied analysis.

Freud's oft-noted aversion to music (1914, p. 211) will be discussed in a later section; in fact, he made little mention of any form of music anywhere in his voluminous writings. Yet despite this conspicuous absence, many analysts and musicologists since Freud have turned their attention to the psychoanalytic themes embedded in music in general, and in opera specifically. Taking the connection between music and psychoanalysis even further, a burgeoning emphasis in more recent psychoanalytic contributions concerns the role and therapeutic potential of "communicative musicality" (Malloch & Trevarthen, 2009) in the consulting room, as embodied and musical forms of communication are increasingly understood to have essential mutative effects.

Origins of the Collection

The collection of essays in this volume emerged from more than a decade of collaboration between the San Francisco Center for Psychoanalysis and the San Francisco Opera in a program known as "Opera on the Couch." Following Sunday matinee performances of selected operas, two psychoanalysts present psychoanalytic discussions of the opera just performed to a group of audience members. The presentations, open to the public at no charge, allow for a substantial period of dialogue with the audience, which typically includes not only psychoanalysts but also individuals from a diverse range of intellectual backgrounds and professions. Over time, the enthusiastic response to our discussions and the interplay between responses from those immersed in psychological theories and those coming from other disciplines became an impetus for this volume. A generative experience for all, a number of participating psychoanalysts were inspired to expand their informal talks into more fully developed papers for publication. This synergy carries over into this book, especially in the final chapter, written by a noted musicologist and distinguished discussant at many national psychoanalytic meetings.

A second inspiration for this collection was the increasing number of compelling psychoanalytic studies of opera published in the psychoanalytic literature, both by authors within our group, and by other psychoanalysts nationally and internationally. Although limited to those published in English language journals, we sought to gather some of the best of these published papers, along with newer unpublished papers by colleagues whose work we knew and admired. The latter, along with the former, constitute the chapters of this book.

Opera on the Couch

Psychoanalytic theories and concepts develop and expand the meanings of an opera at multiple levels that include the creative process of the composer, the nature of the dramatic action, the music and the ways in which music and words interrelate, and the ways in which particular productions emphasize and interpret psychological themes. For example, a psychoanalytic approach can render intelligible the unconscious motivations of central characters, as well as the determinative traumas and other life events that contribute to character formation and interpersonal relationships. A further expansion of meaning might involve illumination of the ways in which the instrumental music constitutes an "orchestral" (S. Goldberg, 2011, p. 58) register of experience that tells a story richer than, and sometimes at variance with, the sung words alone. This musical dimension may amplify, specify, or carry more than what the characters consciously know. The psychoanalytic awareness of multiple voices speaking in multiple registers of consciousness and unconsciousness offers the opera audience a deeper understanding of motivation, character, and conflict – in the drama, and in ourselves.

The breadth of psychoanalytic approaches to putting opera "on the couch" is one of the strengths of this volume. Each of its chapters makes use of one, or more often several, of these psychoanalytic approaches. The following summary will orient the reader to the range of approaches represented here, as well as the specific ones emphasized in each chapter.

The first approach assumes that an opera may be examined in order to discover traces of unconscious wishes, conflicts, and traumas manifest in the creative process of the composer (and/or librettist, director, stage designer), whether consciously intended or not. In this modality, the opera is approached as a psychological expression of the composer's inner life, akin to his/her artistic "dream," and "analyzed" with the aim of understanding the creator's innermost psychic life. In this volume, such an approach is most evident in the chapters concerning Berg's *Wozzeck* (Beaumont), Janacek's *The Makropulos Case* (Tutter), and Bartok's *Duke Bluebeard's Castle* (Balas).

A second approach is to regard fictional operatic characters as if they were actual people, and to view their roles from the vantage points of their unconscious conflicts, motivations, and developmental histories. Questions related to why they feel and behave as they do are particularly amenable to such psychoanalytic inquiry. Why is Don Giovanni manically driven to seduce every woman he encounters? Why is Elektra unable to mourn, and is instead consumed by her passion for revenge? Why is Madame Butterfly so unwilling to face the reality of her fate, and why is her only recourse suicide? Why is Senta devoted to the Dutchman to the point of her death? Why is Tristan's sense of self such a tragic one, even though those around him see him as very much the hero? Each chapter explores such questions with the tools of psychoanalytic insight. Attending to affects, dreams, psychological defenses and inhibitions, creative processes, identifications, and developmental crises portrayed on stage sheds light on the mysteries of how the mind functions and gives rise to the deeper understanding of various motivations, characters, and self-experiences dramatized in the opera. This approach is most emphasized in the chapters on Puccini's *Tosca* (Tyson), *Madama Butterfly* (Goldberg), Strauss' *Elektra* (Mallouh), Britten's *Billy Budd* (Schaefer), Wagner's *Die Meistersinger* (Harasemovich), *The Flying Dutchman* (Keller), *Tristan und Isolde* (Muller), Mozart's *Don Giovanni* (Rusbridger), and Donizetti's *Lucia di Lammermoor* (Nagel).

It is, of course, worth noting that both the first and second approaches deal with people, real and fictional, that are not in an analytic relationship, and the interpretations offered by the analytic writer must remain speculative since there is no actual analysand to react to interpretations in confirmatory manner, as is essential in clinical psychoanalysis (see Frattaroli, 1987 for an in-depth discussion of this theme).

A third approach assumes that successful operas that endure with the public do so because they transcend the particulars of character, setting, and plot to arrive at universal unconscious themes. From this perspective, opera may be approached as a genre of myth or psychodrama in which the characters symbolically elaborate aspects of ourselves within a dramatic and musical narrative. In this sense, regardless of the particulars of character or setting, the opera is a crystallized condensation of complex, over-determined, and enduring emotional themes with which we resonate deeply because it presents an externalized psychodrama of our own internal life. This approach is particularly evident in discussions of Mozart's *The Magic Flute* (Rather), and in Sendak and Knussen's *Where the Wild Things Are* (Hindle).

Finally, a fourth approach examines how opera examines what is now beginning to be thought of as the social unconscious, focusing on ways in which cultural and linguistic givens, reflected in power relationships and differences in race, class, gender, and sexual orientation are internalized and importantly shape the individual unconscious. This approach also explores the inevitable tensions between the individual and the collective, the fundamental challenges of negotiating what Freud referred to as "civilization and its discontents" (Freud, 1930). While this is a theme embedded in each chapter, it is particularly central in those on Mozart's *Don Giovanni* (Rusbridger), Puccini's *Tosca* (Tyson), *Madama Butterfly* (Goldberg), Wagner's *Die Meistersinger* (Harasemovitch), and *The Flying Dutchman* (Keller). Given the growing psychoanalytic attention to the impact of political, economic, and socio-cultural factors on the formation of the dynamics of defense, symptom, and character (e.g., Akhtar, 2018; Cushman, 2019; Dajani, 2017; Gonzalez, 2020; Layton, 2020), we anticipate seeing more of this approach in the future.

While the perspectives outlined earlier are conceptually separate, the reader will find that they are often intertwined in individual chapters according to the inclination of each contributor. In addition, there is considerable variation within each approach in the extent to which contributors use not only the libretto but also the musical score to study the ways in which character and motivation are conveyed. Special attention to the musical score is particularly central in the chapters on Puccini's *Madama Butterfly* (Goldberg), Donizetti's *Lucia di Lammermoor* (Nagel), Wagner's *Die Meistersinger* (Harasemovitch), and *Tristan und Isolde* (Muller).

The Synergy of Psychoanalysis and Opera

As will become clear to the reader, psychoanalytic explorations of opera offer a great deal not only to the opera's audience, but also to those involved in the performance, production, and creation of opera. For opera directors and performers, as well as 20th-century composers and librettists, psychoanalytic understandings of an opera have opened up many possibilities in the areas of drama, stage production, and the interaction of word, gesture, and music. But this is by no means a one-way street. An immersion in opera may offer a great deal to the theory and practice of the psychoanalyst as well.

Freud realized that many of his ideas were anticipated by the great creative artists of the past. As one prominent example, the psychology of the protagonists in Shakespeare's *Hamlet* and in Sophocles' *Oedipus Rex* inspired Freud's formulation of the Oedipus complex. Since Freud, many psychoanalytic writers have traversed a similar path, drawing upon art, literature, and drama to expand psychological understanding. An excellent modern musical example of this trend would be Feder's (1982) deepening psychological understanding of nostalgia in his penetrating study of the music of Charles Ives.

However, of all the arts, Freud was least at home with music. In fact, he considered himself tone deaf, and described feeling suspicious of the ways in which music could evoke emotions in himself that he could not understand (Freud, 1985). Recent scholarship has suggested that Freud's aversion to musical experience stemmed from a defensive need to avoid painful feelings and pre-verbal experiences associated with his earliest childhood, possibly related to preverbal trauma in connection with a problematic relationship with his musically inclined mother (Whitebook, 2017). And yet the picture is somewhat more complex and Freud could be moved by music as long as he could relate it to discrete ideas (Barale & Minazzi, 2008; Nagel, 2013). This is illustrated in his 1897 letter to Wilhelm Fliess in which Freud writes: "The *Meistersinger* recently gave me extraordinary pleasure . . . the *Morgentraumduetweise* [Morning Dream Song Duet] moved me considerably. . . . Real ideas are put into music as in no other opera through association of feeling tones to meaning" (Freud, 1985, p. 238). From this perspective, perhaps Freud's aversion to music stemmed from the fact that he was moved by it deeply but only comfortable if the feelings that were stirred could be easily represented by him with words.

In any case, following in Freud's footsteps, classical psychoanalysts have tended to prioritize the patient's verbal "text" and associations, to the relative neglect of the more embodied and musical qualities of spoken language in its rhythm, pitch, timbre, and tone color. Fortunately, contemporary analysts have benefitted immensely from research into the subtle pre-verbal, essentially musical, "sing-song" exchanges between infant and caretaker that have been so well-studied in modern infant observational research (e.g., Stern, 1985). Such work has catalyzed a correction of the historical tilt toward the verbal text and a move toward attention to the non-verbal.

This dimension of early non-verbal communication is now understood to enhance emotional communication throughout the lifespan, and to play a significant therapeutic role within the clinical psychoanalytic relationship. More speculatively, since each of us went through a developmental period during which sounds and music heard in utero and in the early neo-natal period dominated our proto-consciousness, there exists the potential for both analyst and analysand, in their reveries, to experience sounds and music as emanating unbidden from their unconscious (Grier, 2019, pp. 838–839). Such cutting-edge psychoanalytic thinking has provided a gateway to responding therapeutically to aspects of experience that lie beyond verbally articulated mental content. This exploration of "communicative musicality" (Malloch & Trevarthen, 2009) arose initially in work with infants and children, then became important in work with adult patients unable to make use of verbal interpretation. Gradually it spread as it became clear from clinical practice that such registers of experience are present in all human communication (e.g., P. Goldberg, 2021; Grier, 2019; Grossmark, 2012, 2016; Knoblauch, 2000; Markman, 2020; Pickering, 2020; Purcell, 2019).

With regard to opera, since the layering of the verbal and prosodic levels is so prominent, careful listening to opera has the potential to widen the analyst's listening frame by encouraging greater attunement to the emotional subtleties conveyed by the patient, who accompanies his or her verbal "libretto" with musical elements of melody, timbre, pitch, rhythm, and pacing. With its immediacy of emotional experience, opera teaches the psychoanalyst much about feelings that evade verbal description: "[J]ust as words can describe events we have not witnessed, places and things we have not seen, so music can present emotions, moods, and other embodied experiences we have not felt, passions we did not know before" (Langer, 1942, p. 222).

Listening simultaneously to the multiple conscious and unconscious voices that emerge from the interaction of the libretto's text as it is expressed with subtle vocal musical nuance and underpinned by the multiple layers of the orchestral score helps the analyst develop a perceptual mode that has been variously described as "binocular" (Bion, 1962), "bi-ocular" (Birksted-Breen, 2016), and "bi-auditory" (Grier, 2019). The essential ingredient is that perceptually triangulating the object of attention from more than one perspective enables the listener to move from a simple two-dimensional frame to a complex three-dimensional frame yielding a depth of field that is essential to grasping deeper, more elusive, untranslatable, and unconscious aspects of the patient's communication. As Grier has pointed out:

> It is often the musical aspects of language – the nature and quality of voice, its variability in representing multiple voices, its volume and intensity, rhythmic patterns, and tone color, that stimulate the analyst's bodily experience as well as his visual and/or auditory (and sometimes musical) reveries, which in turn provide access to what is happening unconsciously in the analytic pair at any given moment. At times, the progress of a psychoanalytic treatment can be sensed from shifts in the music of the analysand's utterances.
>
> (Grier, 2019, p. 841)

Such insights are part of a contemporary sensibility in psychoanalytic practice that correctively reverses the unfortunate bifurcation of the verbal and non-verbal modes of communication and of listening in classical analysis (Nagel, 2013). The advantages of re-joining these two modes is especially relevant for work with patients for whom verbal interpretations are relatively unhelpful but who respond well to treatment focusing on affective attunement and "duetting" established through modalities of prosody, gesture, and rhythm of speech. But it goes further than that, as Langer has suggested: "Because the forms of human feeling are much more congruent with musical forms than with the forms of language, music can *reveal* the nature of feelings with a detail and truth that language cannot approach" (1942, p. 235). In the opinion of many contemporary analysts, the music-like duets and certain forms of "accompaniment" to the patient's "solo" (Grossmark, 2012, 2016; Markman, 2020; Purcell, 2019) create embodied feelings of deep connection with another that are in and of themselves mutative and healing, whether or not they lead to subsequent verbal symbolization and interpretation.

Conclusion

As we hope this volume will demonstrate, the great opera composers and librettists offer penetrating psychological insights into the depths of human character, emotion, and psychic life. Unique among the arts, in opera all forms of artistic expression – poetry, text, music, drama, acting, dance, and the visual arts – are brought together. This is what Wagner aimed for in his idealized concept of a "*Gesamtkunstwerk*," a work of art that synthesizes as many possible forms of art to explore the most profound levels of human experience. Wagner may have carried this further than any other operatic composer (even designing his own opera house), but the potential for a *Gesamtkunstwerk* is present in all opera.

Like all serious art, opera is open to multiple interpretations and many levels of understanding. The chapters that follow attempt to illuminate both what the creators consciously understood and intended, and what they may have intuited or captured unconsciously.

While opera composers understand and render desire and emotion in music, drama and words, psychoanalysts create a psychological space in which to discover, formulate, and transform the dynamics of human desire and emotion. This affinity between psychoanalysis and opera creates many opportunities for cross-fertilization and collaboration, enhancing our understanding of the full complexity and dimensionality of human experience. In this way, the chapters that follow represent a collective effort to use psychoanalytic theory and methodology to deepen our understanding of opera and, at the same time, to enlist opera to inspire the continued development of psychoanalytic theory and practice.

References

Akhtar, S. (2018). *Mind, culture, and global unrest: Psychoanalytic reflections.* New York: Routledge.

Barale, F., & Minazzi, V. (2008). Off the beaten track: Freud, sound and music. Statement of a problem and some historico-critical notes. *International Journal of Psychoanalysis, 89*: 937–957.

Bion, W. (1962). *Leaning from experience*. London: Tavistock.

Birksted-Breen, D. (2016). Bi-ocularity, the functioning mind of the psychoanalyst. *International Journal of Psychoanalysis*, 97: 25–40.

Cushman, P. (2019). *Travels with the self: Interpreting psychology as cultural history*. New York: Routledge.

Dajani, K. (2017). The ego's habitus: An examination of the role culture plays in structuring the ego. *International Journal of Applied Psychoanalytic Studies*, 14: 273–281.

Feder, S. (1982). The nostalgia of Charles Ives: An essay in affects and music. *The Annual of Psychoanalysis*, 10: 301–332.

Frattaroli, E. J. (1987). On the validity of treating Shakespeare's characters as if they were real people. *Psychoanalysis and Contemporary Thought*, 10: 407–437.

Freud, S. (1900). The interpretation of dreams. In J. Strachey (Ed. and Trans.), *The standard edition of the complete psychological works of Sigmund Freud* (Vol. 4–5, pp. 339–630). London: Hogarth Press.

Freud, S. (1910). Leonardo da Vinci. In J. Strachey (Ed. and Trans.), *The standard edition of the complete psychological works of Sigmund Freud* (Vol. 11, pp. 59–138). London: Hogarth Press.

Freud, S. (1911). Psycho-analytic notes on an autobiographical account of a case of paranoia (*dementia paranoides*). In J. Strachey (Ed. and Trans.), *The standard edition of the complete psychological works of Sigmund Freud* (Vol. 12, pp. 1–82). London: Hogarth Press.

Freud, S. (1914). The Moses of Michelangelo. In J. Strachey (Ed. and Trans.), *The standard edition of the complete psychological works of Sigmund Freud* (Vol. 13 pp. 210–241). London: Hogarth Press.

Freud, S. (1928). Dostoevsky and parricide. In J. Strachey (Ed. and Trans.), *The standard edition of the complete psychological works of Sigmund Freud* (Vol. 21, pp. 175–198). London: Hogarth Press.

Freud, S. (1930). Civilization and its discontents. In J. Strachey (Ed. and Trans.), *The standard edition of the complete psychological works of Sigmund Freud* (Vol. 11, pp. 57–146). London: Hogarth Press.

Freud, S. (1985). Letter written to Fliess December 12, 1897. In J. Masson (Ed.), *The complete letters of Sigmund Freud to Wilhelm Fliess* 1887–1904. Cambridge, MA: Harvard University Press.

Gay, P. (1988). *Freud: A life for our time*. London: J.M. Dent & Sons Ltd.

Goldberg, P. (2021). The body's way of dreaming: Music and psychical life beyond representation. Unpublished Manuscript.

Goldberg, S. (2011). Love, loss, and transformation in Wagner's *Die Walküre*. *fort da*, 17: 53–60.

Gonzalez, F. (2020). First world problems and gated communities of the mind: An ethics of place in psychoanalysis. *Psychoanalytic Quarterly*, 89: 741–770.

Grier, F. (2019). Musicality in the consulting room. *International Journal of Psychoanalysis*, 100: 827–885.

Grossmark, R. (2012). The flow of enactive engagement. *Contemporary Psychoanalysis*, 48: 287–300.

Grossmark, R. (2016). Psychoanalytic companioning. *Psychoanalytic Dialogues*, 26: 698–712.

Kandel, E. (2012). *The age of insight: The quest to understand the unconscious in art, mind, and brain from Vienna 1900 to present*. New York: Random House.

Knoblauch, S. (2000). *The musical edge of therapeutic dialogue*. Hillside, NJ and London: The Analytic Press.

Langer, S. (1942). *Philosophy in a new key: A study in the symbolism of reason, rite, and art*. Cambridge, MA: Harvard University Press.

Layton, L. (2020). *Toward a social psychoanalysis: Culture, character, and normative unconscious processes*. New York: Routledge.

Lehrman, P. R. (1954). Book Review: *A History of Psychoanalysis in America*, by Clarence P. Oberndorf. MD. New York: Grune and Stratton, Inc. 280 pp. *Psychoanalytic Quarterly*, 23: 263–265.

Malloch, S., & Trevarthen, C. (Eds.). (2009). *Communicative musicality: Exploring the basis of human companionship*. Oxford: Oxford University Press.

Markman, H. (2020). Accompaniment in jazz and psychoanalysis. *Psychoanalytic Dialogues*, 30: 432–447.

Nagel, J. (2013). *Melodies of the mind: Connections between psychoanalysis and music*. New York: Routledge.

Pickering, J. (2020). Harmony of the spheres: Musical elements of couple communication. *Couple and Family Psychoanalysis*, 10: 42–58.

Purcell, S. (2019). Psychic song and dance: Dissociation and duets in the analysis of trauma. *Psychoanalytic Quarterly*, 88: 315–34.

Schorske, C. E. (1980). *Fin-de-Siècle Vienna: Politics and culture*. New York: Knopf.

Stern, D. N. (1985). *The interpersonal world of the infant*. New York: Basic Books.

Whitebook, J. (2017). *Freud: An intellectual biography*. New York: Cambridge University Press.

2 The Internal World of *Don Giovanni*

Richard Rusbridger

Introduction

Mozart's *Don Giovanni* was first performed in 1787 in Prague, and shortly after-wards, in a slightly altered version, in Vienna. His librettist, Lorenzo da Ponte, recast a story that seems to have originated in a play by a Spanish monk under the pseudonym Tirso de Molina (published 1630, perhaps written 1612–1616: see Forman (1981) in Rushton (1981), and which was well known in the eighteenth century in many operatic and other forms. Mozart and da Ponte's version tells how Don Giovanni, a nobleman given to constant seduction of women, kills the father of a woman whom he has been trying to seduce, Donna Anna. He is then pursued by a former lover of his, Donna Elvira, and also by Donna Anna and her fiancé, Don Ottavio. Don Giovanni then attempts to seduce a peasant woman, Zerlina, on the day of her wedding to Masetto. Don Giovanni's manservant and foil, Leporello, accompanies him throughout. Eventually, the ghost of Donna Anna's father appears to Don Giovanni in the form of a statue, commanding him to repent. Don Giovanni invites the ghost to dinner, but steadfastly refuses to accede to his demand that he repent, even while the ghost, the 'Stone Guest', drags him to Hell.

Don Giovanni is an opera full of enigmas. How do we account for its impact on us? Why, although Don Giovanni himself is a murderer, a destroyer of women, is the response of quite a number of women in discussing the opera that they are strangely attracted to him, and of quite a number of men that they would like to be him? What accounts for these reactions of ours? I think that psychoanalytic understanding can help us make sense of these questions.[1]

Contrasting Emotional Worlds

We do not believe any longer in people being dragged to Hell for sexual prom-iscuity, or even for rape or murder. Nor, it seems likely, did Mozart's eight-eenth-century audience (see Fielding, *The History of Tom Jones* (1749), quoted in Allanbrook, 1983, p. 209). And yet the opera has what Kierkegaard (1843), quoted by Bernard Williams (in Rushton, 1981, p. 82), called a 'great and unsettling power'. This is partly due to the contrast of emotional worlds in the piece – between the forbidding intensity of the statue's music; the rich sensuality

DOI: 10.4324/9781032271408-2

of much of the music, particularly that sung by all the women characters; and the farcical elements of the story. These contrasts are not to be explained by, or reduced to, a question of which genre the opera should be assigned to. It is sub-titled by da Ponte a '*dramma giocoso*', a jokey drama (as is *Così fan Tutte*) but it seems to be a comedy in roughly the same sense that, say, *The Winter's Tale* is a comedy (on the question of the opera's genre, see Rushton, 1981, p. 5).

This complexity of response starts right from the beginning of the opera. It arises from the contrast between, on the one hand, the engulfing intensity and darkness of the Stone Guest's music that begins the opera and almost ends it, and, on the other hand, the world of sexualised rush and flight that is so characteristic of Don Giovanni himself, and of the plot as a whole. This division is placed before us immediately at the start, with the Overture: the first two pages of the vocal score of *Don Giovanni* portray utterly different worlds. The first page is ominous and menacing. Mozart uses the key – D minor – that he also chose for the start of his *Requiem* and which seems for him always to be imbued with great seriousness and a sense of the supernatural. Feder suggests that Mozart's five works in this key were all composed at significant moments in his difficult relationship with his father ('works in this tonality appear to cluster around issues biographically related to father, fathering, and fatherhood and affects of rage and vengeance for transgressions against God and father'; Feder, 1993, p. 129), and notes that *Don Giovanni* was written at the time of Mozart's father's death. After 10 bars which evoke foreboding and which establish the key and the pulse, we are thrown into a bewildering world in which all solidity has disappeared. A lurching syncopated figure takes over, and the pulse against which it is set has all but disappeared. We later find out that this is the music of the Stone Guest, the avenging ghost of the Commendatore. Already the music has a force and menace unprecedented in opera. But then after only 30 bars, we are in a different world altogether – in a bright D major, a brisk *galant* comic opera overture in sonata form, with music that does not itself recur, but in a mood that does.

This contrast confronts us again at several points during the opera. It often takes the form of a sudden shift to a minor, sometimes remote, key, in the middle of something rapid and comic. This happens at the death of the Commendatore. The comic patter of Don Giovanni's servant Leporello, typical of the popular comic opera, *opera buffo*, and the rush of the fight give way suddenly to a passage of unearthly beauty in F minor as the trio of characters describe as if in suspended animation the enormity of the death they are witnessing. Then the moment of timelessness is over and we return to the knockabout relationship between Don Giovanni and Leporello. It happens again just after the Quartet in Act 1, when the music suddenly darkens into E flat minor as Donna Anna, the Commendatore's daughter, tells Ottavio, her suitor, about her experience of her father's death. And it happens again right at the end of the opera, where there are two endings – the world of supernatural darkness is superseded by a bright, presto, choric finale in the tradition of what was known as the *lieto fine*, the happy ending, in which the surviving characters rejoice that the bad person has met a sticky end. I shall come back to the question of the two endings later.

How can we understand these contrasts and make sense of our response? This inevitably introduces the question of how we make sense of Don Giovanni himself. Some commentators – Kierkegaard, for example – see him simply as a figure of transcendent vitality. They seem to me to turn a blind eye, just as Giovanni himself would wish, to the fact that he is an extremely cruel serial adulterer who by the end of the play has caused disaster at least in two women's lives; has tried his best to do so in that of a third, and castrated and humiliated men just as compulsively. He can be seen as the epitome of the eighteenth-century literary figure of the libertine (see Conrad, 1990), both challenging the existing status quo in terms of gender and class roles and simultaneously reasserting it at a time when aristocracy and total male power were beginning to seem more tenuous than they once were. I can see that these things are there, and that comedy often had, and has, that function, but these explanations do not seem to me to account for the feeling of intense involvement in the music and the story.

Mania, Guilt and Narcissism

I think that psychoanalytic understanding can help us to make sense of these apparent totally separated worlds – the dark, deadly one, and the world of sexualised flight – as divided aspects of the same reality. We can see the opera as taking us right inside an emotional dilemma and conflict that is also ours, and into a particular outcome of this emotional dilemma that amounts to a catastrophe. It can also help us to understand one of the interesting things that Bernard Williams pointed to, which is that Giovanni is quite blank as a character. Alone of all the characters, he has no self-reflective aria. His only solo aria, 'Fin ch'han del vino' ('Till they have got some wine and are hot-headed' (Act 1, no. 11, p. 100[2]), is a brief, brutally simple, insistent hammering of sexual appetite. He is revelling in the perverse mixing up of roles, boundaries, ages – he orders anarchy, telling Leporello to let all the dances be mixed up and played at once. This in fact happens during the dance scene during the finale of the first Act. (The aristocratic Minuet; the bucolic Teitsch or Allemande; and the middle-class Contredanse, a forerunner of the waltz, are all playing simultaneously, with different time signatures, just before, and prefiguring, Zerlina's screams for help. 3/4, 2/4 and 3/8 are all going on at once – a very classical version of anarchy.) One might think of the pounding pulse of that piece as representing the anxious pounding of a baby's heart where there is no parent to contain or modulate his anxiety.

The split between the two utterly different worlds of the first two pages of the opera starts to make more sense if one thinks of it as conveying crucial information about the characters, especially about Giovanni. He presents himself to us and to the world in the mode of page 2, as one might say – of the rapid, light bustle. He appears as arrogant, intolerant of any boundary or limit or restriction – legal, sexual, or of social class. He is in a rush. He is larger than life. His appetite is boundless. He evacuates pain into the women around him, yet appears to have no guilt. In short, he functions by means of mania, and it is completely essential to him that a sense of being abandoned or depressed is not in him but is in his object. The manic patient – such as Giovanni – is on the run from a side of him or herself that is unbearable, in particular from menacing guilt. Giovanni cannot bear guilt, and becomes furious when accused.

Guilt, the key to mania, comprises both persecutory and depressive elements – both the fear of retaliation by someone we have hurt or damaged; and an identification with that damaged person, accompanied by remorse. If the latter is predominant, the depression that results is acutely painful and difficult to bear for long. One form of defence is to regress to a more primitive, paranoid form of functioning. But an alternative defence is to deny the psychic reality of the damage we have caused. This is the method of mania – Giovanni's method. Because it entails further damage, by the continuing evacuation of pain into others, it is intrinsically both self-perpetuating and self-defeating. In the opera, we can see what would be Giovanni's conscience if he were to stop long enough to let it catch up with him. We especially see it in the form of Donna Anna and Donna Elvira, both treated very badly by him, who pursue him throughout the opera. Elvira in particular arrives on the scene whenever Giovanni's appetite is about to be satisfied, as if both representing the reproach and exhibiting the suffering that he is unable to tolerate. It is notable that Elvira also has the real, vulnerable, personality that Giovanni lacks.

So, Giovanni's emptiness as a character and his inability to tolerate guilt are connected. To understand why this is so, we need to look at what accounts for the level and unbearability of his guilt. His guilt has a murderously intense quality that is exactly and wonderfully shown in the music of page 1, which returns as he is dragged to Hell. This is exactly the murderous punishment that the manic patient is in flight from, and which, when it catches up with them, can lead them to kill themselves – as Giovanni in a sense does. But what has Giovanni done that makes his murderous punishment psychologically justified?

Levels of Guilt and the Oedipus Complex

There are three levels to this, I think. First, if punishment by death is felt, both to us and to Giovanni, to be psychologically justified and appropriate, as I'm suggesting, then he must have killed someone or something. Literally, he has killed the Commendatore – the father of a woman he has tried to ravish. But who or what does the Commendatore represent? The background here, of course, is the Oedipus complex, and it is no coincidence that *Don Giovanni* was Freud's favourite opera.[3] Giovanni's literal murder of Anna's father also represents the symbolic murder of the father principle – the principle of boundaries – which he attacks in various forms throughout the opera.[4] As soon as he sees a wedding about to take place, he tries to take the bride, Zerlina, away from her husband to be, Masetto. In asserting his *droit de seigneur* (an institutionalised version of an attack on the couple) and living out his infantile phantasy that he is the father without constraint or limits, he also breaches a further boundary, one of class.

This world of violent appropriation and equally violent punishment is characteristic of the very early Oedipus complex – of children's play between the ages of two and four, say. In normal development, the violence, and hence the belief that it is felt to be deserved, become modified, defended against and sublimated. If reality, in the form of the child's smallness and dependency, can become more or less accepted, then we can renounce the claim that we *are* our mother or father's partner. In the case of the little boy, if he can then identify with his father – become *like* him, instead of being compelled literally to try to *be* him – ordinary sexual and emotional development can occur. As we know, this achievement takes a great deal of emotional work and pain. The pain derives, in part, from the blow to our narcissism that comes from having to accept our smallness – that we are not It, the all-powerful parent (on smallness and narcissism see Grunberger, 1979). In part, it arises from the guilt about the damage that we believe that we have caused in our phantasies of killing and taking over the father's place. Remorse of this kind – about damage that we have caused – is of a different quality from the deadly, eye for an eye, punitiveness that accompanies the earlier claims to *be* the parent. This more mature guilt also sets in train reparation, a making amends, which is one of the main ways of modifying and making bearable the pain of this stage of development. (for Klein's view of the Oedipus complex, and of differing responses to it, paranoid-schizoid and depressive, see Klein, 1928, 1945; Britton, 1989; Rusbridger, 2004).

If in some way, through trauma, or through innate factors, or through the lack of an emotionally available person to help the child to work through the pain of this stage, and gradual modification and renunciation are not possible, the result can be the perpetuation of very early mental life, with its longings and dangers.

Beneath this layer is a second one. In sexual psychopathy, which we see in Don Giovanni, the same features are prominent, but underneath the central Oedipal wish to take over, control and become the father (by killing him) is an additional level of disturbance that makes an ordinary negotiation of the Oedipus complex even more difficult. This is characterised by immense cruelty to women, disguised as love for women. If one saw a sexual psychopath like Don Giovanni as a patient, and heard of his boasts, his conquests, his one-night stands, one would inevitably think that this was a reversal, in which his victims were taking the place formerly occupied by himself. That is, that the women (and not only the women but also Masetto, Ottavio and Leporello) whom he was attacking in these ways were having to suffer what he had once suffered but could not tolerate – feelings of belittlement, humiliation, rejection, degradation – and possibly, one might conjecture, feelings of being easily displaced in favour of further children, as well as of a father. This reversal is his method of psychic survival. Klein (1937, p. 323) thought that the typical Don Juan is trying simultaneously to prove that his mother is not, after all, indispensable, as she is continuously replaceable; to protect his mother from his dangerous desires; and unconsciously to make reparation to her in the form of other women.

Thirdly, and underlying this in turn, is perhaps the most primitive basis for Giovanni's phallic defence, which is a dread of fusion with the mother. This masquerades as a wish to reunite with her repetitively through sex. His so-called conquests are actually obliterations of each woman's specific identity so that they become merely a number, an entry in Leporello's catalogue. See his 'Catalogue aria', 'Madamina' (Act 1, no. 4, p. 42): 'in Italy, 640, in Germany 230, a hundred in France, 91 in Turkey – but in Spain . . . a thousand and three!' – 2,065 in all. The blankness and precision are perhaps reminiscent of the careful book-keeping of those running the concentration camps, and both conceal and reveal a dread and memory of being conquered and obliterated as a child. And in the eighteenth century, the fallen or abandoned woman was indeed in a serious predicament, and many killed themselves (Lipking, 1990). One can hear how the music – in the familiar and reassuring form of a comic patter aria, with the oom-pah-pah push to its bass – draws us into identifying with Leporello's amusement, sadism, mild remonstration and pride in working for such a man. The statistics in the aria, in which Leporello seems to be in projective identification with Don Giovanni, appear to underline the boundlessness of Giovanni's appetite. In fact, they emphasise the intensity of the underlying terror: for all his talk of needing women like he needs air, it is paradoxically the repeated reassurance of his separateness from each woman he abandons that matters to him. We can see in these deeper levels of the phallic defence the aftermath of a catastrophic beginning in life for him, detectable mainly in its effects on others, rather as the level of background radiation in the universe is thought to be evidence for the occurrence of the Big Bang.

For someone like Don Giovanni, the Oedipus complex is un-negotiable. Renouncing his claims to own, or be, the father's phallus is unthinkable. His manic attempted solution to his dilemma actually compounds the problem, as it inflicts further damage. His belief is that atonement for crimes of this magnitude is impossible. Instead, retribution is the consequence. Even at the level of whole object sexuality, this would take the form of his being castrated – having his penis appropriated in turn. However, at the deeper, more infantile level that I am suggesting is relevant for Don Giovanni, punishment amounts to the very thing that the sexualised defence is meant to protect against – utter annihilation, as punishment for annihilating both his father and his mother. It is this most primitive form of a superego that Don Giovanni is faced with at the end of the opera by the ghost of the murdered father. Rank (1924) suggested that the ghost stood simultaneously for the avenging Oedipal father and for the mother, fusion with whom Don Giovanni both longs for and dreads.[5]

Projective Identification

The leading mechanism in Giovanni's mania is projective identification (Klein, 1946) – and, of course, sex, with its primitive instinctual urges, its bodily connection, and its longings to be in, or filled by, a partner is particularly suited to being the vehicle of projective identification. The phantasy of projective identification has two complementary elements (see Britton, 1998). In one, the subject has a phantasy of evacuating parts of his or her mind into someone else, often accompanied by subtle behaviours in such a way that the object is indeed caused to feel things that correlate with what the subject was in phantasy wishing to expel. In the other, the subject has a phantasy of acquiring the characteristics of the object. Don Giovanni wishes to expel his hated infantile neediness and humiliation into his partners – and also into the male characters (Leporello, Masetto and Ottavio are all attacked, humiliated or cuckolded). At the same time, he wishes to acquire what he unconsciously takes to be the adult potency and invulnerability of both the male and female characters. He tries to acquire the never detumescent power of the father's phallus and at the same time to become the ideal, perpetually needed figure of the mother. The end result of projective identification always tends to seem like a caricature, a mask – to have an unreal, cardboard quality to it – as it is a simulacrum of qualities that are real in the object, the outcome of processes of development, but which are false in the subject; and this is true of Giovanni's so-called potency and invulnerability.

We can work through the Oedipus complex when we feel understood and emotionally contained by another person's mind. Pathology can also carry a striving for health, and that is something that Don Giovanni is perhaps also looking for in his serial conquests – for a woman who will understand this need and not collude with his sexualisation of what is actually much more primitive and infantile in him. It is this that people like Don Giovanni, male or female, are looking for when they come into analysis, and it matters desperately to them that, no matter how they try to seduce their analyst or to sexualise their relationship with him or her, the analyst remains in role as someone trying to understand them. One could think of Don Giovanni as being in ruthless pursuit of a container, of a feminine receptivity that he has had to repudiate and attack in himself and in others. However, because of his very attack, the container, when he makes contact with it, comes to feel full of his projected crushing control, and has to be fled from.

We are now in a better position to see how Giovanni is an adult who is stuck – like many psychopathic or narcissistic patients – with the mind of a very young child, and not only that, but also of a young child using particular omnipotent defences. He is stuck in a world of phallic narcissism.

Don Giovanni Represented in the Music

I now want to go on to think about the consequences for Giovanni as a character and as a seducer. It is no surprise to find that in the opera, Don Giovanni, living in projective identification with the phallus of an omnipotent father, has no character of his own, and that his music, as Joseph Kerman (1990) points out, is quite blank. Although Giovanni alleges that he has transcendent power and individuality, in fact his music depicts him as fitting in with whomever he is with, as wearing a succession of masks. Right at the start, when Anna rushes in gripping Giovanni by the arm and accusing him, he imitates her music rather than having his own. The stage direction at this point is 'Cercando sempre di celarsi' – 'Constantly trying to hide himself' (p. 11). He then re-uses this tune of Anna's during the dark slow-motion F minor Terzetto that I have mentioned (see Kerman, 1990). He adopts the old-fashioned grandeur of the Commenda-tore's music in Act 1 and at the end. He acts the penitent with Elvira when he thinks that that is required; and then plays at being the troubadour, mandolin and all, for her maid. At the start of the Trio in Act 2 (no. 15, p. 164), he is again like a chameleon, playing with Elvira by 'seducing' her in the guise of Leporello, and simply copying the beautiful tune that Elvira has been singing, when he sings 'Elvira, idolo mio' (p. 165). In the nocturnal banquet towards the end of Act 2, when Leporello tries to blend into the background by sing-ing the music from *Figaro* which the band has just been playing, Giovanni in turn fits in and copies him. In the episode of the seduction of Elvira in dis-guise, Giovanni is trying to acquire potency by disguising himself as his servant, Leporello – literally getting into his shoes and his clothes, and adopting both his patter and the *buffa* key of F major from Leporello's initial aria.

Paradoxically, Giovanni's very characterlessness is perhaps the clue to his seductiveness. His two main seductions – that of Zerlina and that of Elvira's maid – seem to indicate as much. In the first – in 'Là ci darem la mano' (Act 1, no. 7, p. 64) ('There, with your hand in mine') – he provides a beauti-ful, rather blank, almost lullaby-like eight-bar phrase. It is entirely self-con-tained and symmetrical, moving somewhat formulaically from the tonic key to the dominant, the most minimal and conventional move possible, a move instantly cancelled by a flattened seventh – and then back to the tonic. In itself it musically stays put: it is Zerlina, not he, who is aroused, takes up this tune, elaborates it and runs with it, conveying that she – not he – is the one who is erotically involved here (they are quickly joined together musically – singing same line three notes apart). What is so interesting is that we can hear and see projective identification in action – how Giovanni elicits in Zerlina, through his lullaby of seduction, his own infantile neediness. This is why his seduction of her seems so shocking – that he is exploiting her deepest vulnerability: her own infantile need. His second attempted seduction, of Elvira's maid – 'Deh vieni alla finestra' – ('Come to the window') with its mandolin accompani-ment, is similarly lullaby-like and lulling in its rocking motion (Act 2, no. 16, p. 174). What we also notice is how very beautiful this song is, how we are lulled and seduced along with her, how we admire and envy someone's capac-ity (Giovanni's, Mozart's) to produce such beauty. We can see how not only is Giovanni's neediness is projected into, and elicited in, his partner and us, but also his envy of the creative capacity of the mother: we and Zerlina are meant to admire his production. At the same time, Giovanni evacuates his jealousy, his dread that someone else has possession of the object, into Zerlina's new husband, Masetto. In the middle of all this, we, like Zerlina, overlook both the song's dangerousness and its odd asexuality. But also, we note the beauty of the music, and how *at the moment*, we are convinced by the reality of the love in it. Not just that, like Zerlina, we want to believe in it, and not just that he is very seductive, though both those things are true. But also, that Giovanni, at the start of each new relationship, perhaps really does believe that this one could be *the* one, the ideal one he has been missing for ever. We can see how music then has – perhaps because of its special quality of corporeality, of acting directly on the body – a particular power to arouse in us the state expressed and depicted so that we identify with it, while at the same time it can enable us to stand back from this emotion by questioning it, ironically commenting on it.

Giovanni's narcissism is conveyed in this – that he is complete and doesn't need anyone else. This has the effect of arousing the neediness – including sexual neediness – in Zerlina that he is tacitly denying and projecting. The people round someone as narcissistic as Giovanni become convinced that if only they could get, or have, him, *their* need would be satisfied. In fact, we know from his own almost animal account of his scenting a woman ('Zitto! mi pare' sentir odor di femmina! (Cospetto, che odorato perfetto!)', Act 1, Recit after no. 2, p. 31); and of needing women as he needs food or air ('Lasciar le donne? . . . Sai ch'elle per me son necessarie più del pan che mangio, più del l'aria che spiro', Act 2, Recit after no. 14, p. 162), that he is profoundly needy, with a sort of oral insatiability like that of a very young baby. As with a very young baby, his interest in women is not in them as whole people but only in parts of them. His hedonism, for all its swagger, is revealed as banal and infantile.

This powerful message to the woman perhaps accounts for the appeal, in the opera as in life, of such narcissistic and psychopathic people. Their message is that here is someone without need, who can satisfy all your own needs. This can also be highly flattering – if the person who has and is everything nevertheless says that he needs you, then you must be filled with even greater perfection. An alternative response to such men may be a maternal one, aroused in women who perceive the despair that underlies the bravado and respond to the infantile appeal for help that is also being transmitted: perhaps they will be the one who can cure or rescue the man. Perhaps the women who write to and marry men on Death Row are operating in this way.

Contrasting Worlds Represented in the Music

Mozart and his librettist da Ponte contrast Giovanni's world of phallic narcissism with other, more complex, worlds. They appose it with the worlds of the women, and, particularly, with the world of the relationship between Zerlina and Masetto. The music of all the women conveys great sensuality, quite unlike Giovanni's. His music either takes the form of a frenetic, masturbatory battering ram ('Fin ch'han del vino'), a lullaby ('Là ci darem'), or, in the case of his serenade to Elvira's maid ('Deh vieni alla finestra'), what may be yet another imitation (of a contemporary folksong).[6] Contrast this with the power of Anna's impassioned cries for help at the start and the strength and sensuality of her aria calling for revenge ('Or sai, chi l'onore' ('He is the one who robbed me of my honour') Act 1, no. 10, p. 90). This exalted march, with its deliberately dated slow two in a bar pulse, suitable for Anna's aristocratic status, is characteristic of a different genre of opera (the more old-fashioned *opera seria*, which typically portrayed noble and mythical characters – as in many of the operas of Gluck and Handel, but also Mozart's earlier *Idomeneo*: Anna could, in terms of the music she is given, be a goddess) (Allanbrook, 1983). The orchestral accompaniment is far more complex than that of any of Giovanni's: the off-beat thrusts of the bass endorse her passion; and the bassoon has an important role in answering, and participating in, her declamations. Mozart demonstrates the complexity of her character by moving, in the middle of this D major cry for revenge, to the distant key of F minor, the key of the Terzetto just after her father's death, just as she talks of seeing his blood covering the ground. She then returns to the declamatory call for vendetta, again in D major, with the F – in its sharpened form, the note that defines D major as a major key – which had been as it were blunted in the move to the other key, conveying a move away from outwardness and defiance to introspection, now once again sharpened. But there is another brief moment later when she sees him again in her memory, conveyed again by flattened F, this time in the context of D minor (p. 93). This telling move to the minor key occurs again in Anna's music during the great Sextet in Act 2 (no. 19, p. 190), where we see her pierced with grief. In contrast with the tonal stasis and predictability of Giovanni's music, apt for the flatness of his personality, her music here is rich and turbulent, rushing in only 17 bars through five keys before settling in C minor, a tone lower than the D minor she had started in, and tonally very remote from it. ('Sola, sola in bujo loca' ('Alone, alone in this dark place' p. 190).)[7]

The intensity of Anna's anger and pain is conveyed in the power of her rushing coloratura scales; and of Elvira's in her jagged arpeggios. This music, like a sublimated scream (Castillo, 1984; Racker, 1951 also writes about music as a 'transformed scream', and Kohut, 1957 also refers to the possible evolution of music from a transformed infantile cry), perhaps reveals what Don Giovanni might express if only he could bear to know about his own rage at being tantalised and abandoned at some very early stage in his life. Exactly because he can't know or process this, he forces his undigested pain into Anna and Elvira.

Perhaps the greatest contrast with the emotional world of Giovanni is in the relationship between Zerlina and Masetto. Their roles come from the tradition of pastoral, depicting the genuine feelings of simple, rustic people – a tradition that had an extra meaning at this point in the eighteenth century, when revolution was in the air throughout Europe and there was an uneasy awareness of the fragility of class relations. Despite this background, Masetto and Zerlina's relationship is not idealised, but comes over as both rich and ordinary. Zerlina, in her aria 'Batti, batti, o bel Masetto' ('Beat me, darling Masetto', Act 1, no. 12, p. 106) conveys not just one emotion but also a remarkable mixture of remorse and flirtatiousness that feels entirely real. The personal, specifically individual, quality of the depiction of Zerlina is emphasised by the solo cello that plays all through this gavotte – one of the features, like the two tempi, that set this apart from the pastoral genre that is ostensibly belongs to by key, metre and style (see Webster, 1991). She deserves punishment, she says, for having yielded to Giovanni, and invites it seductively, particularly when she decorates her melody at the start of the second stanza (p. 107). Her sexual attraction to Masetto is much more convincing, because it is specific and complex in this way, than any of

Giovanni's boasts in the previous aria about having ten women a night (p. 102). Zerlina's love, and her anxiety that Masetto is still angry with her, in the end overflows during the brisk second section of her aria.

All this seems very believable and familiar, as does Zerlina's comforting of Masetto in Act 2, just after he has been beaten up by Giovanni. Her singing here, in 'Vedrai, carino' ('You will see, my dear, if you are good', Act 2, no. 18, p. 184) has a luxuriant sensuality that conveys a psychologically real ambiguity between her maternal wish to soothe his wounds and her sexual wish to hold and caress his body. Very unusually for a comic (*buffo*) aria, and as if to emphasise the emotional significance of this moment, there is an orchestral introduction and also a coda, pastorally simple in idiom (it is in the form of the slow pastoral dance, the siciliano) but rich in texture, with horns and strings. As in her previous aria, a lot happens psychologically during it. She and Masetto are – at least temporarily – reconciled – by the only straightforward seduction in the opera. This stands in a marked contrast with the static, and indeed heartless, monotony of Giovanni's 'Fin ch'han dal vino', where, for all the music's relentless insistence, nothing happens. This juxtaposition points up the difference between, on the one hand, a psychic world where it is possible to retain conflicting feelings within oneself and one's relationship, and to work them through by means of a real interchange with another person; and, on the other, one where conflict has to be dealt with by evacuating pain into someone else.

It is from this internal evidence of the music itself that we can conclude with most conviction that da Ponte and Mozart have experience of these conflicts in themselves. Some external facts support this view but do not of course prove it. Da Ponte had a long and notorious career as a seducer of women and was expelled from Venice because of it: similar tales were told about Mozart after his death (Solomon, 1995). Da Ponte was a friend of Giovanni Casanova, like him a former priest and seducer, who attended the Prague premiere of *Don Giovanni*. Mozart no doubt understood something about the Oedipus complex from his loving but difficult relationship with his dominant father Leopold, whom he had defied when he married Constanze Weber, and who, as already noted, died during the composition of *Don Giovanni*.[8] Ten years before, Leopold had written several letters to Mozart saying that it would kill him if Mozart were to frustrate his will. We may think at the end, where the Stone Guest is ordering Giovanni to repent ('Pentiti!, pentiti' (p. 278)) that Giovanni is at the moment the little Mozart, refusing to give in to his father – which is perhaps also why we also admire Giovanni for refusing to sign up hypocritically to 'goodness', which would have been much more hypocritical than anything else he had done.

The End of the Opera

The end of the opera does not resolve the contradiction between the worlds of manic rush and denial on the one hand, and of suicidal breakdown on the other. There is no resolution within Giovanni himself.[9] Indeed, he refuses any such capitulation, as it would seem to him, and as seems entirely accurate psychologically. Instead, he unflinchingly takes the Commendatore's ghost's hand, in a dark echo of his instruction to Zerlina to link hands, and defies the ghost's orders to repent. The other characters arrive and Leporello tells them what has happened. The harmonic tension, almost unbearable during the music of the Stone Guest (in the tradition of what was called *ombra* music – literally, 'shady', as in evoking the Shades – in C18 opera) rapidly resolves after a dissonant clash between Anna and Elvira's lines (perhaps a last gasp of their conflict and pain). The dramatic tension is further lessened when Ottavio and Anna have a brief, bland *seria* aria, inserted for the later Vienna production. The *buffa* characters then introduce what they call 'the oldest song' ('l'antichissima canzon' Act 2, no. 24.8, p. 202): the final presto chorus, in which all the surviving cast sing 'This is the end of the sinner's game: his life and death are just the same' ('Questo è il fin di chi fa mal', Act 2, no. 24.9, p. 203). The music here is brisk and hard, with just a nod in the direction of a formal *seria* fugal ending. Here the happy ending, the *lieto fine*,[10] attempts to establish, like the choric endings of Greek and Shakespearian tragedies, the continuance of normal order after its rupture during the opera. But the thinness and brittleness of the music convey that developmentally the characters have indeed reverted to the 'oldest song', the most primitive reaction. Giovanni has been able to achieve no insight by the end of the opera, and the other characters in turn adopt his trademark manic stance – everything's fine, the bad person has gone to Hell. Unable to make sense of the ways in which they are left utterly changed, they disown and project their own destructiveness – into Giovanni – just as Giovanni has been doing to others throughout the opera. In this sense, this apparently conventional happy ending is in fact highly unconventional: far from being convincingly happy, it is darkly ironic.

Conclusion

We can now see why the opera is so disturbing. By the rhetorical power of the music, so much of which hints at a world of perverse darkness underneath its beauty, we are invited into identification with Giovanni's empty phallic power; and we are seduced along with Zerlina, Anna, Elvira and Elvira's maid. But we also identify with Elvira's confused love for her abuser; and with Anna's fury – and with Anna's own Oedipal attachment to her dead father, which makes it so hard for her to imagine moving on in her relationship with Ottavio. The greatness of Mozart's achievement is to draw us into these conflicting identifications while avoiding moralising. We understand something about what it feels like to be an abandoned child, a sexual psychopath, who has to use manic phallic narcissism to survive a psychic catastrophe by driving his agony into others. We understand this because the music evokes in us our own abandonment, our own sexual violence, our Oedipal claims and our own remorse. But it also evokes our capacity to live, along with Zerlina and Masetto, in a world in which our internal parents are loved with ordinary ambivalence, and not supplanted. No wonder we are disturbed by this contact with our own deeply buried motives; and no wonder that, because we become excited by and complicit in Giovanni's manic evasions, we want to turn a blind eye and to believe that he is simply the personification of vitality.

Notes

1 There is a huge literature on Don Giovanni and Don Juan (see Williams, 1981; Miller, 1990), though less by psychoanalysts (though see Rank, 1924; Klein, 1937; Gedo, 1997). There is an growing literature on psychoanalytic understanding of music, and of how it can portray psychic conflicts (see Nass, 1971; Feder et al., 1990, 1993; Stein, 2007). As far as I can discover, the depiction in music of a specific defence mechanism such as projective identification has not been described before.

2 Page references are to the Schirmer vocal score of *Don Giovanni* (Mozart, 1961).

3 Freud is reported to have told his patient Joseph Wortis that it was 'the greatest opera there is' (Sterba, 1965, p. 96).

4 Rank writes: 'the many women whom he must always replace anew represent to him the *one* irreplaceable mother; and . . . the rivals and adversaries whom he deceives . . . and finally even kills represent the *one* unconquerable mortal enemy, the father' (1924 [1975, p. 41]).

5 'In the figure of the Stone Guest, who also represents the coffin, appears the mother herself, coming to fetch the son' (Rank, 1924 [1975, p. 96]).

6 Orlinck (1967, p. 312). Though Rushton (1981, p. 18) points out that the source may be the debtor, as it is late enough for it to be borrowed from Mozart.

7 Julian Rushton (personal communication) points out that this aberrant use of C minor in an aria that starts in D minor occurs also in Elettra's first aria in *Idomeneo*, where it leads into the storm scene.

8 His father died on 28 May 1787. The first performance of the opera was on 29 October.

9 In terms of Aristotle's (1996) view of tragedy (350 BC: 1452 a-b), he suffers reversals of fortune (*peripeteia*) but achieves no recognition and insight (*anagnorisis*), as are achieved in *Figaro* and *Così* (see Robinson, 1997; Waldoff, 1997).

10 On the *lieto fine*, see Robinson (1997).

References

Allanbrook, W. J. (1983). *Rhythmic Gesture in Mozart: Le Nozze di Figaro and Don Giovanni*. Chicago, IL: Chicago University Press.

Aristotle (1996). (c.350 BC) *Poetics* (M. Heath, Trans.). Harmondsworth: Penguin.

Britton, R. (1989). The missing link: Parental sexuality in the Oedipus complex. In J. Steiner (ed.), *The Oedipus Complex Today*. London: Karnac Books.

Britton, R. (1998). *Introduction to Belief and Imagination*. London: Routledge, pp. 1–7.

Castillo, F. G. (1984). Personal communication.

Conrad, P. (1990). The libertine's progress. In J. Miller (ed.), *The Don Giovanni Book: Myths of Seduction and Betrayal*. London and Boston, MA: Faber & Faber.

Feder, S. (1993). Mozart in D minor – or, the father's blessing: The father's curse. In P. Ostwald & L. S. Zegans (eds.), *The Pleasures and Perils of Genius: Mostly Mozart*. Madison, WI: International Universities Press.

Feder, S., Karmel, R. L., & Pollock, G. (eds.). (1990). *Psychoanalytic Explorations in Music* (1st series). Madison, WI: International Universities Press.

Feder, S., Karmel, R. L., & Pollock, G. (eds.). (1993). *Psychoanalytic Explorations in Music* (2nd series). Madison, WI: International Universities Press.

Fielding, H. (1749). *The History of Tom Jones, a Foundling.* London: Andrew Miller.

Forman, E. (1981). Don Juan before da Ponte. In J. Rushton (ed.), *W. A. Mozart: Don Giovanni.* Cambridge: Cambridge University Press.

Gedo, J. E. (1997). On the psychological core of opera: Mythic themes in *Don Giovanni* and *Der Rosenkavalier. The Annual of Psychoanalysis,* 25: 49–59.

Grunberger, B. (1979). *Narcissism: Psychoanalytic Essays.* Madison, WI: International Universities Press.

Kerman, J. (1990). Reading *Don Giovanni.* In J. Miller (ed.), *The Don Giovanni Book: Myths of Seduction and Betrayal.* London and Boston, MA: Faber & Faber.

Kierkegaard, S. (1843). *Either/Or* (D. F. and L. M. Swenson). Princeton, NJ: Princeton University Press, 1944.

Klein, M. (1928). Early stages of the Oedipus conflict. In *The Writings of Melanie Klein* (vol. 1, pp. 186–198). London: Hogarth Press, 1975.

Klein, M. (1937). Love, guilt and reparation. In *The Writings of Melanie Klein* (vol. 1, pp. 306–343). London: Hogarth Press, 1975 and Virago Press, 1997.

Klein, M. (1945). The Oedipus complex in the light of early anxieties. In *The Writings of Melanie Klein* (vol. 1, pp. 370–419). London: Hogarth Press, 1975.

Kohut, H. (1957). Observations on the psychological functions of music. *Journal of the American Psychoanalytic Association,* 5: 389–407.

Lipking, L. (1990). Donna abbandonata. In J. Miller (ed.), *The Don Giovanni Book: Myths of Seduction and Betrayal.* London and Boston, MA: Faber & Faber.

Miller, J. (ed.) (1990). *The Don Giovanni Book: Myths of Seduction and Betrayal.* London and Boston, MA: Faber & Faber.

Mozart, A. (1961). *Don Giovanni, Vocal Score.* New York: Schirmer.

Nass, M. L. (1971). Some considerations of a psychoanalytic interpretation of music. *Psychoanalytical Quarterly,* 40: 303–316.

Orlinck, S. (1967). A canzonetta fiorentina in *Don Giovanni? Mozart Jahrbuch, 1967.* Salzburg: Internationale Stiftung Mozarteum.

Racker, H. (1951). Contributions to psychoanalysis of music. *American Imago,* 8: 129–163.

Rank, O. (1924). *Die Don Juan-Gestalt.* Leipzig: Internationaler Psychoanalytischer Verlag (trans. and ed. by D G Winter as *The Don Juan Legend,* Princeton: Princeton University Press, 1975).

Robinson, M. F. (1997). The alternative endings of Mozart's *Don Giovanni.* In M. Hunter & J. Webster (eds.), *Opera Buffa in Mozart's Vienna.* Cambridge: Cambridge University Press.

Rusbridger, R. (2004). Elements of the Oedipus complex: A Kleinian account. *International Journal of Psychoanalysis,* 85: 731–748.

Rushton, J. (1981). *W. A. Mozart: Don Giovanni.* Cambridge: Cambridge University Press.

Solomon, M. (1995). *Mozart: A Life.* London: Hutchinson.

Stein, A. (2007). The sound of memory: Music and acoustic origins. *American Imago,* 64(1): 59–85.

Sterba, R. F. (1965). Psychoanalysis and music. *American Imago,* 22: 96–111.

Waldoff, J. (1997). *Don Giovanni:* Recognition denied. In M. Hunter & J. Webster (eds.), *Opera Buffa in Mozart's Vienna.* Cambridge: Cambridge University Press.

Webster, J. (1991). The analysis of Mozart's arias. In C. Eisen (ed.), *Mozart studies Vol. 1.* Oxford: Oxford University Press.

Williams, B. (1981). Don Giovanni as an idea. In J. Rushton (ed.), *W. A. Mozart: Don Giovanni,* Cambridge: Cambridge University Press.

3   Across the Great Divide

Reflections on the Moral Reversal in Mozart's *The Magic Flute*

Lee Rather

Introduction

There are several ways of bringing a psychoanalytic sensibility to the exploration of an opera. One approach assumes that an opera may be examined in order to discover traces of unconscious concerns and conflicts that have crept into the creative process, whether or not consciously intended. This method follows a tradition begun by Freud in his analyses of numerous works of sculpture and literature (1910a, 1911, 1914, 1928), even if he declared himself tone-deaf and unable to do this with music (1914, p. 211). Yet another approach is to consider the characters as real people with individual inner motivations that could be analyzed as if they were on the couch. This method, itself worthy of discussion (Frattaroli, 1987), has a long and venerable tradition followed by many of the contributors to this volume. A third approach assumes that successful operas that endure with the public will transcend the particulars of characters, settings, and plots, and will tend toward universal unconscious themes. From this angle, opera may be approached as a genre of collective myth or psychodrama in which the characters symbolize aspects of ourselves in conscious and unconscious interaction expressed through dramatic and musical narrative. I will follow this last premise here, focusing more on the dramatic action in examining the enigmatic *The Magic Flute*.

The Magic Flute

The Magic Flute, an opera in two acts with music by Mozart (1756–1791) and a libretto by Schikaneder (1751–1812), has been one of the most popular works of the repertoire, charming many generations of opera lovers since its premier just two months before Mozart's death. It is presented in the form of a *Singspiel*, a genre characterized by spoken dialogue interspersed with folk-like ballads and formal arias in the context of plots that blend serious, comic, romantic, and magical elements often using exaggerated depictions of good and evil in order to present moral lessons.

For a psychoanalyst, the plot of *The Magic Flute* resembles a convoluted, surrealistic, and often confusing dream, complete with abrupt shifts in tone and an abundance of fine-grained detail. At first glance, it seems to be a rambling

DOI: 10.4324/9781032271408-3

fairy tale depicting a hero's quest for true love and wisdom in a world of risks and dangers. As in many fairy tales, one notices a maturational sensibility in which childhood hopes and fears are laid out, worked through, and ultimately conquered. However, in spite of its appeal, *The Magic Flute* remains puzzling because of its enigmatic symbolism, and especially because of a surprising and inexplicable moral reversal that occurs midway through toward the end of Act 1. The enigma of this reversal and its psychological significance is my focus here. But, before moving on, I will present a short synopsis that covers the most salient aspects of the dramatic action I will discuss.

The Story

Tamino, a prince alone in the woods, is calling for help as he flees a deadly serpent. Fainting from fear, he is saved by three ladies who fawn over him before going for their mistress, the Queen of the Night. When Tamino awakes, Papageno, a comical bird-catcher, boasts that he slayed the dragon. The three ladies return, punish Papageno for his braggartly lie, and show Tamino a portrait of the Queen's daughter, Pamina. Tamino falls instantly in love. The Queen arrives in much distress that her daughter has been kidnapped by the wicked sorcerer, Sarastro. Tamino vows to rescue Pamina, and the Queen offers him Pamina's hand if he succeeds. To aid in this perilous mission, Papageno is given a set of magic bells and Tamino is given a magic flute, which was crafted by the Queen's late husband.

However, a surprising twist occurs when Tamino arrives at Sarastro's temple and discovers that the Queen of the Night is an untrustworthy and wicked one, and that Sarastro is actually the high priest of wisdom. A temple priest promises Tamino that the confusion will be lifted during the initiation rites to the brotherhood. He also promises Papageno a wife at this point.

Papageno scouts on ahead and discovers Monostatos, a Moorish slave, trying to force himself on Pamina. Papageno mesmerizes him with the magic bells and he and Pamina escape. The Queen of the Night appears before Pamina and reveals that her late husband was once the owner of the Circle of the Sun temple. When he died, he willed the Queen all his lands and riches but he willed the temple to Sarastro, leaving the Queen weakened and powerless. She tries in vain to convince Pamina to kill Sarastro with the dagger she has given her and sings her famous aria of revenge, *Der Hölle Rache* (Hellish Revenge). Pamina refuses and begs Sarastro to forgive her mother. He reassures her that revenge has no place in his domain.

Pamina and Tamino, protected by the magic flute, pass unscathed through chambers of fire and water. The priests hail their triumph and invite the couple to enter the temple. Papageno, who was previously teased by a haggard old woman who disturbed him by saying she has a boyfriend named Papageno, now feels that he has failed to find his Papagena, but he is advised to summon her with his magic bells. When she appears, the happy couple stutters in astonishment in sing-song bird-like courting sounds as they dream of the many children they will have together.

The Queen of the Night, furious and envious at everyone's good fortune, plots with Monostatos to regain power by destroying the temple. However, all ends well as they are thwarted and cast into the darkness forever as Sarastro declares the dawn of a new era in which day triumphs over night.

Discussion

The most obvious appeal of *The Magic Flute* is first and foremost Mozart's transcendently beautiful music and an astounding collection of captivating arias that include Papageno's "Bird Catcher" aria (*Der Vogelfänger*), Tamino's "Portrait" aria (*Dies Bildnis ist bezaubernd schön*), the Queen of the Night's "Hellish Revenge" aria (*Der Hölle Rache*), Papageno's "Girl or a Woman" aria (*Ein Mädchen oder Weibchen*), Pamina's "Lost Love" aria (*Ach, ich fühl's*) the Papageno-Papagena duets including *Pa-Pa-Pa Papageno*, and finally, Sarastro's "Holy Temple" aria (*In diesen heil'gen Hallen*).

The other major charm of the opera is its fantastical fairy-tale quality: A handsome young prince is saved from a deadly dragon and shown a portrait of a princess with whom he falls instantly in love. Armed with a magic flute, and accompanied by a colorful sidekick, he embarks to rescue a damsel in distress at the behest of a distraught mother who offers her daughter's hand if he is successful. Along the way, trials and tribulations are weathered, wisdom is gained, and, unlike many operas, all ends well. When a production brings all of this altogether with beautiful music, sets and costumes, and, perhaps plays up the comic moments, there's something for everyone. Despite its reputation for having a confusing and jumbled plot, it's no surprise that *The Magic Flute* is often chosen to introduce children to opera, casting its spell on all.

The Enigma of the Moral Reversal

When the final curtain falls and the spell begins to wane, the rather inexplicable moral shift of the fairy tale lingers. While the dramatic direction may have seemed clear early on, the clouds move in quickly. In the first scenes, the Queen of the Night is depicted as a true-hearted mother distraught that her daughter has been kidnapped by the evil villain, Sarastro. But by the end of Act 1, we are thrown a one-two punch and our assumptions are turned upside down. First, when Tamino arrives at the Sarastro's temple, he seems to have forgotten that there is a damsel in distress, and inexplicably begins asking for initiation into the temple's mysteries. Soon after, the moral scales are inverted as Tamino and the audience learn to our surprise that the evil kidnaper is actually a holy man, the High Priest of the Sun, and that the Queen of the Night, who was presented as an innocent victim is actually a treacherous woman who has plotted against him and needs to be brought under control. He has abducted Pamina only to protect her from her mother's bad influence. In Act 2, we learn that Sarastro is actually Pamina's father. Then, before we can think about this moral reversal, we're off on a series of initiation rites whose nature is vague, and we are left to consider what the moral reversal has to do with the quest for mature romantic love and wisdom. As we shall see, there is a moment where some backstory is provided, but what's unexplained is why the moral order of Act 1 needs to be dramatically reversed. As beautiful as it may be, *The Magic Flute* is bewildering with regard to this major shift in the moral characterizations of the Queen of the Night and Sarastro.

While some critics have dismissed the plot as somewhat nonsensical or incomplete, opera goers accustomed to the reality-bending genre of opera might be willing to let it all go by in soft focus, not allowing a seemingly incoherent plot spoil an otherwise wonderful opera. Perhaps they've read that Schikaneder tinkered with the libretto right up until the end, and, given that Mozart fell deathly ill a month before the premier and died two months after, they should forgive a less than totally polished libretto. Either way, we might turn a blind eye to the dramatic inconsistencies and, buoyed by the comic relief offered by Papageno and Papagena, focus on the music and singing.

A more serious opera-goer may have done some further reading (i.e., Chailey, 1982, 1992) and learned that Mozart and Schikaneder were both members of the Freemason brotherhood that emerged in 18th-century Europe after the dawn of the Age of Enlightenment. Freemasonry describes itself as a "beautiful system of morality, veiled in allegory, and illustrated by symbols" (Oliver, 1849/2016), one that embraces a supreme being, but rises above traditional religious orthodoxies. At the core of the Freemason ideology is an appeal for universal brotherhood to replace the class system and religious dogmatism of Europe. Mozart, Schikaneder, Goethe, Haydn, and Liszt were all Freemasons. To step into the substantial literature surrounding *The Magic Flute* is to be persuaded that the symbolism and the dramatic action suddenly make sense in depicting the values and initiation rites of Freemasonry. During the period in which *The Magic Flute* was created, Freemasonry was a controversial subject and Maria Theresa, sovereign of the Hapsburg Empire, ordered the Masonic Lodge in Vienna to be closed over the objections of her husband (Frances, the Holy Roman Emperor), who himself was a member! With this historical context in mind, it is thought that Schikaneder and Mozart took an artistic opportunity both to promote the Freemason's cause and to capture the conflict within the house of Hapsburg. This includes borrowing upon its initiation rituals for the trials of Pamina and Tamino, setting the opera in Egypt where Freemasonry believes its rites originated, and having the Queen of the Night and Sarastro represent the battle between Maria Theresa and the Emperor.

In the modern era, the opera also lends itself to other commentaries from the points of view of gender, class, and racism. For example, William Kentridge, a South African artist who also designs stage sets for opera productions, has exhibited *Sarastro and the Master's Voice*. This multi-media work uses film footage and a recording of Sarastro's aria, *In diesen heil'gen Hallen (In these Holy Halls)*, to critique the abuse of Enlightenment ideals in European colonialism. While a discussion of such diverse interpretive tracks is beyond the scope of this chapter, it can be said that the Masonic interpretation is compelling in explaining much of the deliberate symbolism of the opera and it also offers a historical point of view of the tensions between the Queen and Sarastro. Nonetheless, since the audience for the opera has been far broader than Masons and history buffs, we return to our task of putting *The Magic Flute* on the couch to plumb the depths of its psychological appeal.

The psychoanalytic question remains as to the nature of deeper resonances for opera-goers, beyond beautiful music, fairy tale plots, and Masonic messages. Most particularly, approaching *The Magic Flute* as a psychological allegory, how can we understand the moral shift of Sarastro and the Queen mid-way through the opera? When we, along with Tamino, discover that Sarastro is wise rather than evil, and that the Queen selfishly intent on keeping her daughter away from him, the question arises as to the psychological nature of the gulf between the Queen and Sarastro as well as the developmental task involved as Tamino and Pamina are challenged to make a psychological traversal from the lands of the Queen to the Temple of Sarastro.

Across the Great Divide

The deep structure of *The Magic Flute* is essentially a developmental story of boys and girls needing to situate themselves in relation to mothers and fathers, or more specifically, to maternal and paternal function as elaborated in the following and represented allegorically by the Queen and Sarastro. In this sense, *The Magic Flute* resonates deeply because it portrays the challenging unconscious emotional dynamics involved in individuating away from the mother and encountering the world of the father. Psychoanalysts consider this journey essential as part of growth and maturity.

From the psychoanalytic theoretical viewpoint, the child's first sensual-erotic-love attachment is with the mother (Freud, 1905). Much like the Queen of the Night, she is a powerful presence, a goddess, in the eyes of the child. Both boys and girls initially form themselves within their bond with her. As the natural strivings to separate inevitably emerge, this leads to complications. Traditionally, the boy begins to form his sense of autonomy, gender identity, and masculinity by renouncing aspects of his initial merger with his mother as he is called upon to move across the great divide toward the father for identity. For the boy, this involves the rejection of what is registered personally and culturally as "feminine." The girl's task is differently complex. Since her mother also identifies *with her* more strongly, the daughter's attempts to make the father a love object are complicated by the intense two-way bond with the mother as well as a conflict within both of them concerning how much separation is tolerable. Psychologically speaking, *The Magic Flute* traces Tamino and Pamina's challenges in navigating this journey from the maternal to the paternal world and building a bridge between them.

Readers familiar with psychoanalytic thinking are aware of Freud's interpretation of the Oedipus myth, based on Sophocles' *Oedipus Rex*, as an allegory reflecting the cornerstone of psychological development (Freud, 1897, 1910b, 1925). The traditional Freudian emphasis is on the dynamics of the child's desire, competitive strivings, and the anxieties within the triangular interpersonal space of child, mother, and father. Two analysts after Freud developed additional interpretive approaches that have enriched clinical understanding. First, Melanie Klein (1945) theorized that Oedipal dynamics begin earlier in life and involve the child's conflicted relationship to mother and father as parental couple. Somewhat later, Bion (1963) contributed an additional perspective by highlighting the way the Oedipus myth reflects the human difficulty in balancing psychological curiosity with the dread of full emotional truths.

In contemporary thinking, a growing distinction is made among analysts between the various complexes that may arise, and "oedipality" itself, as a process in which the fundamentals of personality are grounded (Barratt, 2019). It is common among analysts now to refer to *paternal and maternal functions*.

The essence of maternal function emerges from the traditional ideal of close bonding and attachment of infant and mother as a unit. Her body and presence are to be fully available and, in an optimal situation, the child has some experience of a necessary illusion that its needs rather than hers are primary. In this ideal, the mother is content to let her child simply be, to celebrate its unique specialness, and to shield the child from the impingement of demand from the outside world. The mood and ethic is one of merger and unconditional acceptance. Rooted in the romantic sensibility, the child will be encouraged to become its own unique self.

Gradually the father, as a third figure, makes a more definitive entrance into this idyllic simplicity. The father carries the symbolic function of being the "other" who is not the mother, and bringing word of a world beyond the maternal orbit. Paternal function is that which intrudes as the symbolic "third" into the previous dyad of maternal function. In this way, paternal function mediates and influences the child's access to the maternal world. Freud went so far as to pose this as the foundation of the superego, the earliest of which is to say "No" to easy gratifications and merger with the maternal. Clinical explorations suggest a need for a child to construct a symbolic figure who says no even if no actual father is present. This becomes generalized into a range of superego prohibitions under the law of the father. Another dimension is that paternal function is connected with the demand functions of the world external to the mother-child orbit. While maternal function is concerned with *being*, the paternal sphere deals with *doing*, that is, creating and achieving in the world, and gradually arriving at wisdom concerning the greater order of things outside oneself (the law of the father).

It is important to note that, in contemporary psychoanalytic thinking, the terms maternal and paternal function are not discreet roles carried out by actual mothers and fathers, respectively, but rather are symbolic functions that do not necessarily rest on essentialist readings of gender. The function may be carried out by either or both parents depending on time, situation, and personalities. Additionally, the encounter with each function may involve significant figures other than the biological parents. These distinctions are more important than ever in an age when social roles, gender, and family arrangements (i.e., single parents, same-sex parenting, communal parenting) are undergoing radical change.

As social roles and family arrangements have diversified and undergone radical change, it now seems useful to refer to paternal and maternal functions, without in any way applying essentialist concepts to gender. In any case, the general idea is that both maternal and paternal symbolic functions must be provided and then integrated into the child's own relationship to itself and to the world.

Considering this theoretical scaffolding as background, we can note that at the beginning of the opera immediately following the overture, Mozart's stage directions have Tamino running onto the stage carrying a bow, but no arrows. The serpent of male development pursues him, but he lacks the phallic internal strength to deal with it as yet. He needs to be rescued, protected, and loved by the maternal order represented here by the Three Ladies and the Queen of the Night. With their background support, Tamino will be able to set out on the quest for his arrows. Papageno can be viewed as an even younger version of Tamino, a sort of little brother, who lives an idyllic life in a little hut and spends his days playfully catching birds with his little panpipe. He is cared for, nurtured, and fed by the Three Ladies with wine, sugar-bread, and figs. He knows nothing of life outside his little maternal valley and is shocked to learn from Tamino that there is a bigger world beyond the mountain forest he calls home. Papageno's world symbolizes the idealized world of maternal function. Supporting this musically, Mozart provides Papageno with a simple major key folk melody for his introductory aria, *Der Vogelfänger (The Birdcatcher)*. The music is innocent, child-like, and reflects the idealized life of the maternal orbit in sing-song fashion. In fact, only when he asserts some growth instinct, pretending to be more powerful than he really is and claiming to have killed the serpent, does he run into trouble as he is scolded and punished by the Three Ladies. Tamino may be thought of as a more grownup version of Papageno. He has entered adolescence and the music of his love aria (*Dies Bildnis is bezaubernd schön*) reflects a growing experience of the complex tensions of the inchoate feeling of desire triggered by the portrait of Pamina.

As Tamino and Papageno begin to separate from the maternal valley, they are guided by three boys. Their singing subtly forecasts the encounter with the paternal although their voices are pre-adolescent, Mozart has given them a somber, serious, and hymn-like melody. Meanwhile, Tamino and Papageno continue to exhibit their developmental contrast. For example, when Tamino imagines what he would do with a woman like Tamina, he sings: "What would I do? Full of delight, I would clasp her to my fiery breast," alluding to sexual passion. By contrast, when Papageno fantasizes about a "Papagena," he is more innocent and chaste as he sings "She'd fall asleep by my side and I'd rock her to sleep like a child." Papageno seems to envision something more like a play-date than a burning romance. Even the names, Papageno and Papagena, differentiated by a single vowel, suggest a kind of undifferentiated child's world. Of the four young characters, Papagena is by far the least developed, perhaps because she is more a projection of Papageno's childish narcissism than a person in her own right. As they set out to face their initiation trials, Tamino is bold and brave in moving toward the paternal while Papageno is so frightened at

Sarastro's appearance he wishes he were a mouse or a snail so he could crawl back to his hut and hide. As the opera progresses, we get the sense that while Tamino and Pamina strive for enlightenment offered by Sarastro and the temple, Papageno and Papagena want simply to reproduce.

And what about Pamina and Monostatos? In moving across the great divide toward the father-paternal, the young woman has much to deal with. Here, I will omit discussing the latent aspects of racism in portraying Monostatos as a Moor. First, she has to deal with misogyny of men as represented most obviously by Monostatos in his attempts to enslave and molest her. From a psychoanalytic and feminist perspective, the need for the boy to separate from mother too often results in a hyper-machismo posture, and a tendency to demean and dis-empower women. While such a man appears arrogant and domineering on the surface, what lies underneath is a fear of women's power left over from the experience of being a child with a mother (or a Queen). Additionally, his own disowned longings for maternal reunification may also be projected onto the woman who consequently appears as someone who wants to swallow him up or trap him. Such a man may cover over his unconscious fears with behaviors and attitudes of power and dominance aimed not only at degrading women, but often other men as well.

Pamina must not only fight her way through this aspect of men, but she must also sort out her own conflicts and guilt about separating from a mother who is bitter toward men and wants to keep her daughter for herself. This is represented by the Queen of the Night's vengeance toward Sarastro, and her offering her daughter help in the form of a dagger to kill off the paternal. Pamina is now caught between the paternal and the maternal. If she were to kill Sarastro, psychologically speaking, she would be symbolically killing off her future prospects of romantic love (expressed in the aria of loss), so she begins consider suicide rather than suffer such a fate.

In her spectacular aria *Der Hölle Rache*, the Queen expresses her fury and longing for revenge. Mozart chose the key of D minor for this aria, a key often associated with tragedy, and prevalent in his later *Requiem* (1791) that would dominate his thoughts in the weeks following the premiere of *The Magic Flute*. After the opening bars, the music suddenly moves to F major, the relative key of D minor. This key switch signals that the Queen is moving from tragic despair and vulnerability to threatening power. Gathering herself together, she tells Pamina that if she does not kill Sarastro, she will no longer be her daughter. The Queen's power, influence, and trickery over Pamina are well demonstrated by the coloratura vocal heights she achieves. The role requires a soprano of virtuosic capacity with its unusually large leaps between notes that will be recalled in its most famous passages. The recurrent gestures, manic twists and turns, and final ferocious D minor cadence place a thrillingly dark cloud of wrath over Pamina as her mother reaches a series of high Cs before ascending even further to the F above high C. Such a note is nearly impossible to reach and conveys an impression that nothing can stop her.

The Queen's desperate histrionics stand in high contrast to Sarastro's emotional serenity. Musically, Mozart conveys the intense morality of Sarastro best in his aria "O Isis und Osiris." This aria reaches four octaves lower than the highest notes of the Queen's, thereby contrasting her soaring emotional lability with his deep and steady wisdom. Sarastro's basso profondo tones occupy the depths of the bass range and are meant to symbolize the idealized foundational wisdom of the paternal linking the child to the law of the outside world. *The Magic Flute* finally arrives at its destination in the final scene in which the Queen and her maternal world are banished, paternal function and authority prevail, and everything ends happily ever after.

The Absence of a Third Act

Although everything seems to work out in the end, a psychoanalytic reading of the allegory calls this into serious question. In so far as the maturational arc in *The Magic Flute* is a presented progression in which the maternal is finally cast out forever, the moral of the story is the exaltation of the paternal and the banishment of the maternal. What is missing is an integration of the two, and as my following reflections will suggest, it is missing a third act.

The number three is traditionally associated with harmony, wisdom, and understanding, and given prominence in religious traditions. For example: in Christianity, we find the Holy Trinity; in Judaism, the three patriarchs as well as the three parts of the Torah given in the third month of the Jewish calendar by Moses, the third child of his parents; in Hinduism, the three major deities: Brahma, Vishnu, and Shiva; and, in Buddhism, the three jewels of awakened mind: Buddha, Dharma, and Sangha. Likewise, the number three is also repeatedly ritualized in Masonry. A candidate seeks initiation by knocking on the door three times (the so-called Three Distinct Knocks). Upon entrance, there are three degrees of initiation to pass through as the initiate progresses to the ultimate goal of the Masonic Third Degree. And, three Grandmasters preside over the Lodge.

Mozart makes many references to Masonic rituals and symbols with the frequent repetition of patterns of three. This begins with the first chords of the overture, set in the home key of E flat, a key with three flats. This is repeated in the second section of the overture, where rhythmically speaking, the timing of the three chords is identical to that of the Three Distinct Knocks (Thomson, 1977). The triadic pattern is also found throughout Schikaneder's libretto as well as we encounter three boys, three ladies, three slaves, and Tamino's knocks on the three doors at the temple. In this respect, it is notable that *The Magic Flute* lacks an Act 3.

In psychoanalysis, the number three also becomes deeply significant in the theoretical concept of "the third." The idea of the third entered psychoanalysis through Lacan's views on intersubjectivity, in which he considered the symbolic position of third to be that which prevents the relationship between two persons (or points of view) from either rigidifying into power struggles or collapsing into the oneness of merger. The term has since gathered a plethora of nuances, including many ideas about how this third function develops and plays out in relational and cultural configurations. However, for our purposes here, the essence of the concept is that the symbolic third function forestalls polarized and stagnating thinking and fosters generativity of new perspectives.

With reference to the Oedipus situation, the third is grounded in advance from pre-oedipal dyadic relations (mother and child) to triangular oedipal relations (mother, father, child). This move is seen as a major developmental achievement in which the child, by, metaphorically speaking, learning to count from one to three, not only enters the Oedipal phase, but also begins to integrate the sense of a generative parental couple in creative interaction with each other (Rather, 2008; Britton, 1989).

Overall, the third element creates the potential to modulate dissonance and conflict between the first two, allowing emotional processing to become less black and white, and more complex and three dimensional. One could speculate that omnipresence of this truth gives us a sort of intuitive or unconscious striving toward the number three as exemplified in the religious examples given earlier, and the integration of paternal and maternal function in psychoanalytic thinking.

Allegorically, *The Magic Flute* falls short of reaching a third position in integrating the maternal and the paternal. Further psychological evolution movement would be required for a higher state of mind. In this sense, the conclusion of *The Magic Flute* dramatizes a tilted personality development in men and women that is no doubt relevant to considerations of the social construction of gender and the tendency toward the devaluation of women cross-culturally.

It is interesting to contrast this sensibility of Mozart-Schikaneder with that of Richard Wagner. Also in the key of E flat, the opening of *Das Rheingold* (the first opera in the *Ring Cycle*) begins an extended arpeggio (the nature motif) that emphasizes the origins of life in the maternal. Although the *Ring*, too, establishes that one cannot remain there forever, there is much more of a sense that the masculine and feminine are both fully legitimate and also must be integrated for maturity. Along these lines, it is the wisdom of the central female character, Brünnhilde, that brings the *Ring Cycle* to its developmental climax as she integrates her strong nature with her father's will. As Wagner wrote and portrayed more straightforwardly in *The Flying Dutchman*, masculine and feminine must be re-integrated for wholeness in love (Rather, 2014). This lesson seems entirely absent in *The Magic Flute*, as we are never able to bring the Queen of the Night and Sarastro together within the two acts presented.

Given the fact that the Queen is so marginalized, it is fascinating that she alone has any emotional complexity compared with the other principle characters. Tamino's steadfast virtue, Pamina's earnest love, and Sarastro's calm wisdom are all simple, almost cardboard cutouts. Papageno is at least by turns childishly cowardly, sometimes brave, and comically witty, but only the Queen is drawn with more emotional complication and ambivalence. In the first scenes, she appears overcome with grief and worry and her aria, *O zittre nicht mein lieber Sohn* (Oh, do not tremble my dear son), is tender and sad. At the end, we might still wonder whether she was deliberately and cunningly lying in calling Sarastro evil, or whether motherly love and anxiety have twisted her perspective. Interestingly, it is she who enlists the three boys to guide Tamino and Pamina to the temple. The gentle manner and hymns of the boys presage the quiet serenity of Sarastro and perhaps suggest that the Queen may be more complexly ambivalent, resenting Sarastro, but also aware of the need for Pamina to make the emotional link to her father. On the other hand, when she fails to persuade Pamina to kill off the father and return, she even agrees to marry her daughter to the boorish Monostatos if he can bring her back. At the very least, one can say that it seems dramatically incomplete to have banished the most complex character. To play with this idea, it is almost as if the Queen's banishment unconsciously destines her to live on in the minds of the audience, giving them a chance to reintegrate her in a creative third act of their own imagination!

Final Comments

To sum up, *The Magic Flute* is not only one of the most beloved operas in the repertoire but also among the most perplexing with its moral plot shift. The fairy tale plot, the love story, and the mostly light and accessible music have made it one of the more common operas used to entice new generations to the genre. Nonetheless, beneath its charming, simple, and confusing aspects, deeper levels of meaning can be found upon closer examination.

In the imaginative conjectures I have conjured up in this chapter, I do not mean to suggest any conscious or even unconscious intentions on the part of Mozart or Schikaneder. Again, the historical evidence is strong that the manifest content of *The Magic Flute* may be best understood through the rituals of the Freemasons and the historical context of political opposition posed by the Hapsburg court at the time the opera was being created. However, since one of the characteristics of great creative art is its capacity to evoke multiple levels of emotional, intellectual, and psychological response, I have attempted here to examine and play with one strand of psychological resonance which I have proposed is not only implicit but also unconsciously evocative for all who have been moved by *The Magic Flute*.

At times, psychoanalysis and art may converge with regard to the impossibility of arriving at singular or final meanings. Even in psychoanalysis, contrary to popular opinion, there can be no complete interpretations. For example, the very different readings of the Oedipus myth arrived at by Freud, Klein, and Bion suggest that any single reading would be reductionistic given the complexity of unconscious mental life. So, with reference to the dream-like structure of *The Magic Flute* alluded to at the beginning of this chapter, I will end with a passage from Freud's *The Interpretation of Dreams* that captures this sense of almost infinite possibilities of meaning:

> There is often a passage in even the most thoroughly interpreted dream which has to be left obscure; this is because we become aware in the work of dream interpretation that at that point there is a tangle of dream-thoughts which cannot be unraveled and which moreover add nothing to our knowledge of the content of the dream. This is the *dream's navel*, the

spot where it reaches down into the unknown. The dream thoughts to which we are led by interpretation cannot, from the nature of things, have any definite ending; they are bound to branch out in every direction into the intricate network of our world of thought.

(1900, p. 525, emphasis mine)

References

Barratt, B. B. (2019). Oedipality and oedipal complexes reconsidered: On the incest taboo as key to the universality of the human condition. *International Journal of Psychoanalysis*, Volume 100, 7–31.

Bion, W. R. (1963). Elements of psychoanalysis. In *Seven servants*. New York: Jason Aronson, 1977.

Britton, R. (1989). The missing link: Parental sexuality in the Oedipus complex. In J. Steiner (Ed.), *The Oedipus complex today: Clinical implications*. London: Karnac.

Chailey, J. (1982). *The magic flute, Masonic opera*. New York: Da Capo Press.

Chailey, J. (1992). *The magic flute unveiled: Esoteric symbolism in Mozart's Masonic Opera*. Vermont: Inner Traditions International.

Frattaroli, E. J. (1987). On the validity of treating Shakespeare' characters as if they were real people. *Psychoanalysis and Contemporary Thought*, Volume 10 (3), 407–437.

Freud, S. (1897). Extracts from the Fliess Papers (Letter October 15, 1897). In J. Strachey (Ed. and Trans.), *The standard edition of the complete psychological works of Sigmund Freud*. (pp 265–266). London: Hogarth Press.

Freud, S. (1900). The interpretation of dreams. In J. Strachey (Ed. and Trans.), *The standard edition of the complete psychological works of Sigmund Freud* (Vol. 4–5, pp. 339–630). London: Hogarth Press.

Freud, S. (1905). Three essays on the theory of sexuality. In J. Strachey (Ed. and Trans.), *The standard edition of the complete psychological works of Sigmund Freud* (Vol. 7, pp. 125–245). London: Hogarth Press.

Freud, S. (1910a). Leonardo da Vinci. In J. Strachey (Ed. and Trans.), *The standard edition of the complete psychological works of Sigmund Freud* (Vol. 11, pp. 59–138). London: Hogarth Press.

Freud, S. (1910b). A special type of object choice made by men. In J. Strachey (Ed. and Trans.), *The standard edition of the complete psychological works of Sigmund Freud* (Vol. 11, pp. 163–175). London: Hogarth Press.

Freud, S. (1911). Psycho-analytic notes on an autobiographical account of a case of paranoia (dementia paranoides). In J. Strachey (Ed. and Trans.), *The standard edition of the complete psychological works of Sigmund Freud* (Vol. 12, pp. 1–82). London: Hogarth Press.

Freud, S. (1914). The Moses of Michelangelo. In J. Strachey (Ed. and Trans.), *The standard edition of the complete psychological works of Sigmund Freud* (Vol. 13 pp. 210–241). London: Hogarth Press.

Freud, S. (1925). Some psychical consequences of the anatomical distinction between the sexes. In J. Strachey (Ed. and Trans.), *The standard edition of the complete psychological works of Sigmund Freud* (Vol. 19, pp. 241–258). London: Hogarth Press.

Freud, S. (1928). Dostoevsky and parricide. In J. Strachey (Ed. and Trans.), *The standard edition of the complete psychological works of Sigmund Freud* (Vol. 28, pp. 175–198). London: Hogarth Press.

Klein, M. (1945). The Oedipus complex in light of early anxieties. In *The Writings of Melanie Klein* (Vol. I, pp. 370–419). New York: Free Press.

Oliver, G. (1849/2016). *Book of the Lodge*. New Orleans, LA: Cornerstone Books.

Rather, L. (2008). Reuniting the psychic couple in analytic training and practice: Theoretical reflections. *Psychoanalytic Psychology*, Volume 25 (1), 99–109.

Rather, L. (2014). Salvation through love: Reflections on Wagner's *The Flying Dutchman*. *Leitmotiv: The Wagner Quarterly*, Volume 28 (105), 6–9, 22–23.

Thomson, K. (1977). *The Masonic Thread in Mozart*. London: Lawrence and Wishart.

4   Lucia di Lammermoor

An Intersection on the Oral and Aural Roads

Julie Jaffee Nagel

'Twas my hope that death would hide me from a doom of shame and anguish. Comfort is denied me. In despair I must languish. None will counsel me, none will aid me. Heaven and earth have both betrayed me.

(*Lucia in the Sextet, Lucia di Lammermoor by Donizetti, 1898*)

Euripides literary insights (in Medea) point the way to clinical hypotheses that may guide our thinking in situations in which unbearable shame, with no apparent possibility of external or internal resolution or repair drives a hardened vengefulness.

(*Lansky, 2005, p. 462*)

Prelude

When analyzing Donizetti's opera, *Lucia di Lammermoor*, I synthesize musical and psychoanalytic concepts by examining the nonverbal qualities of *music itself*, which have the potential to evoke meaningful emotional experiences for the listener. My leitmotiv maintains that many formal concepts of music (i.e., rhythm, tonality, melody, harmony, consonance, dissonance) and psychoanalytic concepts (i.e., conflict, dissonance, resolution, ambiguity) can be used as psychoanalytic "data" and mutually inform each other. The blending of musical and psychoanalytic knowledge provides an elegant schema for understanding complex nonverbal pathways to emotion.

Freud balked at the suggestion that he appreciated music, claiming he was tone deaf. He famously labeled dreams the "royal (oral) road to a knowledge of the unconscious activities of the mind" (1900, p. 608). While musical innovations and psychoanalysis germinated in the same creative socio-cultural soil, in Fin de Siecle Vienna, they subsequently diverged on a split of **oral** and **aural** roads (my term) to the unconscious.

In 1914, Freud made his famous statement about music:

with music, I am almost incapable of obtaining any pleasure.

(*1914, S. E., Vol. XIII, p. 211*)

When thinking about Freud's disclaimer about music, I suggest his responses, including his "displeasure" (an affect) about music were stimulated, in part,

DOI: 10.4324/9781032271408-4

unconsciously – by the structural and formal properties of music, which resonated emotionally with his psychoanalytic sensitivities. Barale and Minazzi's (2008) important examination of Freud's attitude about music suggests that Freud's alternative route to the unconscious and his detour from music was based on more than his conscious disclaimers. I agree.

Yet at the same time that Freud discounted his acoustic sensibilities, he was reading "The Relationships Between Sounds" in *Grundtatsachen* (1883) by Theodore Lipps (1851–1914), a respected German philosopher. Freud was an admirer of Lipps and admitted "I found the substance of my insights stated quite clearly in Lipps, perhaps rather more so than I would like" (Masson, 1985, p. 325). Lipps made connections between psychic functioning, empathy, and particularly sound as the underpinning of psychic life

A major divergence between Freud and Lipps regarding music is embedded in Lipps' idea that music was a-semantic, a-rational, and had the "capacity to speak directly to the human mind, to inspire affect in it, and to produce potent unifications prior to and beyond any referential language" (Barale and Minazzi, 2008, p. 944). For Lipps, the aesthetic of music was a central feature of psychic life; in fact, music ultimately gave rise to verbal and visual representations. For Freud, working to develop a scientific theory of mental functioning, such thinking was not consonant, even though it apparently resonated with him.

Yet music was believed to be mystical and a-rational and, as German philosopher Theodore Lipps proposed (1883), it tapped into mental *pre*-representations without verbal or visual content. Lipps' theory of psychoanalytic functioning, which included music's capacity to produce powerful emotion, could not accommodate Freud's scientific model of the mind, which relied on uncovering the repressed to make it accessible to verbal and visual representations.

Clearly, to Freud, music was a-scientific, and so there remained a divergence and a split between music and mind on Freud's oral road to the unconscious. Thus Freud's theoretical and clinical path embraced language that could verbally represent "something," rather than music as a language of emotions that conveyed an aesthetic and an affect outside the realm of speech, one that perhaps gave rise to verbal representation. Freud's genius traveled a royal **oral** road to the unconscious. My comments on this "split" – or divergence on two roads – between oral and aural roads, represent both the words and music of *Lucia di Lammermoor*. Future discussions could explore the binary nature of this split or division and examine when the roads cross, are parallel, and if, when, and how they are separate.

A Bridge Between the Aural/Oral Roads

Despite Freud's disclaimers about music and without his benediction, the auditory sphere has long provided fascination to others, including myself, interested in the aesthetics of reception, affect, sound, and nonverbal representation in psychic life (Barale and Minazzi, 2008; Piers & Singer, 1953; Reik, 1953; Kohut, 1957; Ehrenzweig, 1953, 1975; Abrams, 1993; Cheshire, 1996; Noy, 1993, 2009; Lombardi, 2008; Langer, 1942; Feder, 1993a, 1993b; Nagel, 2007, 2008a, 2008b, 2013).

Contemporary psychoanalytic commentary by Noy (2009) and Lombardi (2008) suggests that dichotomies of mental life are not discrete and hierarchical, but rather exist in oscillation; they are dynamic, and both simultaneously contribute to the regulation of contrasting emotions. Ehrenzweig (1953) implies that words are necessary to communicate on a secondary process level about nonverbal, primary-process aspects of music, but – and perhaps most important – his observations also lead to a more inclusive suggestion that both oral *and* aural roads create sonic pathways in mental life, rendering an either/or explanation reductionistic.

Despite divergences, music and psychoanalytic theory convey a language, with one language expressed aurally while the other is articulated verbally. Both modes of communication adhere to a particular canon, that is, a specific set of rules governing style, grammar, and form. Both adhere to theory. Both transcend any single theory.

Given these complex characteristics and parameters, how might one attempt to bridge music and mind, or mind and music? Foremost in crossing the bridge between music and psychoanalysis is the necessity to avoid reductionistic, formulaic, oppositional, "either/or" dichotomies. Embracing an attitude of "also/and" enriches our thinking while simultaneously acknowledging limitations and avoiding exaggerated claims about either music or psychoanalysis, aural or oral. The bridge that spans music, emotion, and mental processes is built upon thoughtful, good enough evidence about how one arrives at conclusions, interpretations, and complex understandings. I attempt to illustrate a good-enough bridge between music and psychoanalysis and unite them in my aural (non-verbal) and oral (verbal) examination of Lucia di Lammermoor.

Lucia di Lammermoor

In the opera, Lucia murders her bridegroom in their wedding chamber on the night of their marriage. She succumbs to madness and dies of a broken heart. Emotionally depleted of internal and external resources, she has been betrayed and coerced (one could say seduced) by her brother, Enrico, into marrying Arturo, a nobleman, who, in exchange for Lucia, will secure her brother's financial and political fortunes in Ravenswood.

ENRICO: The nuptial hour approaches
LUCIA: Ah! No, 'tis the hour of my doom approaches
ENRICO: Spare me thy vain reproaches.
     Listen to what I tell thee:
     Since William lives no more
     Our party is fallen
     Upon the throne of Scotland now will reign the hated Mary
     In this sad hour none can from ruin save me but Arturo
LUCIA: And I am the victim?
ENRICO: Yes, Thou must save me

(Schirmer, 1898, pp. 73–75)

This union will consummate Enrico's vengeance toward his enemy, Edgardo, who is Lucia's forbidden lover. Meanwhile, Edgardo has sworn revenge against Enrico for killing his father and usurping his estate. Murder, madness, and suicide follow Lucia's arranged marriage. This drama, revised by librettist, Salvatore Cammarano from a real life story in Sir Walter Scott's 1819 novel, "The Bride of Lammermoor" (based on a real event that took place in Scotland in 1669), is compelling and gripping. Donizetti's musical treatment of this narrative stimulates the listener's mental processes and illustrates psychoanalytic concepts. An analysis of psychoanalytic ideas and Donizetti's music as it pertains to Lucia's breakdown serves as quasi-clinical material.

Lucia's Shame as Motive for Revenge

The dynamics that underlie self-regulation and self-esteem are pertinent for all of the characters in *Lucia di Lammermoor* (Lansky and Morrison, 1997; Lansky, 1992, 2005; Morrison, 1989; Lewis, 1971). Lucia's early traumatic experiences of her domineering mother contributed to her feelings of narcissistic humiliation, hatred, and rage. Her choice of a forbidden lover, not approved by her status conscious father, unconsciously fueled her real or perceived need for punishment. Shame and its vicissitudes will be the primary focus of my exploration of Lucia's unconscious motivations that led to tragedy, as an admixture of shame and guilt were ever present in her mental life.

When unbearable psychological forces coalesce, one can feel trapped without any possibility of escape. In such instances, the affect of shame can boil over into action without thought of consequences to self or other. Lucia's profound humiliation, hopelessness, increasing detachment from internal or external constraints, and dashed hopes for reunion with Edgardo culminated in her act of violence. Lucia's fantasized reunion with Edgardo that is heard in the music in her Mad Scene suggests unconscious fantasies about destruction of her mother and union with her father.

Lucia's downward spiral and psychic disorganization precede the rise of the curtain. Devalued (offstage) in Scott's novel by her mother, and betrayed in the opera by her brother (perhaps also suggestive of incestuous desire which is not overtly developed), by her trusted confidant/cleric, Raimondo, as well as abandoned geographically and emotionally by her lover, Edgardo (who left for France and who was quick to doubt her faithfulness), Lucia acted. Motivated by conflicted longings for union and destruction, guilt and shame, by despair and rage, by her evil introjects, and by manipulative interpersonal relationships, her adaptive intrapsychic resources became depleted. In Donizetti's musical portrayal through 19th-century musical "language," that is, bel canto operatic style,[1] it is not difficult to *hear* Lucia's defenses and compromise formations increasingly shattered through high notes, stunning cadenzas, and other bel canto techniques as one "locates the shame behind rage . . . or despair" (Morrison and Stolorow, 1997 in Lansky and Morrison, p. 82).

Lucia's marriage to Arturo ultimately brought her to "irreversible disgrace" (Lansky, 2005, p. 439). Lucia increasingly becomes an emotional orphan as she is the devalued – but, ironically, the highly valued – property of her brother.

ENRICO: In this sad hour none can from ruin save me but Arthur
LUCIA: And I am the victim?
ENRICO: Yes, thou must save me.
LUCIA: Oh, brother!
ENRICO: Come to the nuptials.

(Schirmer, 1898, pp. 74–75)

Emotionally depleted and attempting to undo her forbidden strivings for Edgardo and her brother's guilt-laden seduction to marry the man he has chosen for her, Lucia signed the marriage contract to Arturo, sealing her own punishment.

Murdering her husband, Arturo, immediately after their wedding, allowed Lucia psychically to "solve" her intrapsychic losses, longings, disappointments, intolerable rage, shame, and guilt as she metaphorically became the attacking wild boar, introduced in Act I, and identified with her malevolent mother/ brother. With her selfhood continually under internal and external assault, she fulfilled her fantasy of reunion with Edgardo the only way left to her, through hallucination and death. Consequently, Lucia became both victim and aggressor as she felt under attack from within her mind and without from her demanding and demeaning family. She killed her new husband, Arturo. Her irreversible torment is consummated musically in her Mad Scene, which will be discussed subsequently.

An Intersection Between Psychoanalysis, Music, and Affect

Donizetti's orchestral prelude to *Lucia di Lammermoor* evokes an ominous mood before a word is sung. The opera opens in B flat minor with a soft timpani roll evoking distant thunder. This is followed by a solemn phrase for horns which evolves into a mournful melody taken by the clarinets and woodwinds; subsequently a dirge rhythm joins, cumulatively predictive of smoldering intrapsychic and musical storms and actions that erupt throughout the Opera, finally exploding in madness, death (Lucia), and suicide (Edgardo). This opening atmosphere of gravity is abruptly shattered as listeners are jolted by three fortissimo (very loud) chords played by the full orchestra which I suggest musically anticipate the deafening orchestral thunderstorm and Lucia's murderous thunderbolt in Act III. Following these chords, the funeral rhythm, now quickened and modulating to the tonality of B flat major (sonically signifying a shift in mood), is played with agitation by the tympani and horns. It is in this restless tonal and rhythmic musical environment that we hear the first words of the libretto. The brief Prelude conveys in sound Lucia's intrapsychic premonition, "the hour of my doom approaches" (Schirmer, 1898, p. 73).

The Fountain and "Il Fantasma"

Shortly following the opening Prelude, we meet Lucia at the fountain after we learn from a hunter that Edgardo saved her from a wild boar as she was walking on a path, ostensibly mourning her mother's death.

NORMANNO: a sword came brightly flashing, and in a moment slain was the monster.

(Schirmer, 1898, p. 12)

Early in the Opera, the manifest image of the wild boar that was killed not only suggests the malignant revenge motives that become palpable and audible within and among all the major characters, but also permits early clues into Lucia's self – other representations and her intrapsychic disequilibrium.

We discover that the fountain is the place where Lucia secretly meets Edgardo, her lover, who is envied and despised by her brother, Enrico.

ENRICO: torments of hate and vengeance . . . I'll die unless I punish him.

(Schirmer, 1898, p. 13)

Edgardo is a forbidden love object for Lucia. In her aria at the fountain, we *hear* Lucia, who has been soul murdered in Ravenswood, identify with the female ghost who inhabits the fountain as she internalizes her earliest parental empathetic failures, particularly those of her malignant mother. Her terror of "il fantasma" in Act I at the fountain (and again in her Mad Scene Act III) first awakens (and then reawakens) her ambivalent attachment and possibly her unconscious fantasy that some aggressive thought or act of hers has killed her mother as she meets her illicit lover. On one level, her premonitions about "il fantasma" hearken to her perceived Oedipal transgression or fantasies; her sense of doom and punishment portend her own death. The celestial harp introduction at the fountain musically underscores Lucia's otherworldly destination. Gazing into the fountain, her narcissistic mirror, Lucia's terror also reflects pre-Oedipal shame and its underlying affects, which include humiliation, hate, and contempt. This is consonant with Morrison's view that shame is "central to narcissistic disorders . . . rage is a response to narcissistic injury" (pp. 7–8, 1989).

In Sir Walter Scott's novel, Lady Ashton, Lucia's mother, has the reputation of being diabolical, hateful, ambitious, and domineering. She despised her husband and hated Edgardo's ancestors whom she believed more prestigious than her own. She was disdainful of her daughter whom she resented for not wanting to marry the man she chose for her. In Donizetti's and Cammarano's collaboration, Lady Ashton was "killed off" before the opening of the Opera although her presence is clearly felt throughout. While Fisher (2003) surmises that Lady Ashton's absence in the libretto and score reflects the Italian tradition of portraying only "loving Mommas," eliminating her from the libretto does not erase intrapsychic and intergenerational malevolence, which casts a wide shadow upon her offspring. Guilt and shame are timeless in the unconscious and deepen our understanding of Lucia's dynamics. Painful affects and human dilemmas do not vanish beneath the beauty of bel canto operatic style; in fact, they are intensified by these musical techniques. It is clear that Lady and Lord Ashton are intrapsychically as alive as the ghost that inhabits the fountain and the mental life and death of their daughter. Lucia sings about both her mother and her own reflection in the fountain in Act I:

LUCIA: Tis the fountain,
      I tremble whenever I behold it.
      Know'st thou the legend?
      Upon this spot, they say so (*musical instructions: crescendo di forzando*)
      That a Ravenswood slew the maid that lov'd him, (*musical instructions: a tempo*)
      In jealous madness
      The hapless maiden rests in its waters,
      Its tide clos'd over her for ever
      Her wraith once stood before me (*musical instructions: lento over this phrase, ascending vocal line with crescendo*).

(Schirmer, 1898, pp. 31–32)

Lucia's angst is heard *in the music* at the fountain. I bring attention to the end of the first stanza of her aria, "Regnava nel silenzio" (Everything was silent. . .). Lucia's fear is intensified where the word "ecco" ("here") is sung twice which changes the rhythm to emphasize that "here" ("ecco") is where the ghost ("il fantasma") appeared to her. At this place in the *music,* there is a change in tempo from larghetto (slow) to presto (very fast) which, according to bel canto style, suggests intensification of Lucia's affect. Immediately following, when she sings "L'ombra mostrarsi" ("the ghost shows itself") the first syllable is on the *lowest* note of the passage (C natural) and accents are placed above each note in the word "mostrarsi," musically emphasizing/accenting the fright with which Lucia experiences her vision (see Ashbrook, 1982 for a detailed discussion of this passage).

Lucia's aria at the fountain furthers the musical, psychological, and dramatic forces that converge and convey the intrapsychic, interpersonal, and intergenerational tragedy that has begun to unravel in Ravenswood.

Irony and Paradox

Several paradoxes, particularly pertinent to shame dynamics, are present and integral in this Opera from the rise of the curtain. One is the contrast between the beauty of the music with the horrific manifest and latent content and action of the story. This "paradox" can be explained, in part, by the fact that the 19th-century operatic stylistic musical techniques available to Donizetti emphasized beautiful melody, acceleration of tempi, and dazzling vocal displays to convey heightened emotion. Bel canto style, familiar to audiences, conveyed contrasting dynamics and affects.

Act I immediately introduces musical and psychological irony. Lucia responded to Edgardo's request to see her by asking him to meet her at the ominous fountain, her narcissistic mirror, and the wellspring of her terror. Musically, the solo harp's celestial introduction of Lucia at the fountain provides aural commentary about its symbolic importance. In addition to its intrapsychic and dramatic significance, this place was a location likely to be discovered by her suspicious brother. Why, unconsciously, does Lucia invite love, terror, and discovery in this spot? During their meeting, Edgardo offers at first to try to make peace with his avenged enemy, Enrico,

EDGARDO: Ere my departure, I'll seek thy brother. There shall be peace between us, strife be forgotten, in pledge of lasting friendship, I then will ask him for thy hand.

(Schirmer, 1898, p. 44)

Lucia urges Edgardo to keep their relationship secret.

LUCIA: Ah, no, in silence let our love yet be hidden.

(Schirmer, 1898, p. 44)

His response

EDGARDO: He slew my father,
    Will but my life-blood suffice him
    By whose craft I am ruined?
    Eternal hatred he hath sworn me
    Oh vengeance!

(Schirmer, 1898, p. 45)

may move the story along but casts an ominous pall on both his *and* Lucia's motives, which include hardened hatred and envy toward Enrico, who also despises and envies Edgardo. This scene is manifestly problematic and musically interesting. Beneath forbidden love lurks the notion that both Lucia and Edgardo resolve to revenge unfinished, unforgiven business, an unconscious motive for their union. In Act II, why was Lucia so ready to believe Enrico's and Raimondo's lies about Edgardo's unfaithfulness? Why was Edgardo so quick to rage toward Lucia, who, ashen and ashamed, admitted to signing the marriage contract? Further, after the wedding, Enrico ostensibly had achieved his goals yet he left the reception for Edgardo's Castle in Ravenswood, unable to release his loathing:

ENRICO: I to death defy thee . . . Destruction, destruction I have sworn to thee. Come, to the combat. None now shall take vengeance on thee, none but myself who have doom'd thee!

(Schirmer, 1898, pp. 165–166)

A person who is envied also is hated for what is admirable about him. Edgardo and Enrico hate each other and also covet what the other has, that is, Lucia and Ravenswood, suggestive of their unfinished Oedipal business and narcissistic rage. While manifestly trying to escape her psychic heritage, Lucia bows to her brother and the memory of her dead mother in becoming Arturo's bride. At first glance, she appears to become both a victim and disempowered woman, tangled in a web of complex jealous and hateful rivalries. It is not ironic, however, that Lucia is a powerful player motivated by both wishes for restitution and her own hate.

An irony of Lucia's ill-fated relationship with Edgardo is heard in the music. Edgardo's suicide aria in Act III is introduced in *D major*, the concluding tonality of the opera and the parallel major of Lucia's fountain aria, "Regnava nel silenzio," which turns to the key of D minor following its D major recitative and introductory harp prelude. The point emphasized here is that musically their "union" is never consummated in the same tonality. These musical elements, and many others not detailed here, illustrate how Donizetti was sensitive to the internal lives of his characters whom he represented in sound. One does not need to be psychoanalytically or musically sophisticated to experience the potent effect of these musical techniques.

Omnipotence: Another Perspective on Lucia's "Helplessness"

On one level, Lucia's narcissistic vulnerabilities erupt in violence as a Romantic "solution" for humiliating victimization, narcissistic rage, and forbidden fantasies. Yet murdering her bridegroom, Arturo, also provided Lucia an illusion of omnipotence and power over the dominance of manipulating and malignant men, identification with them, and victory over the most important woman in her life, her mother. Her *action* was the antithesis of victimhood and helplessness. Lucia phallically penetrated her bridegroom with a sword (as did the "Ravenswood man who slew a maid"). This chilling climax that leads to the famous Mad Scene consummates Lucia's "triumph" and powerfully unites musical and psychoanalytic concepts. Metaphorically, becoming the "wild boar" from whom she was saved by Edgardo in Act I, Lucia no longer needs rescue by her ego or reliable relationships. With the hindsight of Act III, the "wild boar" emerges as Lucia's counterpoint to her victimization as a female and its companion, her terror, that was displaced onto the slain animal and "il fantasma." The "wild boar" that brings the lovers together in Act I also heralds their undoing, foretelling Lucia's total destruction of Ravenswood, including herself.

Lucia's affects and actions raise complex questions about her intrapsychic motivations and affects, which, like Enrico and Edgardo, also include jealousy, envy, and diminishment, which lie at the wellspring of her inescapable shame, guilt, and her self-destructiveness. In this respect, Lucia parallels the male characters' inability to forgive past hurts and wrongdoings. Lucia's equilibrium is psychically dismantled as her resolution/solution only can be expressed through becoming "mad" enough to resort to murder, an escalation of affect to "instigation" (see Lansky, 2005). Lucia must kill Arturo, because a marriage to him "would be tantamount to forgiveness and complicity with the world of her betrayers" (Lansky, 2005, p. 461). Sonically, Lucia, Enrico, and Edgardo's intrapsychic and interpersonal dilemmas crescendo and accelerando to vengefulness dramatically, emotionally, and musically from the opening tympani in Act I through every cadenza, high note, tempo change, and aria. Murder, for Lucia di Lammermoor, represents psychic dissolution *and* fantasized reunion with loved and hated objects. The heartbreak is that ultimately there are no winners.

Shortly after retiring to the bridal chamber, Lucia reenters the reception hall disoriented and blood stained. She has stabbed Arturo. Her entrance is heralded by a flute (or glass harmonica in the autographed score, an invention of Benjamin Franklin), evoking an eerie and otherworldly effect. It is in the Mad Scene that the flute – *music alone without words* – plays four measures not long after she enters the hall. Shortly thereafter, the flute recalls the opening of her love duet with Edgardo, "Verrano a te" from Act I, which stimulates Lucia's hallucinations of marrying Edgardo, inviting him to come to the fountain to "let us rest there together" (Schirmer, 1898, p. 191). In this chilling scene, the flute repeatedly serves as Lucia's wordless disoriented self/other-self, simultaneously creating accompaniment, establishing mood, and evoking reminiscence. The flute's melody (or glass harmonica) wordlessly precedes Lucia's mournful confusion:

LUCIA: Oh Edgardo, why dids't thou leave me?

(Schirmer, 1898, p. 190)

what shudder do I feel through my veins . . . My heart is trembling, my senses fail . . . come to the fountain, there let us rest together.

(Schirmer, 1898, p. 191)

Following this passage and according to the tradition of bel canto style that conveys heightened emotion, the tempo quickens from allegretto (fast) to allegro vivace (very fast), musically and emotionally conveying increased agitation. It is in this place in the score that Lucia begins to remember – she remembers the ghost "standing between us"; she remembers the ghost that "divides us." Musically, she remembers with vocal octave leaps and short, desperate, clipped phrases.

Above the orchestral tremolo, her growing agitation and disorientation accelerando until she becomes terrified and sings/utters "il fantasma, il fantasma." Donizetti marks this horrifying passage "forte" (loud). Harmonies become increasingly unstable as though both Lucia and tonality are breaking down. The flute's recollection of her love duet has unraveled her. This harmonically unsettled section aurally conveys desperate and pitiful affect as we *hear* the momentum of the intrapsychic torment that has transcended Lucia's mental processes. The music corroborates what the words articulate: the fountain's water has turned into blood; Lucia's impulses have turned into action; Lucia has become blood-stained with murder. She *must* go mad and die; her intrapsychic anguish has been enacted. In the final moments of her collapse and vocal cadenza, Lucia only can sing a reminiscence of the melody of her love song (from Act I) on *wordless* syllables with the flute (or glass harmonica).

Coda: Beyond the Aural Road

Music, like speech, is a form of communication. Although beautiful arias and vocal fireworks in *Lucia di Lammermoor* are most readily apparent to the listener, which can be likened to manifest – or obvious – content, the music *non-verbally* evokes affect and latent – beneath the surface – material that is both psycho-analytic and musical. I suggest music, in general, and specifically here the music examples discussed in Lucia di Lammermoor, activate unconscious processes and latent meanings, intensifying the impact of the libretto (words). According to Lansky (personal communication), there is "something inherently different about music – different from other means of artistic expression that represent something." Citing the philosopher Arthur Schopenhauer, Lansky proposes that music versus literature and painting (which are representational) is a "direct conveyance of the will itself," which he compares to Freud's unconscious wish. Lansky's statement is compatible with Lipps writings about pre-representational aspects of music, affect, and mental functioning with implications about Freud's scientific and affective detour from music. I am in agreement with Lansky, that is, "music is a direct emissary of that force, not a representation of it" (Lansky, 2007, personal communication) and Feder (2004 personal communication, unpublished) that music is a "simulacrum of mental life." The music of *Lucia di Lammermoor* "works" because it has the capacity to bring us in touch with the complexities of the melodies in our own mental lives. Donizetti's music deepens the artistic and affective impact of Lucia's shame and guilt. Should my verbal attempt to convey this idea fall short, Donizetti's music will not.

Note

1 Bel canto literally means beautiful singing and typically refers to the operatic style of vocal embellishments utilized by the Italian composers, notably Rossini, Bellini, and Donizetti. Melodic lines are floridly embellished with vocal virtuosity including trills, high notes, and cadenza-like scale passages. As such, this compositional technique conveyed heightened emotion and was anticipated by music lovers.

References

Abrams, D. M. (1993). Freud and Max Graf: On the Psychoanalysis of Music, in S. Feder, R. L. Karmel, and G. H. Pollock (eds), *Psychoanalytic Explorations in Music* (Second Edition). Madison, CT: International Universities Press, pp. 279–307.

Ashbrook, W. (1982). *Donizetti and His Operas*. Cambridge: Cambridge University Press.

Barale, F. and Minazzi, V. (2008). Off the Beaten Track: Freud, Sound and Music. Statement of a Problem and Some Historico-critical Notes, *International Journal of Psychoanalysis*, 89 (5): 937–957.

Cheshire, N. M. (1996). The Empire of the Ear: Freud's Problem with Music, *International Journal of Psycho-Analysis*, 77: 1127–1168.

Donizetti, G. (1898, renewed 1926). *Lucia di Lammermoor*, Opera Score Editions. New York: G. Schirmer.

Ehrenzweig, A. (1953). *The Psychoanalysis of Artistic Vision and Hearing*. New York: George Braziller.

Ehrenzweig, A. (1975). *The Psychoanalysis of Artistic Vision and Hearing* (Third Edition). London: Shelton Press.

Feder, S., Karmel, R. L., and Pollock, G. H. (eds). (1993a). "Promissory Notes": Method in Music and Applied Psychoanalysis, in S. Feder, R. L. Karmel, and G. H. Pollock (eds), *Psychoanalytic Explorations in Music*. Madison, CT: International Universities Press, pp. 3–19.

Feder, S., Karmel, R. L., and Pollock, G. H. (eds) (1993b). *Psychoanalytic Explorations in Music* (Second Series). Madison, CT: International Universities Press.

Fisher, B. C. (2003). *Donizetti's Lucia di Lammermoor: Opera Classics Library*. Coral Gables, FL: Opera Journeys Publishing.

Freud, S. (1900). *The Interpretation of Dreams*, S.E. IV/V (The Standard Edition of the Complete Psychological Works (SE); trans. from the German under the General Editorship of James Strachey, in collaboration with Anna Freud, assisted by Alix Strachey and Alan Tyson). London: The Hogarth Press.

Freud, S. (1914) *Moses of Michelangelo*, S.E. XIII: 211–236. (The Standard Edition of the Complete Psychological Works (SE); trans. from the German under the General Editorship of James Strachey, in collaboration with Anna Freud, assisted by Alix Strachey and Alan Tyson). London: The Hogarth Press.

Kohut, H. (1957). Observations on the Psychological Functions of Music, *Journal of the American Psychoanalytic Association*, 5 (3): 398–407.

Langer, S. K. (1942, 1957). *Philosophy in a New Key: A Study in the Symbolism of Reason, Rite, and Art*. Cambridge, MA: Harvard University Press.

Lansky, M. (1992). *Fathers Who Fail: Shame and Psychopathology in the Family System*. Hillsdale, NJ: Analytic Press.

Lansky, M. (2005). The Impossibility of Forgiveness: Shame Fantasies as Instigators of Vengefulness in Euripides' Medea, *Journal of the American Psychoanalytic Association*, 53: 438–464.

Lansky, M. and Morrison, A. P. (1997) The Legacy of Freud's Writings on Shame, in M.R. Lansky and A. P. Morrison (eds.), *The Widening Scope of Shame*. Hillsdale, NJ: Analytic Press.

Lewis, H. B. (1971). *Shame and Guilt in Neurosis*. New York: International Universities Press.

Lipps, T. (1883). *Grundtatsachen des Seelenlebens*. Bonn: Cohen.

Lombardi, R. (2008). Time, Music, and Reverie, *Journal of the American Psychoanalytic Association*, 56 (4): 1191–1211.

Masson, J. M. (ed. and trans.) (1985). *The Complete Letters of Sigmund Freud to Wilhelm Fliess (1887–1904)*. Cambridge, MA: Harvard University Press.

Morrison, A. (1989). *Shame: The Underside of Narcissism*. Hillsdale, NJ: The Analytic Press.

Morrison, A. P. and Stolorow, R. D. (1997). Shame, Narcissism, and Intersubjectivity, in M. R. Lansky and A. P. Morrison (eds), *The Widening Scope of Shame*. Hillsdale, NJ: The Analytic Press, pp. 63–87.

Nagel, J. J. (2007). Melodies of the Mind: Mozart in 1778, *American Imago, (Aural Road Edition)*, 64 (1): 23–36.

Nagel, J. J. (2008a) Psychoanalytic Perspectives on Music: An Intersection on the Oral and Aural Road, *The Psychoanalytic Quarterly*, 77 (2): 507–530.

Nagel, J. J. (2008b) Psychoanalytic and Musical Perspectives on Shame in Donizetti's *Lucia di Lammermoor*, *Journal of the American Psychoanalytic Association*, 56 (2): 551–563.

Nagel, J. J. (2013). *Melodies of the Mind*. East Sussex: Routledge Press.

Noy, P. (1993). How Music Conveys Emotion, in S. Feder, R. Karmel, and G. Pollock (eds), *Psychoanalytic Explorations of Music*. Madison, CT: International Universities Press, pp. 125–149.

Noy, P. (2009). *Art and Emotion (Unpublished Manuscript – personal communication)*.

Piers, G. and Singer, M. B. (1953). *Shame and Guilt*. New York: W. W. Norton and Co.

Reik, T. (1953). *The Haunting Melody: Psychoanalytic Experiences of Music*. Madison, CT: International Universities Press, pp. 63–81.

Schirmer, G. (1898). *Opera Score Editions. Gaetano Donizetti: Lucia di Lammermoor Copyright 1898 and Renewed 1929*. New York: G. Schirmer.

Scott, W. (1819). *The Bride of Lammermoor*. London: Everyman's Library (1906).

5 Transformation Through the Other

Senta and *The Flying Dutchman*

L. Eileen Keller

The iconic tale of the Flying Dutchman's arrogance and consequent cursed existence ends in redemption through transformation of the two main protagonists, the Dutchman and Senta. The Dutchman was condemned to forever sail the seas, losing all chance of human warmth and comfort. As is common in mythology, the protagonist's punishment for his grandiose claim – in the Dutchman's case, to rule the sea – is tempered by mercy. Every seven years, he has a chance to win the love of a true and faithful woman and be released from his travail. Of course, if she fails to be true, she dies, and The Dutchman returns to the seas.

In this essay, I focus on Senta, the romantic heroine who is transformed through her relationship with the painting of the Dutchman during the overture, as staged by the San Francisco Opera in 2013, long before she takes the stage in Act II. I find Senta's character to be much more than just the "faithful woman," and I explore her as a fuller and more complex person in this essay. After describing Wagner's creation of this opera, and summarizing the plot, I explore Senta's development, her position as a motherless child, and the realities of her situation as a girl of her time, and differentiate her sacrifice from masochism by articulating the concept of surrender (Ghent, 1990). Finally, I address the Dutchman's achievement of the developmental milestone of *care for the other*. In this opera, each hero transforms the other.

The Flying Dutchman

Wagner considered this opera to be his step up from "a mere concocter of opera texts" (Wagner, 2008/1851). In his 1851 essay, "A Communication to My Friends," Wagner claimed that the Dutchman represented a new start for him: "From here begins my career as poet." Indeed, to this day the opera is the earliest of Wagner's works to be performed at the Bayreuth Festival and, at least for that theater, marks the start of the mature Wagner canon. He based the story loosely on a combination of folktales, myth, and a story by Heinrich Heine, a satire called "The Memoirs of Mister von Schnabelewopski," published in *Der Salon* in 1834. In Heine's tale, the narrator watches a performance of a fictitious stage play on the theme of the sea captain cursed to sail forever for blasphemy. Heine introduces the character as a sort of nautical Wandering Jew,

DOI: 10.4324/9781032271408-5

and also added the device taken up so vigorously by Wagner in this opera: the Dutchman can only be redeemed by the love of a faithful woman. In Heine's version, this is presented as a means for ironic humor; however, Wagner took this theme literally, and in his version, the woman is faithful unto death.

In Act I, Senta's father, Captain Daland, is forced by a storm to shelter seven miles from home (note Wagner's mirroring of the Dutchman's seven-year reprieve). Daland sees another ship appear. The ghostly ship carries the Dutchman, coming once again to search for a faithful woman. The Dutchman hears that Daland has an unmarried daughter named Senta, and he asks for her hand in marriage, offering a chest of treasure as a gift. Tempted by the gold, Daland agrees to the marriage. The kindly south wind blows and both vessels set sail for Daland's home.

Act II begins with Senta, in a room of women spinning and working at other household tasks, dreamily ignoring the pleas of Dame Mary, the housekeeper, to stop mooning over a portrait and get to work on spinning. Then she begins singing the ballad of the Flying Dutchman. Though her local suitor, Erik, tries to caution her, Senta becomes convinced that she will be the faithful woman sought by the Dutchman. Daland enters the room with the Dutchman and, in his avaricious way, introduces Senta to her betrothed, oblivious to the starstruck silence of both Senta and the Dutchman. They fall in love and Senta promises herself to the Dutchman.

In Act III, that evening the local girls bring Daland's men food and drink. They invite the crew of the strange vessel to join in their merrymaking, but in vain, as the ghostly crew cannot respond. Senta arrives, followed by Erik, who reproaches her for deserting him, as she had once loved him. When the Dutchman, who has been listening, hears these words, he is overwhelmed with despair, as he thinks he is now again lost and condemned to continue his hopeless sailing for another seven years. The Dutchman summons his men, tells Senta of the curse, and to the consternation of Daland and his crew, declares that he is the "Flying Dutchman." As *The Dutchman* sets sail, Senta throws herself into the sea, claiming that she will be faithful to him unto death. This is his salvation. The spectral ship disappears, and Senta and the Dutchman are seen ascending to heaven.

Senta as Tragic Hero

Wagner's *The Flying Dutchman* carries complex elements of our human experience, including passion, jealousy, avarice, love, and longing. In the San Francisco Opera's 2013 production, Senta's dream to rescue the Dutchman takes center stage. During the overture, we see her gazing into the portrait of the Dutchman, and we feel her dreamy rapture through the music. As I studied the libretto, I began thinking about the teenage girls who put posters of male icons on their walls, gazing at them with the same dreamy rapture that Senta shows. Psychoanalysts might interpret these deeply felt though impossible loves as a developmental passage, a way that young girls can safely, in fantasy, explore their own emerging sexuality and passions. The desired and loved idol can safely contain a girl's love for her father and her growing interest in boys without plunging her too quickly into the real world of developing boys. The idealized male of the painting is a safe repository for her romantic fantasies.

In Senta's recognition of her wish to save the Dutchman, we can see a wisp of her illusion that she is "the special one." She will be the woman who is perfect for him, better than all the other women who have failed him and died. Her triumph, as she imagines herself the "one" to save the Flying Dutchman, hints to a psychoanalyst that Oedipal wishes are surging. The daughter's identification with her mother and her wish to outdo her mother are both contained in Senta's triumphant declaration.

What partially drives Senta's own grandiose declaration is the reality of her position as a motherless girl, tied to hearth and home with no real scope for her romantic, passionate longings. Her mother figure, Dame Mary, has no patience for supporting any dreams of the richer, fuller life that Senta might have. Dame Mary's wish is for Senta's conformity to the drudgery of housework, while Senta longs for something more, a reason for her own existence. We can all identify with Senta's search for true meaning in her life. This is one of the ways Wagner brings us into sympathy with her.

Each of these elements contributes to Senta's unwavering commitment to save the Flying Dutchman, but I propose there is something more – something that grows beyond a transitional developmental stage into a genuine capacity to submerge her own subjectivity into the other's desperate need. We learn early on that Senta, to the dismay of her mother figure, the housekeeper, languishes in sorrow and pain as she gazes on the Dutchman's portrait, thinking of his agony, doomed to sail forever unless the curse is lifted. The workaday world encircles her, but she is absentminded and dwells in another world, dreaming of the tragic fate of the Dutchman. She begins to sing of the Dutchman, and in a beautiful, lyrical ballad, "A Ship the Restless Ocean Sweeps," enchants her audience with his story as she sings the tragic tale. Her audience is deeply moved, as is she. All bemoan the fate of the Dutchman, and Senta is struck with inspiration: *She will be the one to rescue him!* Here we see Senta transported by the glorious idea of being the one true woman who can save the Dutchman from eternal pain.

> I would be she, who by her love will save thee!
> Oh may the angel hither guide thee!
> Through me may newfound joy betide thee!
>
> *(Wagner, 1925, pp. 107–108)*

We understand that she is enchanting herself as well as us. Some have interpreted Senta as mad; to our modern sensibilities, the sacrifice of one's life to another implies a kind of failure of selfhood. Others might take for granted the sacrifice of a woman to a man and view Senta as the eternal woman; a principle, rather than a person. I argue for a fuller understanding of Senta, one that recognizes her selfhood – with all of her complexities, developmental pressures, losses – and what she makes of herself in the course of the opera, including finding within herself the human capacity to transcend the narrow interest of the self at times of great crisis or danger.

Senta's passionate desire to save the Dutchman grows as she meets him in reality and they fall in love. First, we see the realization of Senta's dream of romantic love when her father brings them together, glibly and coaxingly introducing them as they gaze at each other struck to silence. He finally notices their enthrallment with each other and leaves them. They sing together in a beautiful romantic duet, the Dutchman, singing of Senta: "dare such as I to name of love the yearning?" (Wagner, 1925, p. 148) and she of him: "he tells me all his mingled hope and fear" (Wagner, 1925, p. 150) reminding me of Shakespeare's (1597/1997b) Romeo speaking of Juliet:

> O. she doth teach the torches to burn bright.
> It seems she hangs upon the cheek of night
> As a rich jewel in an Ethiope's ear.
>
> *(Romeo and Juliet, I:V)*

The first hint of Wagner's redemption theme arrives in this duet as the Dutchman cautions Senta about her terrible fate should she love him. Here we see the Dutchman thinking of Senta,

> realizing the danger to her, perhaps for the first time in all his years of ruthlessly taking women to try to save himself. Senta brushes the danger aside and claims her place as the woman who will save him. Another Shakespeare (1622/1997a) play comes to mind: "She loved me for the dangers I had passed and I loved her that she did pity them."
>
> *(Othello, I:III)*

In his paper "Masochism, Submission, Surrender," psychoanalyst Emmanuel Ghent (1990) describes surrender not as defeat but as a transcendent experience that is with "all one's heart, with one's soul, and with all one's might" (Eigen, quoted in Ghent, 1990, p. 109). For me, Ghent's description captures the ecstatic certainty Senta brings to her betrothal. Ghent seeks in his paper to differentiate the concept of surrender, so foreign to the Western mind, from masochism. While the psychoanalytic literature articulates many subtleties in understanding masochism, the important distinction Ghent makes – and Eigen (1981) also discusses – is the quality of joy. "It is an all out, nothing held back, movement of the self-and-other feeling . . . a floating freely in a *joyous shock of difference* (Eigen, 1981, p. 416).

Wagner's duet between Senta and the Dutchman captures this sense of transcendent joy! For Senta, it's an experience of complete fulfillment: surrendering herself to the loss of her earthly life in service of releasing the Dutchman from his curse. Not just the release but also the *transformation* of the Dutchman, which becomes fully real when he declares his joy and relief that Senta does not have to die, as so many others have before her. Both are transformed through their love and recognition of the other. Of course, other issues are present, too:

Senta's avaricious father, who plans to sell her to the highest bidder, and her local suitor, who would tie her to the life of drudgery we witness in the women of the household. We can understand her attraction to the mysterious stranger, and we could blame it all on young recklessness and romanticizing.

Wagner takes the story beyond these more ordinary, recognizable themes. In giving herself to the Dutchman, Senta becomes a heroine – the one woman, through her ultimate sacrifice, who can save him from his sad, despairing wandering and the recklessness that brought the curse on his head. I am reminded of another woman in history, Joan of Arc. She began hearing voices early in adolescence that she believed were messages from God telling her to save France, then the underdog in the Hundred Years' War between England and France. Against all odds, Joan of Arc persuaded a court to permit her to defy her father's arranged marriage for her, and she traveled to seek an audience with the failing king. She led a small army against the Anglicans and ousted them from Orleans. Though she was captured, tortured, and executed for witchcraft by the English in 1431, Joan was eventually cleared and then canonized (Harrison, 2014). Again, Joan's sacrifices – her courage and conviction in subjugating and then losing her individual life to the greater good of freeing her people from the yoke of the English – is unfathomable to the modern mind. Her passionate conviction and courage remind me of Senta.

The Flying Dutchman

Madame Marie Bonaparte (1949), in her book on Edgar Allan Poe, gives one interpretation of the Flying Dutchman legend. In this version, the punishment is attributed to the wicked obstinacy of the mariner who insisted on attempting to double the Cape in spite of contrary winds. The impious Dutchman is said to have exclaimed, "I will try, even if I go on trying until the Day of Judgment." Providence took him at his word, and he was forced to go on sailing without respite. His crime of arrogance, denying both the father and the mother, lands him and his crew in the tragic fate of sailing forever, with only the slim chance of redemption every seven years (Loewenstein, 1945).

He sings:

Ha! haughty ocean!
A little while and thou again shalt bear me!
Thy rage subsideth, but endless my despair!

(Wagner, 1925, pp. 30–31)

The Dutchman's words show his lack of regard for or recognition of any other's existence. Wagner continues to make the Dutchman's arrogance and grandiosity clear, and we understand how he landed in such trouble. We learn about the innumerable women who have lost their lives by promising and failing to secure the Dutchman's redemption. He has callously risked their lives and, when they die, only regrets his own fate. It isn't until he sings to Senta that we begin to hear a growing awareness of her and her warm, human life, along with his fear for her and his hopes for himself. "Ye angels, who once forsook me, now strengthen her heart and keep her true!" (Wagner, 1925, pp. 168–169)

Here, the Dutchman develops something beyond arrogance. He began by asking Daland if there was a marriageable daughter available, offering gold with faint hopes of getting what he needed. Now we hear a hint of awareness of Senta as he prays for her heart to strengthen. This theme – the Dutchman's growing recognition of Senta as a separate person rather than a tool of his salvation – continues when, following his fear of her betrayal, he sings of his gladness that she will survive:

> Now hear and learn the fate from which thou wilt be saved!
> Condemned am I to bear a frightful fortune.
> Ten times would death appear a brighter lot!
> A woman's hand alone
> the curse can lighten.
> If she will love me, and till death be true.
> Still to be faithful thou hast vow'd,
> yet has not God thy promise heard: this rescues thee!
> For know, unhappy, what a fate is theirs who break the troth
> which they to me have plighted: Endless damnation is their doom!
> Victims untold have fall'n beneath this curse through me.
> Yet, Senta, thou shalt quite escape! Farewell!
> . . . Oh help her! Let her not be lost!
>
> *(Wagner, 1925, pp. 240–241)*

The Dutchman is now able to feel joy that she will not die, that she is spared the "fate of countless others," and he departs to again hopelessly sail the seas for seven more years.

Concern for the Other

For a psychoanalyst, this awareness of others, a capacity for concern for the other, is a crucial development for children. It cannot be taken for granted but is contingent on the "good enough" environment of the family (Winnicott, 1965). Eigen (1981), exploring the "area of faith" in Winnicott, articulates the developmental leap of the infant in achieving the recognition of the other as a separate and whole person, thus making possible, simultaneously, the recognition of the self. Winnicott describes this development as placing the object outside the area of personal omnipotence. Remember that omnipotence was the destructive force in the Dutchman, causing his downfall and accursed existence.

As a child therapist, helping children heal in the context of their parental relationships, I have witnessed this transformation – the bringing of tea or some kind of pretend food or reparative hugs and kisses to a mother. Research on toddlers shows that offering tea to mommy is a marker for the recognition of her as something more, a person in her own right who can be fed and nurtured by the baby. In this opera, Wagner shows us two different versions of this development. First, the adolescent Senta looks beyond her own dreamy preoccupations with the romantic figure of the Dutchman to behold him in reality with her concern for his plight. Senta's care for him results in her decision to sacrifice herself willingly to save him. For the Dutchman, we see his tired arrogance in Act I, as he desperately seeks to succor himself with salvation without apparent regard for all the girls who have failed him and lost their lives. When he meets Senta and falls in love with her and feels her pity for his hardships, something in him softens, allowing a recognition of her as other, an other whom he does not want punished and lost. In spite of his despairing recognition that he has failed again to find salvation, he feels care for her. He has gained a core quality of being human, the recognition and care for the other, Senta, outside his own narrow, self-centered desire to break the curse.

In my psychoanalytic work, this kind of ordinary recognition of another's humanity and the development of concern is a breathtaking change; it demonstrates the dissolution of the narcissistic, grandiose misuse of others and being heedless of the harm done that marks perverse relationships. Wagner brilliantly captures this movement in the Dutchman. In the midst of his own despair, he is able to feel joy for Senta, who will live. The Dutchman, condemned by his arrogant conviction that he and he alone can master the world, denying all whom he relies on – his sailors, the sea, his own mother and father – enters into relatedness through the birth of love between him and Senta. For the first time, the fate of the other matters to him. Senta, through her passionate, joyful surrender of her physical life to the Dutchman, saves him and his crew from the horrible fate of endlessly wandering the stormy seas.

In our modern culture, the idea of self-sacrifice is deemed masochistic and unhealthy. We can hardly fathom a sacrifice such as Senta's and easily fall into the trap of thinking of her in current terms as a girl who fails to think of her own interest, who doesn't see the danger to herself, who is blinded by passion in her acceptance of the Dutchman. Or, as someone who, in the grip of masochism, in her denial and subjugation of the self, sees suicide as the ultimate murder of the self. We live in an age where the actualization of the self as an individual self is idealized. To us, recognizing the claims of the other is considered masochistic. Since the 1970s, philosophers have explored the widespread effects of this cultural shift (Lasch, 1979).

The Dutchman's original arrogance in claiming super-human abilities has been redirected toward a ruthless search for the woman who will save him, utterly disregarding that woman's personhood. His capacity to be glad that Senta will live signals his growth, hard won over centuries and achieved through transformation in his love for Senta and hers for him. This is the true redemption: that the Flying Dutchman has become human.

How much is our real, essential dependency on others reversed to deny any claims others might have such that Senta's suicide is inevitably seen as a failure to value her own life over that of others and, thus, pathological? Consider the following clinical example. A young financial advisor, a partner in her firm, had a teenage daughter who was psychiatrically hospitalized for depression after a suicide attempt. My patient chose to reduce her hours at the office in order to be home after school when her daughter was released from hospital. When bonus time came, she offered to reduce her share and her male partners agreed. During the same year, one partner had a health problem and was fully out of work for over half the year but neither offered nor was asked to consider reducing his share. His leave was not considered optional. I asked her, *Would any of us want to live in a world where a mother's care for her child was optional?*

All of us rely on others' care but are conflicted about acknowledging that care. All of us depend on others – at the very least, as infants, we are completely dependent for our survival. The Dutchman's omnipotent claim that he could sail around the cape in a singular way denies the very reality, for example, of his crew, without whom he could not even try. In the myth, interestingly, the crew has no personhood but is only tied to the Dutchman's fate. How much of our cultural reluctance to acknowledge the sacrifices mothers make to care for infants – our need to assume entitlement to those sacrifices and our resulting social expectations that mothers make it work on their own without social supports – is tied to a denial of dependency?

I would argue that Senta's pity for the Dutchman, her passion to release him from his endless sailing through her love, can be seen in the transcendent terms of surrender: the surrender of her narrow self-interest in life to the sublime wish to save her lover from his cruel fate. Like Senta, Joan of Arc saw herself as part of a larger good, her life made meaningful through sacrifice to a greater good. The differentiation of surrender from masochism is subtle and yet not:

> It is an experience of being "in the moment," totally in the present, where past and future, the two tenses that require "mind" in the sense of secondary processes, have receded from consciousness.
>
> . . . Its ultimate direction is the discovery of one's identity, one's sense of self, one's sense of wholeness, even one's sense of unity with other living beings. This is quite unlike submission in which the reverse happens: one feels one's self as a puppet in the power of another; one's sense of identity atrophies.
>
> . . . Resignation accompanies submission; it is heavy and lugubrious. Acceptance can only happen with surrender. It transcends the conditions that evoked it. It is joyous in spirit and, like surrender, it happens; it cannot be made to happen.
>
> (Ghent, 1990, p. 111)

Summary

In the opera, as often in art, development is foreshortened. Senta is first presented as a dreamy adolescent girl, brushing aside her mother figure's requests to help with the housekeeping by continuing to gaze at and dream of the distant figure of the Dutchman like a starstruck girl. Then we see the shades of her Oedipal longings and fantasies as she suddenly conceives of becoming the Dutchman's savior. As a psychoanalyst, I would say the transference figure of the Dutchman brings to light her Oedipal wishes to be the perfect woman for her father. When she meets the Dutchman, we see romantic love blossom in both of them, a transformative love for each other, as the Dutchman experiences for the first time a wish to protect the other rather than only a narrow, self-centered, singular wish to get what he needs. Senta, for her part, cements her wish to be the faithful woman who will free him from the curse, thus establishing a kind of maternal protectiveness and generosity toward him.

Returning to the idea I sketched earlier, Wagner's libretto carries a theme of redemption in the Dutchman's emerging ability to think of Senta not just ruthlessly (as he always had done in the past), but with understanding that she is sacrificing herself to his hopeless longings. Though he was angry at first, when he overheard Erik courting Senta and believed her to have betrayed him, something transformational happens to the Dutchman and in Wagner's musical score. The Dutchman sings to Senta that too many have died for him, and he cannot bring himself to condemn her to death and everlasting torment. The Dutchman is glad that she is not bound by the curse since final vows had not been taken. Here we witness his empathy and identification with Senta as a separate person for whom he can feel love and give up something of himself.

Unlike the past, when he had ruthlessly used any woman he encountered to attempt his release from the curse without concern for her terrible fate, the Dutchman now sings that he is glad Senta has been spared this fate, even though it is so harsh for him, returning to the endless seas. He is changed through his love for Senta and his experience of her as a separate person rather than a tool for his salvation. Senta doesn't know that her sacrifice will bring him relief and unite them in heaven, but she boldly and freely casts herself over the cliff with belief, not knowledge, and Wagner unites the lovers as the ghost ship disappears, sending all who strove for so long into peaceful oblivion.

References

Bonaparte, M. (1949). *The life and works of Edgar Allan Poe: A psycho-analytic interpretation.* London: Hogarth Press.

Eigen, M. (1981). The area of faith in Winnicott, Lacan and Bion. *International Journal of Psycho-analysis, 62*, 413–433.

Ghent, E. (1990). Masochism, submission, surrender – Masochism as a perversion of surrender. *Contemporary Psychoanalysis, 26*, 108–136.

Harrison, K. (2014). *Joan of arc: A life transfigured.* New York: Doubleday.

Heine, H. (1834). The memoirs of mister von Schnabelewopski. *Der Salon.* Hamburg: Hoffman und Campe. Retrieved from: *https://en.wikisource.org/wiki/The_Works_of_Heinrich_Heine/Vol._1/The_Memoirs_of_Herr_von_Schnabelewopski*

Lasch, C. (1979). *The culture of narcissism.* New York: W. W. Norton & Co.

Loewenstein, R. M. (1945). A special form of self-punishment. *Psychoanalytic Quarterly, 14*, 46–61.

Shakespeare, W. (1997a). *Othello. The Riverside Shakespeare* (p. 1257). Boston, MA and New York: Houghton Mifflin. (Original work published 1622)

Shakespeare, W. (1997b). *Romeo and Juliet. The Riverside Shakespeare* (p. 1112). New York: Houghton Mifflin. (Original work published 1597)

Wagner, R. (Composer & Librettist). (1925). *Der fliegende Holländer* [The Flying Dutchman]. *Opera Score Editions*. New York: G. Schirmer. (Original work published 1840)

Wagner, R. (2008). *A communication to my friends*. London: Dodo Press. (Original work published 1851)

Winnicott, D. (1965). The development of the capacity for concern. In D. W. Winnicott (Ed.), *The maturational processes and the facilitating environment: Studies in the theory of emotional development. The International Psycho-Analytical Library, 64*, 73–82. London: The Hogarth Press and the Institute of Psycho-Analysis. (Original work published 1963)

6 The Orpheus of All Secret Misery

The Expression of Profound Grief in Wagner's *Tristan Und Isolde*

John J. H. Muller IV

Prologue

After I had given a lecture on Wagner's *Die Walküre*, a psychoanalyst who was fairly new to opera approached me and exclaimed, "I love Wagner! His operas are so realistic!" I thought to myself, only a psychoanalyst would make such a statement. Normally when one thinks of realism in opera, works such as *Carmen*, *La Bohème*, or *Pagliacci* come to mind, and yet, I understood what the person meant. On the surface, the legendary and mythic settings of Wagner's works can seem far removed from reality, but these stories contain elemental truths of human behavior, and Wagner demonstrated a penetrating insight into the inner lives of his characters. Nietzsche recognized Wagner's gift and referred to him as an "alienist," a 19th-century term for a psychiatrist. Robert Gutman writes, [In Tristan] "Wagner devoted himself to depicting the mental attitudes of his characters and could happily tarry in that world of protopsychology in which he was most at home" (Gutman, 1968, p. 167). Never was Wagner's understanding of psychology more apparent than in *Tristan und Isolde*, and this is especially evident in his portrayal of Tristan himself. *Tristan* is truly an intra-psychic music drama; almost nothing happens on the stage in terms of traditional action. Adolphe Appia, the revolutionary scenic designer of the early 20th century, acknowledged that "the action involved is an entirely inner, spiritual one" but he goes on to add, "Nevertheless, *Tristan* is a work written for the theater, intended for the stage, and one that can be realized only in performance" (Wagner, 1964, pp. 377–378).

Tristan is generally viewed as the greatest operatic testament to love, a love so all-consuming that it can only be fulfilled in death. To be sure, it is hard to deny the power of love expressed in the work, nor do I intend to. From the yearning expressed in the Act I Prelude to Isolde's rapturous hymn to Frau Minne (the goddess of love) in Act II, and from the Act II duet, which portrays so many nuances of love, to the concluding *Liebestod*, Wagner created a world of insatiable longing and eroticism unparalleled in music history.[1] The composer himself explained to Franz Liszt, "As I have never in life felt the real bliss of love, I must erect a monument to this most beautiful of all my dreams, in which, from beginning to end, that love shall be thoroughly satiated" (Wagner, 1897, p. 54). I believe, however, that the true subject of the opera is actually grief, a profound,

DOI: 10.4324/9781032271408-6

persistent grief that has colored Tristan's entire life, from the time of his birth, and I will focus on the musical expression of this grief. The first sound welling up out of the orchestra in the cellos is a leitmotif often identified as Grief,[2] and Tristan's very name, clearly related to the word *tristesse*, identifies him as a man of sorrows (Vazsonyi, 2013, p. 590). To quote Nietzsche once again, he saw Wagner as "a master at finding the tones in the realm of suffering, depressed and tortured souls, at giving language even to mute misery. . . . *Indeed, as the Orpheus of all secret misery he is greater than any*" (emphasis mine) (Nietzsche, 1959, p. 663).

It is important to remember that Wagner had extensive practical experience in the theater, and wrote both the words and music for his operas. Therefore, the connections between a character's thoughts and how these are expressed musically are unusually strong. Wagner's music is the very embodiment of a character's emotions. The music does not merely underline or highlight the words; it is their tonal equivalent; it depicts and enacts the text.[3] All elements of music, among them, theme, harmony, and orchestration, are employed to this end, and the resultant synergistic effect is overwhelming. Wagner seemed to be aware of the dangers of *Tristan* when he wrote to Mathilde Wesendonck, his muse,

> This Tristan is becoming something *terrible*. This last act!!! – I fear the opera will be forbidden – unless the whole is turned into a parody by bad production – : nothing but indifferent performances can save me! Completely *good* ones are bound to send folk crazy, – I can see nothing else for it.
>
> *(Wagner, 1905, p. 119)*

Wagner's Life

Before proceeding further on *Tristan* itself, it is necessary to summarize briefly some of the formative events of Wagner's own life, specifically those relating to parental loss, to see what these might reveal about his choice of subject matter and his manner of treating it.

Six months after Wagner's birth, his father, Carl Friedrich, died, and less than a year later, his mother Johanna married Ludwig Geyer, a family friend and actor. When Wagner was eight years old, Geyer died, leaving Wagner fatherless at an early age for a second time. There has long been speculation that Geyer was Wagner's biological father, but despite some intriguing circumstantial evidence to support that view, the issue remains open (Millington, 1992, pp. 2–3). Nevertheless, up until age 14, Wagner used the surname of Geyer (i.e., well after he had died). During the period that his mother was married to Geyer, Wagner competed for the attention of his stepfather with his older siblings. Both before and after Geyer's death, he was sent away to live with other families from time to time, and suffered inconsolable homesickness. Young Wagner had a very active imagination, and even inanimate objects would appear to come to life and terrify him (Köhler, 2004, pp. 15–21). Biographers have disagreed about Wagner's feelings toward Geyer. At one extreme, Joachim Kohler states that Wagner was afraid of him, and had nightmares about Geyer into his adult-hood (Köhler, 2004, pp. 21–23). Although Wagner's mother lived until 1848, she was a remote figure, emotionally unavailable to him as a child. Many biographers have discussed the difficulties Wagner endured in his formative years, but in Köhler's view, his childhood was positively traumatic.

Considering these early experiences, it should not be surprising that the theme of parental absence and loss is a recurrent theme in a number of Wagner's works. In *Die Walküre*, Siegmund's father (actually Wotan, king of the gods) disappears when he is a child and never returns. In the sword narrative of that opera, Siegmund cries out to his father in his hour of need, to no avail. Siegfried, the son of Siegmund, was born after his father's death, and Gamuret, the father of Parsifal, died in battle before his son's birth. Some works contain scenes of father/son conflict. Wotan has to allow his son Siegmund to fall in battle. Indeed, it is Wotan himself who shatters the sword he had promised to his son. In *Siegfried*, the title character eventually lops off the head of Mime, the evil Nibelung who had reared him, and later destroys Wotan's spear and with it, the power of his grand-father. One could cite the relationship between Alberich and his son Hagen, portrayed with such chilling malignancy at the start of Act II of *Götterdämmerung*.

The conflict between Amfortas and his father Titurel in *Parsifal* is not vio-lent, but nevertheless leads to great emotional pain, and in the opera under discussion, Marke has played the role of a father figure to Tristan. (In fact, the theme of paternal loss can be traced back as far as Wagner's drama *Leubald*, written when he was a teenager).

Maternal loss is arguably of even greater significance. Siegfried is deeply moved when Mime describes his mother's agonizing death in childbirth. Later, in a tender scene in Act II of the opera, he wonders if all mothers die giving birth, and comes to realize that his mother was an actual human woman, not an abstraction. When Siegfried encounters the sleeping Brünnhilde in Act III and finally learns fear, his first reaction is to call out to his mother, and when he finally awakens Brünnhilde, he briefly wonders if his mother might also be asleep. In *Parsifal*, Wagner creates an idealized mother in Herzeleide, who dies of heartbreak when her son leaves home. She would appear to be the opposite of Wagner's real mother. As I will show, parental loss, especially maternal loss, is at the core of Tristan's grief.[4]

Brief Synopsis

At an American Psychoanalytic Association session in 2010, I presented on *Tristan und Isolde* with Carol Rubin. She remarked that, as with psychoanalysis, much has already happened in the opera before it even begins. Although this is true of Wagner's other works as well, her observation is especially apt in the case of *Tristan*. Continuing the analogy, in analysis, material is presented in a non-linear manner, and only over time and much probing does a fuller picture emerge. In *Tristan*, we first learn of his immediate past from Isolde and only gradually does Tristan himself reveal the earliest events of his life. With each act, there is a greater focus on Tristan, as he delves more deeply into the causes of his grief. The monologues in Act III are a veritable self-analysis on the part of the character. This structure makes for a compelling drama, but poses a challenge to the writer. In order to explore Tristan's character in this study, it is necessary for the reader to be familiar with events of his life that are only revealed in later stages of the work. The following is a short synopsis:

Act I is set on a ship sailing from Ireland to Cornwall. Tristan is going to deliver Isolde, an Irish princess, as bride for his uncle, King Marke. Tristan avoids Isolde during the journey, which enrages Isolde. In a narrative, she explains to her maid Brangäne that sometime earlier, she had tended to a grievously injured knight, only to discover that he was Tristan, the man who killed her betrothed, Morold. She raised Tristan's sword to kill him, but the gaze of the helpless man stopped her. This explains the source of her anger, and her desire that the ship be lost in a storm. The man she fell in love with has betrayed her. Tristan finally agrees to meet with her, and Isolde has Brangäne prepare a death potion. They toast one another and believing they will die, rapturously confess their love. Unbeknownst to them, Brangänge had substituted a love potion. At the end of the act, Isolde is presented to Marke, but she is in a daze, unaware of her surroundings.

Act II is set in a garden in King Marke's castle. Marke and his retinue have ostensibly gone hunting, and we hear the horns in the distance. Isolde is impatient to give Tristan the signal for their assignation, but Brangäne counsels caution. She believes Tristan's friend Melot has betrayed him, but she is unable to dissuade her mistress, and Isolde extinguishes the torch. The love duet runs the gamut of amorous expressions, as Tristan and Isolde feel inseparable and long for night and death. At the climax of the duet, the lovers are caught by Marke. The hunt was indeed a ruse. Marke cannot understand how Tristan could hurt him this way, and Tristan has no answer. He explains to Isolde that his mother died in childbirth, and asks if she will join him in his true home, death. When Isolde agrees, Tristan drops his guard and allows Melot to strike a mortal blow.

Act III takes place in Kareol, Tristan's ancestral home in Brittany. Kurwenal, his loyal servant, has brought him here, and they await Isolde. A shepherd plays an old, sad tune as a disoriented and delirious Tristan gradually awakens. During a series of monologues, he contemplates his life, from the recent past and his love for Isolde to his childhood memories and the death of his parents. Learning of Isolde's arrival, he tears off his bandages to greet her and dies in her arms. Marke's ship lands shortly after, and Kurwenal slays the treacherous Melot but is then killed in turn by Marke's men. Marke had forgiven Tristan and Isolde. Unaware of her surroundings, Isolde enters a transfigured state and dies.

Tristan's Profound Grief

A major concept of *Tristan und Isolde* is Wagner's presentation of multiple views of reality, one external and the other an inner, dream-like state, or using the terminology of Schopenhauer, the world of phenomena and the world of noumena. The imagery of light and dark, day and night, and ultimately, life and death, is evoked throughout. Clearly, Tristan is in conflict with the role he plays in life and his desire to escape into a world of night and death. This conflict with his outer and inner self is portrayed with great power in the section of the Act II love duet immediately following the lovers' ecstatic greeting. He has wrestled with his place in the outer world. Day is deception, day is delusion. He remarks to Isolde in the Act II duet, "Is there one grief or pain that it [daylight] does not awaken with its light?"[5] Tristan was duty-bound to sing Isolde's praises in court, and to maintain his honor, he presented her to Marke. "How could Isolde be mine in the shining light of day?"[6] We should consider, therefore, how others see him, and how he sees himself. Most of the characters only perceive the outer manifestation of Tristan. To them, he is a hero. Early in Act I, Brangäne describes him as "That wonder of all kingdoms, that highly vaunted man, that peerless hero, the crown and embodiment of fame." Shortly after, Kurwenal calls Tristan a hero, "a lord of the world." As he mockingly describes the death of Morold, Isolde's beloved, he again proclaims Tristan a hero, and the ship's crew echoes his words. Even King Marke, after catching the lovers in Act II, recites a list of Tristan's qualities, and although he does not explicitly use the term hero, it is certainly implied. Tristan is the "Truest of all true men . . . staunchest of friends." He was thought to embody noble qualities of loyalty, honor, and virtue. At the end of the opera, Marke laments the death of "Tristan my hero."

Isolde shows more insight into Tristan's self-image; she senses a part of the character that was missed by the others. After all, she tended to him when he was at his weakest physically. In Act I, she periodically refers to him as a hero, but always in a sarcastic manner. To her, he is a coward for refusing to meet with her on the ship, and for sending evasive explanations through Brangäne.

Externally, Tristan truly is a hero. He defeated Morold, who had been exacting tribute from the Cornish, in battle. Presumably, there had been similar examples of his knightly prowess to gain such a heroic reputation. Yet Tristan's own self-image is very different. Until late in the work, Tristan neither refers to himself as a hero, nor does his music suggest such a status. Wagner's other heroes, such as Lohengrin, Siegfried, and even the passive hero Parsifal, have musical themes that follow a traditional heroic topos. Such themes are fanfare-like, martial in nature, and outline the notes of a triad, thereby emphasizing the tonality. Such a musical Gestalt conveys strength and stability. When Tristan makes his first appearance to Isolde in Act I, after avoiding her, we hear an oppressive, brooding theme, one that changes key with each repetition. Elsewhere in the opera, Tristan's themes relate to sickness or to his anguish. Not until his anticipation of Isolde's return in Act III, after an entire act of self-examination, does Tristan identify himself as a hero.

> Tristan the hero, exulting in his strength, has snatched himself from death's grasp. . . . She who will close my wound for ever comes to me like a hero, to save me. Let the world pass away as I hasten to her in joy.
>
> *(Libretto, p. 34)*

In his mind, he has risen to heroic stature in preparation for his death. (This section will be discussed in greater detail later in the chapter.)

How does one account for the discrepancy between Tristan's outer and inner self? We learn a possible answer to this psychic conflict at the end of Act II, and it is explored with far greater detail in Act III. Tristan's father died before he was born, and his mother died in childbirth. The trauma of parental loss could have left him with feelings of abandonment and guilt, and consequently, a lack of self-worth. This could explain why he would deliver Isolde, a woman he had fallen in love with, to his uncle King Marke, even though Marke was not looking for a bride.[7] Why should Tristan seek fulfillment in life, when all he has known since birth is sorrow? Moreover, in Tristan's view, his parents dwell in the world of night, and since childhood, he may have fantasized a reunion with them in death. This desire for a reintegration of the family may have been transferred to his feelings for Isolde, and could explain his striving for death with her.[8]

Acts I and II

After drinking the potion in Act I, Tristan and Isolde are free to express their true feelings since they believe they are going to die. In the short love duet that follows, they leave the world of reality and are oblivious to what is taking place around them. The surging chromaticism of their music stands in bold relief to the bright C-major fanfares announcing the presence of King Marke and the arrival in Cornwall. This removal from reality continues into Act II. Despite Brangäne's concerns that the hunting horns are still too close, Isolde hears what she wants to hear, rustling branches or the rippling of a fountain. Wagner expresses this beautifully, as the horn calls give way to a gentle tremolo in the strings or a fluttering in the clarinets. With the extinguishing of the torch, the love duet of Act II represents their ultimate immersion into a world of night and death. In one of the duet's moments of quietude (detumescence?), the lovers ruminate on "this sweet little word 'and'," which binds them. "But this our love, is it not called Tristan and Isolde?" Then moving towards the climax of the duet, Tristan sings, "Thus we might die, undivided, one forever without end, never waking, never fearing, embracing namelessly in love." The music of this concluding section is recapitulated, in the same key, in Isolde's *Liebestod*.

As Tristan and Isolde are caught by Marke and his retinue in the throws of their ecstasy, Kurwenal cries out, "Save yourself, Tristan!" Tristan, however, has a different goal, and remarks, "For the last time, the dreary day." He wants no more part of the world of reality, and is prepared to leave it. After a long lament, discussed later in this chapter, Marke asks Tristan to explain what has happened. Before he utters a word, the opening of Act I Prelude is recapitulated, but with a striking change in orchestration. Instead of alternating strings and winds, Wagner employs only the winds, in particular, double reed instruments. The opening gesture, the Grief motive, is given to the English horn, and I believe this is a timbral foreshadowing of the English horn solo of Act III, which embodies Tristan's entire life of sorrow.

Tristan has no answer for Marke, and as he turns to Isolde, we hear a striking contrast in orchestral color, as a motif from the love duet is played with the warm glow of the strings. He asks, "Where Tristan now is going will you, Isolde, follow him?" He elaborates upon this question, and we learn the source of his life of sorrow:

> To a land, Tristan means, where the sunlight never shines; it is the dark land of night from which my mother sent me forth when he whom in death she conceived in death she let go into the light: there where she bore me, which was the refuge for her love, the wondrous realm of night from which I first awoke, that Tristan offer you, where now he goes on ahead; let Isolde now tell him if she will follow, loyal and gracious.
>
> *(Libretto, p. 29)*

Tristan's father died before he was born, and his mother died in childbirth. He has been born into death, and sees death as his true ancestral home. This passage hovers between A-flat minor and major, the latter the key of the central section of the previous love duet ("Oh sink down upon us, night of love"). It even includes the pulsing, off beat chords from that scene. Does Tristan associate lovemaking with death?

Isolde understands the message, and sings "Isolde will dwell where Tristan's house and home is: now show Isolde the way that, loyal and gracious, she must follow." Her music also references the key and characteristics of the duet, until broken off by Melot. With her assurance, Tristan lets his guard down, allowing his false friend Melot to deliver a grievous wound with his sword.

Act III

The Prelude to Act III presents a scene of desolation, a bleak landscape of the outer world and a soulscape of Tristan's psychic emptiness. Wagner works with three motifs in the Prelude, which are often identified as Despair, Solitude, and Languid Suffering.[9] The harmonic movement in the bass of Despair suggests finality, a sense of hopelessness, while the rising line is clearly a diatonic version of Desire, the second motif heard at the very start of the opera. Wagner starts this rise on the lowest string of the violin, an open g, that creates a cold, stark, hollow sound. As the Solitude motif evaporates into the upper register of the violins, a depiction of the vast sea on the horizon, but also of the loneliness Tristan feels. The opening measures span over five octaves. In contrast to these two themes is that of Languid Suffering, whose shifting, sinking chromatic line embodies Tristan's sorrow. As the curtain rises, the Shepherd's Old Tune emerges, significantly heard at first from the stage, not the orchestra pit. This famous unaccompanied solo for English horn, an instrument often regarded as the most lamenting in the orchestra, unfolds over a period of about three minutes, and the melancholy timbre along with the highly chromatic character of the tune convey Tristan's isolation and loneliness even more than the Prelude. At this moment, the Old Tune captures the sadness of this specific scene, but its global significance for Tristan will be revealed later in the act.

Much of Act III is devoted to Tristan's Delirium.[10] This lengthy scene can be divided into two monologues, the first of which climaxes with Tristan's illusory anticipation of Isolde's arrival, and the second of which leads to his final, fleeting moment with Isolde and death. The first monologue is concerned with the events of the recent past and his love for Isolde, as Tristan blames an external agent, the day, for his predicament. The second monologue is more probing, as Tristan returns to his birth and examines the events that shaped him, ultimately realizing that the agent is internal, that all his life experiences have shaped him. During the act, moments of lucidity weave in and out of his delirious state.[11]

Over the course of these monologues, Wagner will draw upon all his musical resources to portray Tristan's growing self-awareness. One memory leads to another in a kind of free association. Particularly important is the interplay of leitmotifs. In his essay on Ludwig Schnorr von Carolsfeld, the tenor who created the role of Tristan (and who died a little more than a month after the premiere, in 1865, at the age of 29), Wagner gave the best explanation possible on the role of the leitmotifs. He advises one to listen closely to the orchestra, from the start of the act up to Tristan's death.

> Follow carefully the ceaseless play of musical motives, emerging, unfolding, uniting, severing, blending anew, waxing, waning, battling each with each, at last embracing and wellnigh engulfing one another; then . . . reflect that these motives have to express an emotional-life which ranges from the fiercest longing for bliss to the most resolute desire of death, and therefore required a harmonic development and an independent motion such as could never be planned with like variety in any pure-symphonic piece.
>
> *(Wagner, p. 343)*

In other words, the motivic density embodies the very texture of Tristan's life, as overlapping and contrapuntal combinations of motifs become the norm.

First Monologue

At the start of the act, Tristan has been awakened by the Old Tune and is disoriented, while fragments of the tune begin to appear in the orchestra. Kurwenal attempts to explain that he is in Kareol, his ancestral home, but this is simply a reference to Tristan's physical location. Tristan knows better. Gradually, Wagner's music conveys a man in a delirious state, coming out of a haze, attempting to account for where he has been. The texture is sparse; Tristan's vocal line is broken up with rests as he tentatively starts his narrative. "Where I awoke, I did not stay; where I stayed I cannot tell you." Between these fragmentary lines, the low strings play the rising Despair motive heard in the Prelude to Act III. Tristan realizes that he has been in a liminal state, at the threshold of death, and as his line grows more melodic, he sings the same music from Act II (and in the same key, A-flat) that he had used to tell Isolde that his true home was death. Now in Act III, he reflects, "I was where I had been for all time and where for all time I shall go, in the vast realm of universal night. But one knowledge there is ours – divine, eternal, total oblivion." With increased animation, he realizes he has come back from death because Isolde still lives, radiant in the sunlight. With this thought, the orchestral texture becomes much fuller, with references to music associated with the love scene of Act II. The section culminates with Tristan exclaiming, "Accursed day, with your glare!"

Tristan relapses with the words, "When will night come to the house?" and imagines he is awaiting Isolde's signal from the garden. With Kurwenal's assurance that she is on the way and will heal him, Tristan erupts with anticipation. "Isolde coming! Isolde drawing near!" This is expressed with an extraordinary transformation of the Languid Suffering motif, as Tristan's frenzied music climbs sequentially higher, along with that of the orchestra, suggesting a man feverous and light-headed with expectation. Tristan's question, "Kurwenal! Do you not see it?" is answered initially by the Old Tune, not heard in the first monologue, and then by Kurwenal's dejected "No ship is in sight yet!" The tremolo in the upper strings suggests not just the vastness of the horizon but also the void within Tristan's soul. This emotional plunge is one of the most devastating moments in all of opera.

Second Monologue

In the self-analysis that follows, Tristan takes apart his psyche so that he can reintegrate it. The Old Tune, still played onstage, initiates Tristan's recollection of long-past events. (Gutman trenchantly observed that it "serves as Tristan's Proustian 'petite madeleine,' helping him to summon the past" (Gutman, 1968, p. 251), and Karol Berger has made a similar connection (Berger, 2017, p. 272). Indeed, tastes, smells, and sounds can be powerful triggers of past memories. We now realize that this tune is not merely an expression of Tristan's current state and separation from Isolde, but rather it is the leitmotif of his entire life, his inheritance of grief. Tristan poignantly describes how it sounded when he learned of the deaths of his parents.[12] Indeed, it had served as a tune of mourning during their lives as well. As Roger Scruton states so eloquently, "Tristan stands peering into the great well of grief that he bears within, and the shepherd's melody takes hold of his thoughts and weaves them into a continuous narrative of pain and isolation" (Scruton, 2004, p. 67). With its reappearance here, it is worth reflecting again on the first unaccompanied statement of the Old Tune, at the start of Act III. It suggests a gradually revealed narrative of suffering, as every turn of phrase, change in melodic direction or rhythm, conveys an event in the sorrowful history of this family.

Fittingly, the tune dominates this entire section, threading its way through Tristan's recollection. He cannot escape his past. Fragments of the tune begin to appear in the orchestra, suggesting bits of memory that are returning. He asks, "to what fate was I destined. . . . The old tune tell me again: – to yearn and die!" Tristan leaves the past and considers his future. The tune is taken up in full by the orchestra and combined with the Day motif, conveying the all-encompassing sorrow of the character, the grief from his past and present. He exclaims, "Dying, still to yearn, not of yearning to die!" Tristan's thoughts now return to the recent past as he recounts how Isolde found the wounded Tristan and nursed him back to health. The Old Tune reverts to the English horn on stage, once again with fragments of it in the orchestra. Thus, the spatial separation of stage and orchestra pit creates a temporal dimension, delineating Tristan's past and present. He is engulfed by his history of sorrow.[13]

Tristan continues to ponder his initial encounter with Isolde, and in the midst of this, Wagner combines four motifs at once; two sections of the Old Tune, Day, and the Sick Tristan. As the Old Tune is repeated with greater urgency, he curses the drink with the words, "The potion! The potion! The terrible draught!" Tristan's entire being, body and soul, is racked with pain, and Wagner's dissonant, chromatic harmonies and frenzied rhythms embody this pain. He has pushed the musical language of the mid-19th century to the breaking point.[14] Two sections of the Old Tune and Desire combine in a climactic moment, and the reality of his life's history and his love for Isolde collide. Tristan now understands that all his life experiences have shaped him. With a new motif, he exclaims, "I myself did brew it."[15] This motif rises sequentially with unbearable intensity in the orchestra while Tristan elaborates

> From father's grief and mother's woe,
> from love's tears through the ages,
> from laughing and weeping, rapture and grief,
> did I distil the draught's poison!
> Accursed be that fearful draught
> that I brewed, that flowed into me,
> that I quaffed with endless delight,
> and accursed be he who brewed it!
>
> *(Libretto, p. 33)*

Tristan has become an analyst and analysand, and with this revelation, there is one final *ff* statement of the Old Tune. It has served its purpose, and is not heard again in any of Tristan's music. (Fragments of it are repeated after Tristan's death, but this is in connection to Kurwenal and his battle with Marke's men).

In the first monologue, Tristan's curse of day led to a brief relapse, where he awaited night and union with Isolde. Now, after this extended curse in the second monologue, Tristan's collapse is so deep that Kurwenal momentarily believes he is dead. In a section of chamber-like scoring, introduced with solo woodwinds and a tender violin solo, Tristan hallucinates that Isolde has actually arrived and will release him from his torment.[16] Tristan's sense of repose is expressed in the lyricism of his melodic line and the tonal stability of the passage. It is based on the motif of Love's Peace from the Act II duet. Here it is extended and peaks on Tristan's words, "Ah, Isolde, Isolde! How fair you are!"

Tristan's reverie is broken by a new, joyful tune and Kurwenal's announcement that Isolde's ship truly is in sight.[17] His anticipation of her arrival is depicted with an impetuous treatment of motifs from the love duet and frequent shifts of meter. Now, after deep self-examination, he sees himself as a hero, exclaiming

"Tristan, the hero, rejoicing in his strength." Just as the anticipation of the first cycle featured a transformation of a motif, Languid Suffering, now it is Love's Peace, which undergoes the change. Normally very languorous, here it embodies Tristan's frenzy, and is stated in 5/4 meter, uncommon during this time in music history. Ernest Newman suggested there is now a touch of madness in this motif (Newman, 1949, p. 272), but is he really "mad," or is he expressing the joy of his realization? As Isolde calls to him from offstage, Tristan imagines himself in the garden once again, waiting for the torch to go out. A climax for full orchestra combining three themes, Ardour, Bliss of Night, and Consecration of Death, is gradually reduced to a recapitulation of the opening measures of the Act I Prelude, through a final statement of the Gaze motif in the cellos, as Tristan dies. This moment marks a beautiful symmetry in the work. Outside of the Act I Prelude, where it bore no particular connotation, the Gaze motif was first heard in its entirety during Isolde's Act I narrative, as she described the moment when their eyes met, and she was unable to kill the helpless Tristan. It is played by a solo viola whose quality captures the tenderness and intimacy of the moment. The motif was also heard when they confessed their love to each other in Act I, exchanging the names "Tristan" and "Isolde." Now, the dying Tristan looks into Isolde's eyes one last time, sings her name, and expires as the motif dissolves into an arpeggiated, unresolved chord, never to appear again.

Isolde's Grief

Although Tristan's grief is the focus of this study, his actions and death precipitate grieving on the part of other principal characters as well. We know much less about Isolde's background than that of Tristan. Early in Act I, Brangäne conveys her worry over Isolde's apparently emotionless departure from Ireland. There were no tears when she left her parents and homeland, and she has been withdrawn, not eating or sleeping, during the voyage to Cornwall. We also learn that she lost her betrothed, Morold, in combat with Tristan. We witness Isolde's fury toward Tristan directly, and of her plan to kill them both with a death potion, but once they confess their love (a love that preceded the start of the opera), she exists in a state of ecstasy. At the close of Act I, she seems unaware of her surroundings, fainting onto Tristan's breast. After the lovers are caught by King Marke in Act II, she responds only to Tristan. Act III, as we have seen, is essentially Tristan's act. Although his longing for Isolde dominates much of his music in the act, she makes a physical appearance only at the end, where she has two contrasting scenes. The *Liebestod* (or Transfiguration, as Wagner called it) closes the work, and is one of the most famous scenes in all of opera. However, it is in her first scene, "Here I am! It is I, dearest friend!" immediately after Tristan's death, in which she mourns for him with searing intensity. Wagner captures the complexity of her grief and its non-linear quality. She has come as quickly as possible to nurse his wounds and marry him (i.e., in death), and she is stunned at his death. She calls to Tristan, wondering why he could not remain just one more hour. At times, she almost seems angry that he could not wait for her.

Rather than accepting the reality of his death, she believes he awakes, and at this moment, her transfiguration begins, well before the *Liebestod*.

Wagner's music embodies Isolde's grief in a number of ways. The scene alternates between recitative-like outbursts and long, sustained lines, and the soprano's line gradually rises higher and higher. One hears reminiscences of several motifs from the love duet, as Isolde revisits a joyous memory of the past, as well as Languid Suffering. Wagner introduces a new motif in this scene, sometimes referred to simply as Death, which moves toward a cadence before being broken off. This seems to be the musical equivalent of the character attempting to comprehend Tristan's death, but being unable to accept it. There is a particularly eloquent statement of the motif wherein Isolde asks for a single, eternally short, last worldly joy. Here, the vocal line is drawn out, as if she cannot bear to let Tristan go. At the close of "It is I," this Death motif finally does cadence, but into the theme that will later begin the *Liebestod*. (Indeed, this theme has already been heard earlier in her lament.) Wagner even uses the same warm scoring of soft trombones that he will use at the start of the *Liebestod*. Clearly, the transfiguration has already begun, as she sinks down senseless upon his body. Isolde is oblivious to the tumult that follows, with the arrival of Marke and the death of Melot and Kurwenal.[18]

King Mark's Grief

King Marke also grieves, after catching Tristan and Isolde *in flagrante delicto*. It is striking that all of his pain is addressed to Tristan, not Isolde. His sorrow is not over the loss of his young bride, but rather, the loss of Tristan and the intensity of that relationship. The lament is in several sections and introduces two new motifs in the bass clarinet. Up to this point, that instrument has not played a significant part in Wagner's orchestration, but here, its lugubrious timbre dominates the scene. It becomes the voice of Marke, conveying a grief beyond words. He saw Tristan as the embodiment of noble qualities – loyalty, honor, and virtue, but with Tristan's betrayal, he believes these knightly attributes simply do not exist. Marke's world-view is shattered. "This, Tristan, to me?" He was not seeking a wife; only after Tristan threatened to leave the court did he agree to accept Isolde. Marke does offer a loving description of her, but it is from an emotional distance, as if he admires her from afar. I have to question whether this marriage was ever consummated. Marke becomes more agitated, and asks "If I can win no heaven, why this hell for me?" Tristan, as we have seen, has no answer.

This monologue is one of moving, deep expression, and yet can be overlooked, since it follows the emotional extremes of the 30-minute-long love duet. Kurt Moll, a famous interpreter of the role, remarked

> If the bass isn't careful, he will find that his audience has fallen fast asleep by the end of it. You can stand there in your beard, and that beard will seem to get longer and longer as you sing.

He added that the singer must "Externalize what is essentially inward – give the monologue variety, color, nuance" (Cooper, 2017, p. 23). Moll is acknowledging the challenge Appia referred to earlier. How does one bring to life on the stage a psychological drama that unfolds in the orchestra?

There is a continuation of his grieving at the end of the opera. He journeyed to Kareol to let Tristan know he was forgiven, and he was prepared to bless a marriage to Isolde. Instead, he blesses the dead.

Epilogue

In the *Liebestod*, it might seem that Wagner has given the final word to the singer, as Isolde floats out her final words *pianissimo*, "unconsciousness, supreme bliss." Fittingly, however, it is the orchestra that brings an end to Tristan's grieving and unites the lovers. Two oboes and the English horn intone the rising four-note motif of Desire, but as the English horn drops out, the oboes carry the theme up two more pitches, bringing about a resolution. The entire orchestra cuts away, leaving just the two oboes holding a note in unison, a magical moment in the opera. As the orchestra settles on the final chord, every instrument of Wagner's orchestra is sounding – with the exception of the English horn. The cycle of grief has ended, as Tristan attains the world of endless night with Isolde.

Tristan und Isolde is a work of endless fascination, not only one of the most influential works in the history of music but also one that carries a tremendous emotional impact. Wagner himself put it best: in a letter to Mathilde Wesendonck, he wrote, "*Tristan* is, and remains, a marvel to me. I am more and more unable to understand how I could produce such a thing."

Notes

1 Robert Bailey points out that when the Prelude to *Tristan* was performed as an excerpt, Wagner entitled it "*Liebestod*." For Wagner, the concluding scene of the opera was the *Verklärung* (Transfiguration) (Bailey, 1985, pp. 36–43). However, to most opera-goers the close of the work is known as the *Liebestod*, and I will follow this convention for the sake of clarity.

2 See later footnote on the labeling of leitmotifs.

3 This view of music's function was one stressed by Prof. William Kimmel, whose classes I attended at Hunter College and the Graduate Center of the City University of New York. It has strongly influenced my own work, and I have tried to pass the interpretation down to my students.

4 Elsa in *Lohengrin* also suffers from multiple losses. Both of her parents have died and her younger brother has disappeared under unexplained circumstances, which causes Telramund, her ward and future husband, to leave her. Is it any wonder that she would fall prey to Ortrud's intimations that Lohengrin might vanish as mysteriously as he appeared?

5 All quotes from Wagner's libretto are taken from Lionel Salter's (1966) translation which accompanied the Deutsche Grammaphon recording from the 1966 Bayreuth Festival.

6 Out of concern for the tenor's stamina (and the audience's as well), this section of music, running about eight minutes, is often cut in performance. Not only does such a cut damage our understanding of Tristan, it also unbalances the overall structure of the duet.

In order to fully appreciate the bliss of the section that follows, "O sink down upon us, night of love," we need to hear how oppressive reality and day are to the lovers.

7   Karol Berger considers Tristan's behavior towards Isolde in the context of *fin'amor*. (Berger, 2017, p. 205).

8   Tristan's need to revisit the traumas of his life, and how this relates to concepts of Schopenhauer and Freud, is explored in Linda and Michael Hutcheon's article "Death Drive: Eros and Thanatos in Wagner's *Tristan und Isolde*" (Hutcheon and Hutcheon, 1999).

9   An explanation on leitmotifs and their labeling is in order. Wagner did not invent the term leitmotif, and he rarely assigned names to these recurring themes. There is no such thing as a master list of leitmotifs from the Master. However, he certainly acknowledged the use of such motifs, most notably in his major theoretical work *Opera and Drama*, where he referred to them as "signposts of the emotions." For the purposes of discussing the music, it is useful to have a convenient method of identifying the motivic material of the work. Nevertheless, an overly literal approach to the labeling of leitmotifs is a danger. First of all, their significance lies not in their mere presence but in the ways they embody musically a character or emotional state. Moreover, Wagner's ability to develop and transform motifs, to combine them and subtly "morph" from one to another, is remarkable. Labeling motifs in *Tristan* presents special problems. Many of the *Ring* motifs refer to concrete objects such as Spear, Sword, and Tarnhelm, but in a work that is so psychologically oriented, coming up with a definitive name is more difficult. We see this at the very start of the opera. The opening two motifs (whose intersection creates the famous "Tristan chord") are usually identified as Grief and Desire. Yet other analysts have called them Longing and Mystery (or Magic). Furthermore, the Act II love duet introduces a number of themes expressing the lover's passions; is it necessary or advisable to distinguish Ardor, Ecstasy, and Love itself? In this essay, I am using the leitmotif names commonly encountered in the English language literature, but I do not claim fidelity to any one source.

10   In his influential study, *Opera as Drama*, Joseph Kerman offers a structural model for Tristan's Delirium. He discerns two monologues (or cycles), each of which follows a pattern of recollection, curse, relapse, and anticipation (Kerman, 1988, pp. 165–166). This view informs my approach to the scene. More recently, Eric Chafe has suggested that the Delirium scene comprises three monologues (Chafe, 2005, p. 238).

11   I can think of only two other scenes in Wagner that approach the remarkable level of insight found here. One is the final scene of *Siegfried*, which portrays the transition of the title character and Brünnhilde into early adulthood. The other is Kundry's attempt to seduce Parsifal in Act II of *Parsifal*. Both of these were composed after *Tristan* and involve the interactions of two characters.

12   Wagner's composition sketch shows that he reworked this important passage over and over until it suited his purposes (Geck, 2013, pp. 248–249).

13   Using the terminology of film scores, one could call the off-stage English horn solo diegetic music, that is, music heard by, and affecting, the characters in the drama. The rest of the score is non-diegetic. In this particular example, the diegetic music becomes non-diegetic. In film music, a classic example is found in *Casablanca*, where "As tears go by" is first heard by the lovers diegetically, and is then developed in the score (composed by Max Steiner) as non-diegetic music. (In *Tristan*, the Steersman's song at the start of Act I and the off-stage horns at the start of Act II are also examples of diegetic music.)

14   Theodor Adorno stated that such passages stood "at the threshold of modern music" (Groos, 2011, pp. 118–119).

15   The first interval of this Curse theme, an ascending fifth, is the same as that of the Shepherd's Old Tune, suggesting that the tune has sparked this moment of insight.

16   The oboe and clarinet actually play a much-softened version of the Curse theme (Groos, 2011, p. 65). There is no end to the subtle transformations of leitmotifs in *Tristan*, and their dramatic implications.

17   Although scored for the English horn, Wagner indicated in a footnote that he actually wanted this passage, so different from the Old Tune, to be played on a natural-sounding instrument, something along the lines of an Alpine horn. Any number of exotic wind

instruments has been employed in performances, from the heckel-clarina to the tárogató (the latter originally used in Hungarian folk music).

18 In an otherwise drab and de-eroticized Bayreuth production directed by Christoph Marthaler and first performed in 2009, this moment was handled beautifully. Tristan has languished in a hospital bed for most of the act, and died on the floor in front of it. As Isolde concludes her grieving, she climbs into the bed and falls asleep. She later emerges from the bed to sing her *Liebestod*. Marthaler's direction seems to acknowledge that the transfiguration had begun before the *Liebestod* and that this change of state took place in sleep, as she is moving from consciousness to unconsciousness.

References

Bailey, Robert, ed. (1985). *Richard Wagner: Prelude and transfiguration from "Tristan and Isolde."* New York: W. W. Norton and Company.

Berger, Karol. (2017). *Beyond reason: Wagner contra Nietzsche.* Berkeley, CA: University of California Press.

Chafe, Eric. (2005). *The tragic and the ecstatic: The musical revolution of Wagner's "Tristan und Isolde."* Oxford: Oxford University Press.

Cooper, Michael. (2017). Kurt Moll, bass, dies at 78: Found humor and menace in an array of opera roles. *New York Times*, March 12.

Geck, Martin. (2013). *Richard Wagner: A life in music* (Translated by Stewart Spencer). Chicago, IL: University of Chicago Press.

Groos, Arthur, ed. (2011). *Richard Wagner: "Tristan und Isolde."* New York: Cambridge University Press.

Gutman, Robert. (1968). *Richard Wagner: The man, his mind, and his music.* New York: Harcourt, Brace, and Jovanovich.

Hutcheon, Linda, and Michael Hutcheon. (1999). "Death drive: Eros and Thanatos in Wagner's *Tristan und Isolde.*" *Cambridge Opera Journal*, Volume 11, 267–293.

Kerman, Joseph. (1988). *Opera as drama.* New and revised edition. Berkeley, CA: University of California Press.

Köhler, Joachim. (2004). *Richard Wagner: The last of the titans.* Translated by Stewart Spencer. New Haven, CT: Yale University Press.

Millington, Barry. (1992). *Wagner.* Revised ed. Princeton, NJ: Princeton University Press.

Newman, Ernest. (1949). *The Wagner operas.* New York: Alfred A. Knopf.

Nietzsche, Friedrich. (1959). *Nietzsche contra Wagner.* In *The Portable Nietzsche.* Translated by Walter Kaufmann. New York: Penguin Books, pp. 661–683.

Salter, Lionel. (1966). English translation. *Tristan und Isolde*, by Richard Wagner. Orchestra and Chorus of the Bayreuth Festival, conducted by Karl Bohm. Deutsche Grammaphon Stereo 2713 001.

Scruton, Roger. (2004). *Death-devoted heart: Sex and the sacred in Wagner's "Tristan and Isolde."* Oxford: Oxford University Press.

Vazsonyi, Nicholas, ed. (2013). *The Cambridge Wagner encyclopedia.* New York: Cambridge University Press.

Wagner, Richard. (1897). *Correspondence of Wagner and Liszt.* Vol. 2. Translated by Francis Hueffer. New York: C. Scribner's Sons.

Wagner, Richard. (1905). *Richard Wagner to Mathilde Wesendonck.* Translated by William Ashton Ellis. New York: C. Scribner's Sons.

Wagner, Richard. (1964). *Wagner on music and drama: A Compendium of Richard Wagner's prose works.* Translated by H. Ashton Ellis. Selected and arranged by Albert Goldman and Evert Sprinchorn. New York: E.P. Dutton.

7 The Dark Matter of Wagner's Dream

Chaos and Creativity in *Die Meistersinger von Nürnberg*

Jeanne C. Harasemovitch

Casting his net of musical sound over 16th-century Nürnberg, Richard Wagner transports us into his dream world and the dreams of its inhabitants. Die Meistersinger von Nürnberg is Wagner's creative dream. Constructed as a dream, the opera is built upon the fertile soil of unconscious desire: the latent dream form experienced in the unstable harmonies, in the recall of Tristan and Isolde, and in the movement from darkness and chaos toward the light of consciousness where Wagner's dream is transformed. Wagner creates a dream within his dream to cast his conviction that it is the task of the artist to dip deeply into the chaos of the unconscious and transform its dark matter into a work of art. Young knight Walther's morning dream, born out of unconscious desire and a midsummer evening of rioting, is harnessed by Walther and Hans Sachs, and wrestled into the daylight of consciousness, the dream's dark beauty realized as the luminous Quintet of Act III.

Die Meistersinger von Nürnberg embodies Wagner's fundamental belief that all acts of creation are wrestled up out of darkness and confusion. Temporally and musically punctuating the opera with a riot scene at the end of Act II, Wagner creates the catalyst for Walther's morning dream and its transformation, and he creates the dark permutations that penetrate the latter half of the opera, infusing Act III with the musical beauty and emotional depth that elevate and transform Wagner's dream opera into a work of great art.

Dreams in Die Meistersinger von Nürnberg are rich composites of the intellectual and aesthetic inheritance of 19th-century German thought. Rooted in Kant's "dark map of the mind" – the dark and obscure desires and sensations of which we are not conscious – (Nicholls and Liebscher, 2010, p. 12), the works of Goethe, Schopenhauer, and Nietzsche influenced Wagner's conception of dreams as a source of creativity and as an illumination of the chaotic and far reach of an as yet undiscovered world. A world ruled by laws entirely different from those governing conscious thinking, dreams were a perfect alchemy for Wagner's operas: housing contradiction, transcending time and space, and dissolving boundaries of reality and illusion, dreams surrender to the poetic, the mythical, and the impossible.

In the fall of 1856, stirred by reading Schopenhauer's (1818/1969) *The World as Will and Representation*, Wagner incorporated and reworked Schopenhauer's

DOI: 10.4324/9781032271408-7

theories of aesthetics, dreaming, and somnambulistic clairvoyance, enacting his newly formed version in his dramatic operas. Germinating during this period of discovery, Die Meistersinger von Nürnberg reflects Wagner's developing theories of dreamlife and his use of Schopenhauerian insights of passion, desire, unconscious motive, and the comingling of desire and suffering. Not surprisingly, Thomas Mann (1933/1957, pp. 202–203), uniting the line of descent of these turbulent human truths, was summoned to make this comparison: "Wagner the psychologist. . . [is] in remarkable intuitive agreement with another typical son of the 19th century, the psychoanalyst Sigmund Freud." Wagner's theories of dreamlife presage Freud and contemporary psychoanalysts who, expanding Freud's theory of dreamlife, considered the composition of the dream, whether asleep or awake, as a psychological function of the human mind and as an aesthetic object. Dreams serve as the guardian of sleep, as Freud suggested, and dreams are the instigator of psychic health and creativity (Bion, 1962, 1970, 1992; Civitarese, 2013; Grotstein, 2009; Meltzer, 2008; Ogden, 2007, 2010).

Wagner conceived music as having the character of a dream and as a vital bridge between our conscious and unconscious worlds. Music evokes images and emotions, giving life and form to emotional experience beyond our conscious awareness. Wagner intuited that as listeners we were enraptured in a dreamlike quality of clairvoyance, a state of being Wagner imagined as outside time and space. In this dreamlike state, we are engaged in the strange and rich primary processes that Freud (1900) considered the realm of the illogical, where

> temporal and spacial logic and its limitations are suspended: the passage of time and space may be accelerated, held still, experienced as past present or future. The self may be represented at all ages or compressed into the briefest moment of time.
>
> *(Harasemovitch, 2011, p. 1186)*

Wagner heightened the experience of the musical dream by hiding the orchestra from sight, allowing sound to emerge out of a timeless and spaceless darkness. Wagner (1870/2014, p. 69–71) describes how music becomes the theater for the mind when the waking mind enters a dreamlike state:

> as sympathetic listeners in a concert hall we are no longer consciously aware of our surroundings . . . we now attain with open eyes a condition resembling . . . the clairvoyance of a sleepwalker . . . it is truly only in this condition that we become directly involved with the musician's world. From this world . . . the musician weaves his sound . . . nourishes our powers of perception . . . to incapacitate us, as if by magic, for perceiving anything but our own inner world.

Wagner's clairvoyant sleepwalker dreams while awake.

Wagner's Dream Opera

The Overture

The Overture builds the scaffolding for Wagner's dream opera and the dream's relation to the creative process. As in a dream, the Overture generates and underscores the tension between the manifest and latent, the frame and the dynamic, the dream and its ongoing translation. Wagner introduces motifs and then skillfully modifies, intertwines, and reinterprets them. The Meistersingers, an association of amateur poets and musicians, primarily master craftsmen of trade, are presented in the historical grandeur, honor, and tradition of C Major, while young knight Walther's unformed Prize song swirls passionately in E Major, the chromatic harmonic chords and their progressions, textures, and contrasts infiltrating and transforming the diatonic C major. As in dreams and their interpretation, through the magic of association, the overture's latent structure emerges, and joining the manifest dream, the overture looks back and moves forward, creating music always in a state of becoming.

Act I

Act I continues to build upon the dream structure of Die Meistersinger von Nürnberg. Eva's waking dream appears as a state of being when in love; Walther "waking from a dream" composes his renegade trial song with its fresh harmonies; and the recall of Tristan and Isolde at the end of Act I kindles the dark matter of Sachs' waking dream in Act II and Sachs' lament in Act III, resoundingly articulating the opera's latent dream structure.

As the curtain rises in Act I, we hear the congregation of Saint Catherine singing a Lutheran chorale in C Major. Standing behind a church pillar, Walther, a young, impetuous aristocrat, resettling in Nürnberg, exchanges glances with Eva, the daughter of a wealthy goldsmith and Meistersinger. Walther and Eva met the day before at her father's house. Their impassioned love at first sight is threatened when Eva's father offers her hand in marriage to the winner of a Meistersinger song contest the following day. Walther's outsider status and Eva and Walther's endangered love summon the tension that Wagner requires psychologically and musically. Wagner's musical score contrasts the uprising of Eva and Walther's emotions with the rules they are to obey. The E major chromatic love theme introduced in the prelude breaks through the rule bound world of the diatonic as solo violoncello and viola become the emotive voice accompanying Eva and Walther's silent gestures of excitement and passion. Clarinets and oboes play strands of the love theme during intervals of the chorale and joining the orchestra's fermatas, transform the traditional form of the chorale, almost overtaking it. Exploring her subjective experience kindled by a portrait of David by Albrecht Dürer, Eva tells her maid Magdalene, "I feel as if I were in a dream" (all libretto quotes are from Wagner, (1867). As the music touches on the key of E flat, the oboe captures Eva's waking dream – not a portrait of an old and bearded King David, as maid Magdalene imagines, but of a young, conquering David who felled Goliath.

Upon learning Eva's father has offered her hand in marriage to the winner of a Meistersinger contest among the bachelor members of the guild, Walther decides to audition. The Meistersingers abide by strict rules of form, and to become a member Walther must present a poem/song that passes exacting conditions. David, Magdalene's lover, is encouraged to help Walther learn the rules. As the apprentices gather to set up the meeting for the Meistersingers, David sings of the many rules Walther must learn and the hard work necessary to become a Meistersinger. Walther's unbound intuitive talent is the counterpoint to David's memorization of rules and devotion to tradition. Walther embodies the transition from the old and established to the inspired and aesthetic modernity. Musically, Wagner develops the deep connection between these seemingly opposite positions. Walther's first aria, *Am Stillen Herd* (*At the quiet hearth*), begins with a similar melodic line as the Meistersinger meeting and roll call. Walther claims the legendary poet Walther von der Vogelweide and the birds in the forest as his teachers, each grounded in the same poetic tradition as the Meistersingers. Walther's trial song follows a similar path, beginning with an identical melodic line and in the same key of F major. The inheritance Walther shares with the Meistersingers recedes as Walther's song travels toward the unknown. Driven by desire and passion − "love rising deep inside me, waking me from a dream" − Walther's poetic dream leaps from the path, leaving rules and tradition behind as the chromatic uprising of the strings throb with harmonic freedom.

Shaken by the naked intuitive power of Walther's song, the Meistersingers roar their dissent. Meistersinger Beckmesser, whose task as marker is to record each mistake, and who hopes to win Eva's hand, exacts his role with relish; his white chalk marks engulfing the entire blackboard. Moved by the strong emotional authority of Walther's song, Meistersinger Hans Sachs rises above the fray protesting: "His song was new, not confused. He left our usual paths, but he went his own way quite firmly." The Meistersingers, unconvinced, and Walther, angry and frustrated, abandon the meeting. Roused by the spirit of Walther's song, Sachs remains behind, musing on the song's effect. In the silence, transcending time and space, overlapping past with present, a lone Tristan figure played by the oboe erupts from the orchestra, sounding the dream's latent structure. The emotional potency of Walther's trial song, full of desire and longing, will haunt Sachs in Act II.

The Dark Matter of Wagner's Dream

> Its innermost composition . . . can in fact be apprehended only by an ear that is willing to cast itself, as the music does, into uncertainty.
>
> (Adorno, *2002/1963, p. 591*)

Act II and the Riot

Wrestling up out of darkness and confusion, the riot scene of Act II brings to light Wagner's investigation of the dark and hidden realms of the human psyche. Wagner, who saw darkness as an illumination of the human soul, unveils the intensity and breadth of the human desire to obtain pleasure, and the challenge desire must confront – the renunciation of personal and individual self-interest for the sake of social stability. The riot scene enacts the violent play of contrasts between unconscious desire and renunciation and suffering – that which lies beyond reason, engages the senses, the body, the world of emotions, and reveals itself "as the personal creation of truth" (Mann, 1938/1957, pp. 255–257). In Act II, the deep affinity and contrasting aim of desire and renunciation are expressed musically in tonal instability and psychologically in the fragility of social order.

It is the Eve of St. John's Day, a time of the summer solstice, known to some as the Witches Sabbath. In German folklore, on Midsummer Eve, the primal forces of Spring are unbound and witches and warlocks cast their spells. Bon-fires are ignited, kindled from "the friction between two different woods," the height of the flame closely aligned with the reap of the harvest and one's future fortune or misfortune (Frazer, 2012/1940, pp. 160–171). In the city of Nürn-berg, a riotous outburst of its citizens erupts. The backdrop for this disturbance is the inner turmoil of its inhabitants who generate an evening of illusion and deception, passion and love, chaos and confusion.

Meistersinger Beckmesser, in pursuit of Eva's hand, and old enough to be her father, is on his way to serenade Eva. When Eva learns of Beckmesser's plan from her maid Magdelene, she instructs her to impersonate Eva by dress-ing in her garments. Alone, sitting under the elder tree outside his cobbler shop, preoccupied with the strange effect of Walther's trial song, Sachs lifts his face skyward, losing himself in a waking dream, the Tristan theme infusing his reverie with its timeless restlessness and sadness. As the violoncellos delicately recall the melody of Walther's song, Sachs sings:

> And yet that song won't leave my mind. I feel it, but I don't understand it, I can't get a hold of it, yet I can't forget it, and even if I grasp it, I can't measure its worth. But then how can I measure what seems so limitless. It sounded old . . . yet so new.

Sachs' reverie becomes ever more poignant when Eva joins him and Sachs learns the strength of Eva's feelings for Walther. A father figure who has known Eva since she was a baby, Sachs has consciously abandoned wooing her, but uncon-sciously his desire and passion toward Eva are alive. Eva would prefer to marry Sachs over Beckmesser, yet her romantic love lies with Walther, who, failing his audition to become a Meistersinger, lost his bid for Eva's hand. Eva and Sachs' conversation, full of conflict and desire, grows emotionally complex and con-fused as Sachs and Eva struggle with the meaning and fate of their relationship.

Eva and Walther, fearful of the danger to their future, make plans to elope. When Sachs overhears their conversation, he decides to help them and prevent their flight. Illuminating the night with his lantern, Sachs forces the young lov-ers to remain hidden in the shadows, unable to flee. Waiting in darkness with Walther, Eva hears the anguish Sachs' feels as he sings his lusty cobbler song. Meanwhile, Beckmesser arrives to serenade Eva and finds his plan disrupted by Sachs' raucous hammering and singing. At Sachs' instigation, Beckmesser agrees to have Sachs mark any broken rules of style in his song with his cobbler's hammer, reminiscent of Beckmesser's role in Walther's audition. Sachs' frequent, interrupting hammer strokes sound loudly through the night as Beckmesser haltingly recites his serenade to Magdalene who is impersonating Eva. Awoken by this cacophony of folly and deception, Magdalene's lover David dashes onto the street, wildly attacking Beckmesser, whom he believes is wooing Magdelene. Roused from their sleep, the night-shirted men and women of Nürnberg spill out onto the street, exchanging blows, and joining the pandemonium, now a full-blown riot. Wagner accompanies the insurrection with a vocal and instrumental fugue of extraordinary texture and complex beauty, built upon Beckmesser's simple song.

The night watchman blows his horn. The rioters disperse. The evening's mayhem has ended. The citizens of Nürnberg are safely in their beds. Wagner introduces a repose – in the silence, the night watchman's sings "Guard your fires and keep warm/Let no one come to harm." The chaotic undomesticated fires of passion and madness are contained. Yet, like the dream, they are always urging toward presentation and expression. "Will this madness be transformed into a noble work?" asks Sachs in Act III. As we shall hear, the midsummer evening's madness is not vanquished. Wagner placed the riot scene in a pivotal position in relation to Die Meistersinger's emotional and artistic development, elevating and transforming its chaotic dark matter in Act III.

The psychoanalyst Hans Loewald (1978, pp. 188–189) suggests that we need an intimate yet not too close relationship with the creative destructive flame of the unconscious. Too close to its fire and we cannot dream and cannot create – our experience devolves into a nightmare. Too distant a relationship to the unconscious and human life is no longer vibrant, nor warmed by its fire, the flame extinguishing itself. The riot scene and its afterlife in Act III record the fragility of social order and the potential within chaos as the source of creativity. Wagner, a revolutionary, was amnestied in 1861 after living in exile for twelve years. In November of that year, perhaps not coincidentally, Wagner's 1845 sketch of Hans Sachs significantly changed, revealing a more psychologically complex character incorporating new dimensions. Sachs' unexpressed love for Eva, and his questioning of his own accomplishments, are linked to what Schopenhauer describes as character having a certain trace of silent sadness. Schopenhauer further elaborates this sadness as "a consciousness that has resulted from knowledge of the vanity of all possessions and of the suffering of all life, not merely of one's own (Schopenhauer (1818/1969, p. 396).

Wagner's Dream Opera Transformed

> [Wagner] . . . knows a sound for those quiet, disquieting midnights of the soul, where cause and effect seem to be out of joint and where at any moment something might originate out of nothing.
>
> (Nietzsche, 1888/1968, p. 663)

A constant precondition of Wagner's dream opera is his conviction that chaos is the matrix of creative rebirth and unconscious desire the kindling for the flame of creativity. Wagner uncovers an invisible universe living side by side with the one we thought we knew, where deeply felt, unreasoned, and hidden truths live, and reality's handcuffs of logical linearity and divided temporalities do not exist. The powerful, violent, intoxicating lawlessness of the riot stirs and awakens the depth and breadth of desire and passion heard throughout Act III: in the *Prelude*, in Sachs' cry "Wahn, –Überall Wahn!," in Walther's morning dream, in Sachs' and Eva's lament, echoed in the dissonant Tristan chord, and in the waking dreams of the Quintet. Sounding the depths of the unruly unconscious, Wagner enlarges the sphere of human experience, unearthing psychic localities that house waking and sleeping dreams and states of mind that encompass desire, suffering, estrangement, and reconciliation. Holding disorder in dialectical tension to order, Wagner transforms the discordant world of the riot musically and through the character of Hans Sachs. Reconciling the opposing forces of creation and destruction, the latter half of Wagner's dream opera achieves unexpected and novel musical, emotional, and poetic vitality.

The Prelude of Act III

The Prelude of Act III registers the musical and emotional alteration of Die Meistersinger von Nürnberg; its dark permutations envelop the second half of the opera. Emerging from the Prelude is the centrality of love for Wagner, who arouses us by exposing the ways that love, dreams, and art are deeply destabilizing yet essential in creating fresh ways of thinking and becoming. The Prelude presents a complex psychological portrait of poet-cobbler Hans Sachs. Full with melancholy, grace, and love, the Prelude embodies Sachs' deeply rooted emotional life. The violoncellos voice the passionately felt and hidden truths of Sachs' inner world, his conflicting strivings and loyalties. They sound "the music of a burdened soul" (Mann, 1933/1957, p. 215). This is the Hans Sachs who has not yet surrendered his claim on Eva. The woodwinds play achingly low as the strings join in, and the violins in response to the trombones expand the mood of anguish. Rising above the melancholic atmosphere, strands of gratitude, resignation, pain, and loss burst forth. The Prelude of Act III holds the dark truth and timelessness of human emotion, and Wagner in his genius musically conveys all the sensuous details of those emotions. Wagner's virtuosic system of motifs has transformed music into an instrument of psychological truth, music pregnant with unconscious longing and desire.

Bernard Shaw (1893–1898/1961, pp. 48–53) observed that Wagner learned from Beethoven, who called himself a "tone poet," how to musically inscribe inarticulate emotions that surge through us. Unbound from classical form, expressing what is felt but not yet known, Beethoven's symphonies and late quartets crossed a musical threshold, plumbing the depths of the unconscious to create music that aroused emotional affects and complex states of being beyond our conscious awareness. "After the symphonies of Beethoven" wrote Shaw "it was certain that the poetry that lies too deep for words does not lie too deep for music" (p. 51).

In his essay entitled *Beethoven*, Wagner (1870/1995, pp. 96–98) compares the genesis of music as an art to the phenomenon of the dream, choosing "the marvellous tone-piece," Beethoven's C Sharp Minor Quartet as his example. Wagner describes the lengthy opening Adagio as "surely the saddest thing ever said in notes," the Allegro's longing as "sweet and plaintive," and the Allegro finale as "the dance of the whole world itself: wild joy, the wail of pain, love's transport, utmost bliss, grief, frenzy, riot, suffering." Beethoven the musician and *Beethoven*, Wagner's 1870 essay, an elaborate thesis on dreams and their relation to creativity, are viscerally present in the Prelude and throughout Act III where Wagner inscribes the deeply conflicted, tragic, and sublime expressions of being human.

Wahn

As the orchestra plays the final notes of the Prelude of Act III, the curtain rises on St. John's Day. Moving from the dark night of rioting into the calm of the morning light, we find Hans Sachs in his workshop, a book of world history held in his hands, musing on an element of human nature difficult to define: *Wahn*. The impossible to translate German word, *Wahn*, appears as the madness that drives human passion: a tangle of unruly emotions, the collective illusions of the human condition, and for Wagner, a life force that drives and contributes to dreams and art. Sachs laments, "Wahn, Überall Wahn!" – "Madness, Everywhere Madness!" Who can give it a name? When it awakens, who can restrain it? I search all of the history books looking for reason." *Wahn* is the unbidden, unreasoned madness of life that demands translation. Sachs determines to undertake the task – "let it help the extraordinary which are achieved only with a touch of madness . . . Now it's Midsummer's Day. Let us see if Hans Sachs can transform madness into a noble work."

The ability to transform *Wahn* for Wagner and Freud means turning back toward inner life; turning away is at one's peril. Sachs transforms *Wahn* into a well of loss, aging, and generation. In the scenes that follow, Sachs and Walther will transform an old man's folly and the hot blood of youth – *Wahn* – into a noble work. Wagner believed it is the artist's responsibility to create illusions that help us grasp and face truths that are otherwise unbearable, and it is the task of the artist to elevate and transform the dark matter of Wahn and dreams into works of art.

Warrack (1994, pp. 111–136) suggests Die Meistersinger von Nürnberg takes its musical language from the tension between and within order and disorder, and that this tension is represented by "the chord of Wahn" (pp. 116). The *Wahn* chord, containing C and F sharp, represents two aspects of *Wahn* – creation and destruction; C Major is the key of established civic order and artistic achievement and opposing that order is F sharp, the *diabolus in musica*, or devil in the music. The note's challenge to order is both creative and destructive.

(The night watchman's horn sounds F sharp during the riot scene of Act II.) Warrack considers Wagner's use of the chord as among the most potent devices of the opera. Connected harmonically to C as part of the chord of the diminished seventh, F sharp-A-C-E flat, the chord of *Wahn* is an "illusory chord" (pp. 116) in that it has no root and can modulate in any direction. Joined together, the orderly and the destructive are given a discipline and a freedom that each alone would not be able to achieve. The *Wahn* chord finds its fullest expression in the harmonic soil of Act III.

Walther's Morning Dream and Its Interpretation

> The beautiful illusion of the dream worlds, in the creation of which every man is truly an artist . . . afford him an interpretation of life. . . [for] the serious, the troubled, the sad . . . the whole divine comedy of life, including the inferno.
>
> (Nietzsche, 1872/2000, pp. 34–35)

In Scene 2 of the Act III, Wagner creates an image of the psychoanalyst at work in collaboration with the dreamer. Hans Sachs and Walther bring interpretation and form to dreamlife's boundless chaos and lawless confusion, demonstrating the creative interplay of dreaming and reality.

During the evening of midsummer madness, Walther has been dreaming. Upon awakening the following morning, Walther enters Sachs' workshop and tells him, "I had a wondrous dream." "That bodes well! Tell it to me!" urges Sachs. Walther responds, "I hardly dare think of it, for fear it will vanish." Walther gives voice to the anxiety that thought and language cannot grasp the ineffable dream, the dream that lives beyond the reach of reason and words. Foreshadowing Freud, Wagner (2014, p. 73) describes in poetic richness the realm of dreamlife that remains inaccessible to consciousness, "What it here has seen, no tongue can impart." Freud's concept of the dark mystery of the dream that defies interpretation found expression in another bodily image:

> There is often a passage in even the most thoroughly interpreted dream which has to be left obscure; this is because we become aware during the work of interpretation that at that point there is a tangle of dream-thoughts which cannot be unraveled. This is the dream's navel, the spot where it reaches down into the unknown.
>
> (Freud, 1900, p. 525)

Wagner's and Freud's conception of dreamlife was not limited to a dark, ineffable realm. Again, anticipating Freud (1900, 1915), Wagner (2014, p. 73) conceived dreams as an exchange between our conscious and unconscious worlds, envisioning the dream that is accessible to the world of "waking consciousness through translation into the language of a second, an allegoric dream, which immediately precedes our wakening."

Sachs encourages Walther to reveal his dream, inviting him on a journey of recovery and discovery, where "man's deepest madness" can be interpreted and transformed.

"My friend, says Sachs, it is exactly the poet's task to record and interpret his dreams. Believe me man's deepest madness is revealed in his dreams and poetry is the only true interpretation of dreams." Sachs suggests, "Begin with your morning dream. Use the art of poetry, it helps recover what was lost." Sachs' counsel mirrors Freud's (1900, pp. 277–508) "dream work." The art of the psychoanalyst who interprets dreams – condensation, displacement, secondary revision, and symbolization – is the art of the poet creating verse. Psychoanalyst and poet strive to recover the dark and obscure, what lies outside conscious awareness. Wagner and Freud conceived dreams as a reservoir of lost connections. What appears lost to the dreamer is rejoined and transformed in creative association with the listener, continually reborn in the work of translation.

Walther asks Sachs, "So it might not be a dream but poetry?" Sachs answers, "The two are good friends. They support each other." Poetry and dreams are inseparable for Wagner. Their union in musical drama creates a perfect oneness where feeling and intellect do not override one another; rather they join in aesthetic creation. Much like the interplay between conscious and unconscious, poetry and dreams simultaneously disrupt, reorganize, and revitalize one another. The dream for Wagner, Freud, and contemporary analysts is both a chaotic and reorganizing experience that when worked upon in consciousness comprises an aesthetic power.

The psychoanalyst Hans Loewald (1960, pp. 250–251) writes of the relations between conscious and unconscious experience and the vital necessity of their dynamic exchange in creative expression and in all aspects of life:

> the unconscious needs present day external reality and . . . present day psychic reality . . . for its own continuity, lest it be condemned to live the shadow life of ghosts or to destroy life . . . The opening of barriers between unconscious and preconscious, as it occurs in any creative process, is then to be understood as an internalized integrative experience – and is in fact experienced as such.

The pure associative power of the dream is communicated to Sachs, a call and response between dreamer and listener. Seeking Walther's inner dream vision, Sachs carefully inscribes and comments on Walther's dream. Walther and Sachs' dream collaboration recall Freud's (1900) technique of dream interpretation and Freud's (1905, p. 161) theory of the "day's residue" or psychic intensities – those occurrences that escape our conscious awareness yet hold deep psychic meaning and association; fragmentary and unfinished, they wend their way into our dreams and await translation.

Walther's dreamlike flowing narrative moves with ascending wave-like crests as the orchestra swirls romantically around the melody. Situated in Walther's dream universe, we hear the intimate details of Walther's sensual experience – a lush erotic garden infused with the woman he loves, who offers him "succulent fruit to quench his desire." The woodwinds and horns carry a feeling of deep structure beneath the play of strings, rendering an emotional immediacy to Walther's subjective experience that words alone cannot provide.

"I can't tell what you composed and what you dreamed," says Sachs. This may be a reference to Wagner's belief that we dream while awake, and that waking dreams or reveries are portals of creativity. Wagner gives the famous example of a waking dream as creator of the Overture to Das Rheingold. Wagner (1880/1983, p. 603) writes in his autobiography that on September 5, 1853, during a trip to Spezia Italy, suffering from an attack of dysentery and desiring sleep which did not come, "I fell into a kind of somnolent state, in which I suddenly felt as though I were sinking in swiftly flowing water." The rushing sound soon became the chord of E flat major and the mesmerizing wave-like aqueous movement of the Overture. Wagner writes, "I at once recognized that the orchestral overture to the Rheingold, which must have long lay latent within me, though it had been unable to find definite form, had at last been revealed to me."

Walther and Sachs continue to dream his composition into existence. Sachs tells Walther his trial song made the masters uneasy: "It is with such fire of poetry and love that our daughters are seduced to adventure. For long blissful wedlock, other words and melodies are invented." Sachs is not only speaking to tradition and rules of conduct, but he is also speaking to the creative necessity for the fire of passion to be contained within form. Walther's dream demands form. Sachs, aware of the rules of the Meistersingers and of their limitations, responds to Walther's concern that he does not know the rules, with this advice: "Make up your own and follow them." Form arises from a compelling necessity that originates from within. The tender dream poem is not to be coerced into arbitrary form. Dreams and their interpretation are the magic of the poet and the psychoanalyst, their arrival in waking and sleeping life a creative force and source of inspiration.

Sachs' and Eva's Lament and the Tristan Chord

Throughout Wagner's dream opera, we encounter the red thread of *Tristan and Isolde*, its latent trace woven into musical figure, motif, single chord, compositional style, allusion, and quotation. Disrupting and joining the traditional diatonic, dissonant *Tristan and Isolde* disassembles and deconstructs the manifest dream, restoring the unknown and the unfamiliar. Unmasking the infinite longing and desire of the unconscious, Wagner sounds the Tristan chord in Scene 3 as Eva and Sachs confront love and loss.

Eva arrives at Sachs' workshop dressed for the Mastersinger contest. Sachs welcomes Eva and tells her "You'll dazzle both young and old. You've never looked more beautiful." Eva, clearly unhappy, complains that the shoes Sachs made for her do not fit properly and she is unable to walk comfortably. It is not difficult to perceive that Eva is frightened of having outgrown the "shoes" she has worn in her relationship with Sachs. As Eva and Sachs struggle to "repair" the shoes, we witness the intimacy of their relationship; the love they feel for one another is palpable. The child Sachs held in his arms is now a grown woman. Sachs' role as surrogate parent and unconscious lover is usurped by Eva's passionate feelings for Walther. This psychic shift becomes evident when Walther, surprising Eva, enters the workshop, and at the sight of him, Eva's face radiates with joy.

Sachs' growing disappointment is evident even as he encourages Walther to sing the newly formed trial song for Eva. Hearing Walther sing the song, Eva is overcome by emotion. Torn between her love for Walther and her loyalty and affection for Sachs, Eva falls into Sachs' arms. Sachs quietly turns Eva toward Walther, gently guiding her toward him. Sachs' grief is visible as he sings his woes as a cobbler and a widower, a song of frustration, suffering, and unrequited love. Eva, moved by Sachs' despair and her love for him, sings of her gratitude:

> My friend, you dear man, How can I repay you. What would I be without your love? I would have remained a child if you had not awakened me. I learned what a soul is . . . You allowed me to bloom.

The love and loss Eva and Sachs feel are unmistakable. Eva once more thrusts herself into Sachs' arms, pressing her head against his breast. In this moment of longing, love, and loss, the Tristan Chord sounds, displacing time and space. Sachs tells Eva: "My child, I know the sad tale of Tristan and Isolde. Hans Sachs is too wise to want the role of King Mark." Unlike King Mark, who was betrothed to a much younger woman who loved another, Sachs recognizes the boundary of generation and Eva's love for Walther. Acknowledging his emotional kinship to Eva, Sachs once again tenderly guides Eva into Walther's waiting arms. An immense compassion permeates this scene, conjuring the powerful image of parent and child, the origin of love, and the painful psychological necessity to relinquish unconscious incestuous ties. The rite of passage from love of a parent to mature love reveals an inner Oedipal world of conflicting loyalties and an intimacy of contradictory feelings. When Freud (1900, pp. 263–266) incorporated the Oedipus myth into psychoanalytic theory, he wrote "it seizes us because each of us was once in germ or fantasy such an Oedipus." The Oedipus myth, well known to audiences of Sophocles and of modernity, continues to arouse fear, anxiety, and recognition. Freud conceived Sophocles' play as portraying the primeval wishes of childhood fulfilled: sexual wishes and feelings of rivalry. Like Oedipus, who unwittingly killed his father and married his mother, these primeval wishes are an aspect of our unconscious world, ones that we would consciously shrink back from in horror. We live, as did Oedipus, in relative ignorance of their existence. Hans Sachs' sudden awareness of his psychological position relative to Eva and Walther instills the sounding of the Tristan chord and Sachs' allusion to *Tristan and Isolde* with unconscious emotional depth. Uniting the psychological and the mythical, Wagner bestows Act III of Die Meistersinger von Nürnberg with a power analogous to ancient tragedy.

The Tristan chord, a cluster of notes dark and delicate – F, B, D#, and G# – and their restless undertow, uncovers the dynamic compositional tension within Die Meistersinger von Nürnberg; a tension between rules and spontaneity, the old and the new, love and loss, longing and satisfaction, a tension resembling the psychological tasks of the Oedipal parent and child who must relinquish their claim upon one another, must make way for the new while keeping the old, must bear and integrate loss – and must transform their love.

The Radiant Quintet

> Have I only dreamed my life or is it real?
>
> *(Walther von der Vogelweide, (1170–1230)/2018, p. 92)*

Wagner celebrates the birth of the dream in Act III, Scene 4. Walther's morning dream, sprung from his love of Eva and a midsummer evening of madness, is born into the world as a work of art. The lovers Magdalene and David join Eva and Walther in Sachs' workshop where Sachs baptizes Walther's dream. Sachs tells them a child has been born – "Now let his name be chosen." Sachs names himself and Eva the dream's godparents, names Walther's song *"The Blessed Interpretation of a Morning Dream,* and invites Eva to give the song her blessing. Here begins the sheer beauty of the lyrical counterpoint of the Quintet as each member, voicing a deep inner emotional life, enters their waking dream. Eva's solo, twelve bars of ascending lines, is entwined by oboe and clarinet. The melody of Walther's prize song sounding, Sachs softly enters the waking dream with a rising phrase of love for Eva. Walther enters the dream pianissimo, and David and Eva join, singing their contentment. Their voices, separate yet conjoining, dream one another, moving us as listeners to our deepest being. Eva returns to the original melody and Walther and Sachs sing the ascending woodwind phases echoed by David and Magdalene. As all five sing their happiness (Sachs' imbued with gentle regret), the Quintet moves toward the resolution of differences, leading to a radiant climax of voices – "a sublime dream." The achingly beautiful Quintet unveils the creative interlacing of dreaming and reality as each voice asks, "Am I awake or is this still a dream?"

The question, "Am I awake or is this still a dream?" brings us to the epigram earlier by the poet Walther von der Vogelweide, the legendary mentor of Walther and the Meistersingers. In a poem entitled *Alas! Where Have All the Years Gone?* von der Vogelweide asks, "Have I only dreamed my life or is it real?" Across time and space, von der Vogelweide's question occupied contemporary poets and psychoanalysts. Reading the poem centuries later, the poet Jorge Borges' (1980/1984, pp. 29–40) responds to von der Vogelweide's question about dreaming and reality, suggesting there is no difference between the two – that all of waking is a dream. Psychoanalyst Wilfred Bion (1962, 1970, 1992) theorized that dreaming occurs throughout the day and night, whether we are awake or asleep, and is synonymous with unconscious thinking. Borges and Bion join the extended reach of Wagner's dreamlife and his belief in the creative unconscious. Mirroring Wagner's account of the clairvoyant sleep-walker who dreams while awake, Borges corroborates that we are the theater, the spectators, the actor, and the story (1980/1984).

Die Meistersinger von Nürnberg's deep accord with psychoanalysis is found in the centrality of dreamlife, in the unearthing of unconscious desire and inner conflicts, and in the feeling that we have crossed over into another universe where dreams and the imagination are set loose. Wagner's genius as musician, poet, and "psychologist" resides in recognizing waking and sleeping dreams as the psychological presentation of our innermost being and as the origin of creativity.

Die Meistersinger von Nürnberg is Wagner searching after form, not form we easily recognize, themes and harmonies with which we are familiar; rather those uncanny experiences we find in our dreams, asleep and awake; emotive and disruptive and still in states of chaotic formlessness. Wagner's dream opera refuses to foreclose the fragmentary and feral nature of psychic life; the dark matter of Wagner's dream is where art arises, where love and longing, joy and pain, and the ineffable, live in dark allure, and where meaning and its creation – verbal, tonal, non-representational – is inexhaustible, forever a flame to be ignited.

References

Adorno, T. W. (2002). Wagner's relevance for today. In *Essays on Music*, pp. 584–602 (Trans. S. H. Gillespie, ed. R. Leppert). Berkeley, CA: University at California Press. (Original work published 1963)

Bion, W. R. (1962). *Learning from Experience*. London: Karnac, 1984.

Bion, W. R. (1970). *Attention and Interpretation*. London: Karnac, 1984.

Bion, W. R. (1992). *Cogitations*. London: Karnac.

Borges, J. L. (1984). Nightmares. In *Seven Nights*, pp. 26–41 (E. Weinberger, Trans.). New York: New Directions Books. (Original work published 1980)

Civitarese, G. (2013). *The Violence of Emotions*. London: Karnac.

Frazer, J. G. (2012). *The Golden Bough, Volume 10: Balder the Beautiful: The Fire Festivals of Europe and the Doctrine of the Eternal Soul* (3rd Edition). New York: Cambridge University Press. (Original work published 1913)

Freud, S. (1900). The interpretation of dreams. In J. Strachey (Ed. and Trans.), *The Standard Edition of the Complete Psychological Works of Sigmund Freud* (Vol. 4/5). London: Hogarth Press.

Freud, S. (1905). The relation of jokes to dreams and to the unconscious. In J. Strachey (Ed. and Trans.), *The Standard Edition of the Complete Psychological Works of Sigmund Freud* (Vol. 8, pp. 159–180). London: Hogarth Press.

Freud. S. (1915). The unconscious. In J. Strachey (Ed. and Trans.), *The Standard Edition of the Complete Psychological Works of Sigmund* Freud (Vol. 14, pp. 166–204) London: Hogarth Press.

Grotstein, J. S. (2009). Dreaming as a "curtain of illusion:" Revisiting the "royal road" with Bion as our guide. *The International Journal of Psychoanalysis*, 90(4), 733–752.

Harasemovitch, J. C. (2011). (A)temporal dialectic: Creative conversations between time-lessness/time and transference. *Journal of the American Psychoanalytic Association*, 59(6), 1183–1200.

Loewald, H. (1980a). Primary process, secondary process, and language [1978]. In *Papers on Psychoanalysis*, pp. 178–206. New Haven, CT: Yale University Press.

Loewald, H. (1980b). The therapeutic action of psychoanalysis [1960]. In *Papers on Psychoanalysis*, pp. 221–256. New Haven, CT: Yale University Press.

Mann, T. (1957a). Schopenhauer. In *Essays by Thomas Mann*, pp. 255–302. (H. T. Lowie-Porter, Trans.). New York: Vintage Books. (Original work published 1938)

Mann, T. (1957b). Sufferings and greatness of Richard Wagner. In *Essays by Thomas Mann*, pp. 197–254 (H. T. Lowie-Porter, Trans.). New York: Vintage Books. (Original work published 1933)

Meltzer, D. and Harris Williams, M. (2008). *The Apprehension of Beauty: The Role of Aesthetic Conflict in Development, Art, and Violence*. London: Karnac.

Nicholls, A. and Liebscher, M. (2010). Introduction. In *Thinking the Unconscious: Nineteenth Century German Thought*, pp. 1–25 (eds. A. Nicholls and M. Liebscher). New York: Cambridge University Press.

Nietzsche, F. (1968). Nietzsche contra Wagner. In *The Portable Nietzsche*, pp. 661–683 (ed. and Trans. W. Kaufman). New York: Viking Press. (Original work published 1888)

Nietzsche, F. (2000). The birth of tragedy: Out of the spirit of music. In *Basic Writings of Nietzsche*, pp. 30–144 (ed. and Trans. W. Kaufman). New York: Random House. (Original work published 1872)

Ogden, T. (2007). On talking as dreaming. *The International Journal of Psychoanalysis*, 88(3), 575–589.

Ogden, T. (2010). On three forms of thinking: Magical thinking, dream thinking, and transformative thinking. *Psychoanalytic Quarterly*, 79(2), 317–347.

Schopenhauer, A. (1969). On the vanity and suffering in life. In *The World as Will and Representation*, pp. 573–633. (Trans. E. F. J. Payne, Trans.). New York: Dover pp. 573–633. (Original work published 1818)

Shaw, B. (1978). Wagnerism. In (L. Crompton (Ed), *The Great Composers, Reviews and Bombardments*, pp. 40–61. (ed. L. Crompton). Oakland, CA: University of California Press, pp. 40–61. (Original work published 1893–1898)

von der Vogelwiede, W. (2018). In *Walther von der Vogelweide: Ein altdeutscher dichter, geschildert von Ludwig Uhland*. Frankfurt am Main: Outlook Verlag GmbH (original published 1822). (The poem "Ouwe" is translated by Stefanie Nickel-Rather & Ronka Nickel).

Wagner, R. (1867). *Die Meistersinger von Nurnburg*. Deutsche Grammaphon. 2004. James Levine, conductor; Sonya Friedman, translator.

Wagner, R. (1983). *My Life* (Trans. A. Gray, ed. M. Whittall). New York: Cambridge University Press. (Original work published 1880)

Wagner, R. (1995). Beethoven. In *Actors and Singers, Richard Wagner's Prose Works, Vol. 5, 1896*, pp. 57–126 (Trans. W. A. Ellis). Lincoln, NE: University of Nebraska Press. (Original work published 1870)

Wagner, R. (2014) Beethoven. In *Richard Wagner's Beethoven (1870): A New Translation* (Trans. R. Allen). Woodbridge, Suffolk: Boydell Press. (Original work published 1870), pp. 29–200.

Warrack, J. H. (1994). Wahn, words and music. In *Richard Wagner: Die meistersinger von Nürnberg*, pp. 111–134 (ed. J. H. Warrack). New York: Cambridge University Press.

8 Evil as Sadistic Perversion in *Tosca*

Amy Tyson

Introduction

What is evil? Is it the farthest point on a behavioral continuum of cruel behavior? Or is it uniquely different from the wide range of self-serving unkindnesses humans impose on one another? And where do we look to fathom its origins? I will explore this question by examining the nature of the male rapist character in Puccini's opera Tosca, who is considered to be one of the opera's most evil protagonists.

Scarpia's psychology is timeless and well worth understanding. Increased public pressure for transparency, fostered by case after case of sexual abuse receiving widespread publicity, makes us wonder more specifically why some powerful, successful men are motivated to assault women. Opera is filled with themes of human malfeasance amazingly relevant today when seen with a modern perspective, and the character type exemplified by Scarpia remains universal. As the villain aptly dramatized in this opera from 1900, he's clearly identifiable as a remarkably accurate portrayal of a person for whom the modern diagnosis of psychopathy and sadistic perversion can be made. Even if Puccini didn't have these terms at hand, he and his librettist intuited the sadist's internal world and described it precisely. This may be one reason, apart from the beauty of Puccini's music, why the opera doesn't seem dated and continues to be one of the most popular operatic works performed worldwide. Tosca speaks to something deeply troubling that hasn't gone away. Sexual abusers were around then and they are still around. The difference is that we now, belatedly, recognize them for how their behavior operates in a culture that allows it. A psychoanalytic lens can add greater insight into the predator's motivations.

Tosca is not just the story of victim and evil perpetrator, since rape is shown as an intolerable violation which Tosca violently resists. It's also the story of a man's internal world that leads him to dominate with manipulation and violence; of a woman fighting back and not allowing herself to be victimized; of the darkest consequences of their brutal encounter. As an audience, we're invited to enter into Scarpia's malevolent internal life and be thrilled by the catharsis of Tosca's rebellion.

DOI: 10.4324/9781032271408-8

Synopsis

The opera, sung in Italian, is set in Rome during a time of political unrest in the year 1800. The story unfolds over twenty-four hours. In brief, Rome is controlled by the kingdom of Naples and ruled by Baron Scarpia, the politically powerful chief of police who suppresses all dissent. He dominates the lives of the populace, but Napoleon's impending invasion threatens his power. Scarpia lusts after Floria Tosca, a famous opera singer in love with the painter Mario Cavaradossi. He manipulates her emotions as he simultaneously pursues his political ends. When he summons her to extract information in his pursuit of Angelotti, a political fugitive Mario has hidden at his home, he forces her to listen to Mario's screams as he is tortured. In anguish, she gives him the information. The sadistic Scarpia then pressures Tosca to submit to him sexually in exchange for a promise to release Mario, who he plans to execute the next day. When Scarpia learns Napoleon's troops are marching on Rome, threatening to overthrow his rule, his advances on Tosca grow more menacing, rising to attempted rape. Desperate, she finds a knife and stabs him to death. She then runs to the prison for a brief, joyous reunion with Mario. But the next morning, Tosca tragically discovers that Scarpia's promise to allow Mario to survive was a lie. She is devastated as she witnesses her lover's death by firing squad instead of his survival by way of a promised sham execution. Grief-stricken and certain that capture and punishment await her, Tosca leaps to her death off a parapet.

Rape and Opera

How did audiences react to this story of attempted rape and resistance when the opera premiered in Rome in 1900? At the time, Tosca was considered a political thriller about Napoleon's coming liberation of Rome. The political unrest that embroiled late nineteenth- to early twentieth-century Europe disposed audiences to view Scarpia's domination of Tosca primarily as a representation of political tyranny (Plotkin, 1994). Rape was a metaphor, not necessarily recognized as an abusive act. However, over time, critics also objected to the opera's perversity and sensationalism. Tosca was famously called a "shabby little shocker" by Joseph Kerman, author of the classic text *Opera as Drama* (Kerman, 1988, p. 208). It seems that the sadomasochistic themes surrounding the attempted rape made people uncomfortable, and the second act of Tosca has been seen as the "locus classicus of opera sadomasochism" (Englund, 2020, p. 135) in which power, violence, and desire intersect.

A contemporary audience will likely have a jolt of recognition witnessing a woman being forced to have sex by a powerful man, now that the widespread sexual abuse of women is more clearly evident and increasingly prosecuted.

> When the Me Too movement exploded during the autumn of 2017, it came as no surprise that opera was profoundly implicated . . . as a workplace, the

opera house is itself a structure defined by rigorous hierarchies . . . gender inequality and sexual harassment.

(Englund, 2020, p. 119)

Englund goes on to give examples that abound in the professional opera world internationally: hundreds of singers signed an open letter testifying to abuse, perpetrators were investigated and when credible allegations found, fired. The line between the fantasy sexual themes of opera and the reality of the working opera world has long been blurred.

That men have not always been held fully accountable for rape has historically rendered the act invisible. Treated judicially as an unprovable crime, the victim's testimony is seldom believed. Women are frequently blamed for their behavior or appearance that allegedly provokes a rape, and when they do fight back, they're often held liable. Even if vindicated on the grounds of self-defense, women still must be viewed as broken or crazy. The "not guilty by reason of insanity" defense has been used to acquit them for self-preserving attacks on their abusive husbands. (Sorrentino et al., 2019; Balas, 2019). Gender bias has long been a factor in how we conceptualize sexual violence and culpability, but now the chilling power of Scarpia's character and the social support for his actions can be fully understood, rather than obscured by historical invisibility and the drama and beauty of the opera. As laws, punishments, and education about consent make their way into our consciousness, we strive for a change in the culture such that the enabling social context of Scarpia's behavior will no longer exist. Still, a key question remains: though cultural change may restrict predatory behavior, will it change the psychology behind it?

Rape has been a central theme in art since ancient Greek times; mythic and biblical rapes have proven popular subjects, and the violent extremity of the act has often been minimized. Art historians describe how throughout history, depictions of "heroic rape" in art portrayed an expected social and sexual capitulation of women through romanticized, eroticized paintings. Such paintings were objects owned by the aristocracy and supported the aristocratic ethos of sexual and political conquest. Yet there have also been images that contradict the heroic tradition and depict rape as a shocking, unacceptable act of brutality and violence (Zarrucchi, 2000). Rape has been both glorified and condemned in art. As a recurrent theme in opera, rape is not always portrayed as a violent act, but instead often disguised euphemistically as "seduction." But the problem with this portrayal is that it disguises a violent act as a titillating seduction.

In the art of opera, themes of rape, pushing limits, and crossing boundaries are often explored. Are these shown as violent, or glorified? Perhaps these themes can be seen as similar to BDSM (bondage/dominance/sadomasochism) sexual practices, which is held to be a kind of play, exciting but not real. Although the BDSM agreement is to maintain safe limits, in this practice boundaries are in fact crossed. Englund (2020) suggests that the possibility of boundary violation is exciting. He shows that opera "habitually plays with an eroticization of cruelty and humiliation, inviting its devotees to take sensual pleasure in the suffering of others" who "come to the opera house to hear extreme suffering voiced in stylized, high-pitched cries" (p. 152). The audience is a complicit observer in the boundary violations of opera, such as Scarpia's creation of the scene of physical and psychological torture as foreplay to attempted rape.

Opera is an expressive dramatic vehicle for portraying characters' internal worlds in all their baffling and unconsciously motivated complexity. Though uniquely, blatantly evil, Scarpia is not the only rapist character depicted in opera. We meet entitled narcissistic rapists, such as Don Giovanni, the titular character of Mozart's opera, who enjoys what he views as playful seduction and feels entitled to forcefully rape when his charms don't suffice. In Verdi's Rigoletto we meet the Duke of Mantua, shown flirting with many women including Rigoletto's daughter Gilda, who falls in love with him and whom he then forcibly abducts and rapes while treating it as a joke with his courtiers. These characters force sex for different psychological reasons than Scarpia. These narcissists need to believe they will be admired and loved, and even when they use force they can't imagine they aren't desired.

In contrast, Scarpia makes no attempts to flirt and seduce, but instead enjoys being hated by his victims. He is a callous serial perpetrator who views women as objects to be brutally taken whenever he wants. He doesn't fool himself into believing they want him; his thrill is obtained when they resist and despise him. There can be no doubt about this, as when he sings:

> For myself the violent conquest has stronger relish than the soft surrender.
> *(Libretto, p. 12)*
> *(This and subsequent libretto quotations from*
> *Puccini, G. 1900/1953)*

We wonder what he is trying to prove to himself by his compulsion for repeated sexual violence, and what the meaning is of his desire to evoke revulsion.

Evil and Perversion

Opera is full of unstable, unpredictable individuals who commit terrible acts. But are they evil or mentally ill? In his book *Disordered Heroes in Opera*, John Cordingly (2015) explores the question by writing about the genre's personality disordered male protagonists. He observes that in the nineteenth century, "operatic madness was gendered" (p. 11). Women's insanity was often set in motion as a reaction to loss, whereas male protagonists who appeared "mad" were more likely unhinged by guilt. However, Scarpia does not fit this profile; he feels no guilt and is not "mad" in an easily recognizable way. Cordingly explains that in the nineteenth century the idea of "moral insanity" was used to describe people who were "perverted or depraved, but there was no apparent mental illness; they were bad, but not mad" (p. 13). But contemporary psychoanalysts would disagree that perversion is not mental illness. Perversion is often a component of the character disorder of psychopathy, which is a kind of mental illness disguised behind a veneer of normalcy. One writer called it "the mask of sanity" noting that the psychopath (or sociopath, which he uses interchangeably) can mimic normal behavior, hiding the lack of internal personality structure and the inability to feel normal emotions, which led to purposeful destructive behavior (Cleckley, 1964). Psychopathy, which includes the components of chronic antisocial behavior, deficient affective experience with the inability to feel empathy, and aggressive, arrogant narcissism, is a strong predictor of sexual offending (Maloy, 2002).

Scarpia's profile, comprising psychopathy and perversion, must be included with those of opera's mentally disordered male protagonists. His destructive desires drive all the dramatic action and emotions in Tosca. He creates mayhem by fomenting jealousy, torture, attempted rape, murder, betrayal, and suicide. He torments others, but appears to feel only sadistic glee himself, and the audience clearly views him as evil. In fact, in one performance I saw, the audience hissed when the singer who played Scarpia appeared for a curtain call! They hadn't yet relinquished the suspension of disbelief in his villainy. Scarpia is one truly bad, if not overtly mad, character; however I maintain that he is both evil and mentally disordered. He is considered to be one of the most evil characters in all of opera. But we must wonder what evil means from a psychological point of view.

Philosophers have long approached the concept of evil as they tried to understand the most horrendous atrocities. Evil was initially wrestled with as a religious concept, as theologians tried to understand why an all-powerful God is powerless against the forces of evil. Later philosophers turned to a secular concept of evil. Since humans are moral agents, it seemed that only the concept of evil could capture the immorality of humans who perform the worst imaginable acts. Hannah Arendt tackled the secular problem of evil when trying to understand the Holocaust. She thought the perpetrators' motives were "banal" in that they didn't think deeply about what they were doing; rather, they were superficial, thoughtless functionaries of a totalitarian regime. Later thinkers disagreed, arguing that evil acts involve the perpetrator's intention that the victim suffer, or taking delight in causing harm. These ideas move toward a psychological understanding of evil acts, and the role of psychopathy began to enter the discussion. More contemporary philosophers called this "evil personhood" meaning that an evil person has a fixed character with a disposition to do evil (Calder, 2020).

So what sort of human has the capacity to commit acts so bad, causing horrible suffering to other human beings, that they are viewed as evil? In his book *The Science of Evil* Simon Baron-Cohen (2011) argues that lack of empathy, or what he calls "empathy erosion," characterizes evil. He defines empathy as the ability to keep another person's mind in view as well as one's own. "Empathy is our ability to identify what someone else is thinking or feeling and to respond to their thoughts and feelings with an appropriate emotion" (p. 16). When empathy is switched off, you think only about yourself. "Treating other people as if they were just objects is one of the worst things you can do to another human being, to ignore their subjectivity" (p. 8). Baron-Cohen developed a measure for empathy and found that it exists on a spectrum. On the low end, no reference to another person's thoughts and feelings exists, but various pathological states can be found, including antisocial personality disorder. Such people or characters are also known as psychopaths or sociopaths. He notes that the causes of these personality disorders vary, but include severe childhood abuse and neglect, as well as genetics.

That Scarpia lacks empathy is clear. We can deepen this insight to see how the tortured internal experience of this problem is vividly illustrated in his character. In one study exploring the nature of evil from a psychological viewpoint, the psychoanalyst Fred Alford (Alford, 1997) maintains that evil is related to a feeling of dread. From his extensive interviews with violent inmates, Alford found that they consistently began by defining evil in terms of maliciously taking "pleasure in hurting and a lack of remorse" (p. 21), but then went on to describe, in very personal terms, their own suffering from a terrible inner feeling of losing themselves and their separate identity. This profound, inchoate feeling of dread so overwhelmed them that they tried to inflict it on others in an attempt to be rid of it. They wanted to feel like God to the other person's utter vulnerability, as that person begged for his or her life. In that moment, these abusers experienced themselves as powerful and strong, and the other as little and weak. Alford compellingly argues that

> evil is an experience of dread. Doing evil is an attempt to evacuate this experience by inflicting it on others, making them feel dreadful by hurting them. Doing evil is an attempt to transform the terrible passivity and helplessness of suffering into activity. This is, in the end, how I came to interpret the relationship between the experience of dread and the concept of evil.
>
> *(p. 30)*

This kind of terrifying internal experience is also described by other psychoanalysts. Thomas Ogden notes that the analyst Bion called it "nameless dread," but Ogden suggests that "formless dread" is a more apt term for the fear that the self is dissolving (Ogden, 1989a, 1989b). In other words, evil stems from a person's deep internal experience of dreading an existential threat to the self, one that is alarming, intolerable, destroys all meaning, and therefore must be expunged at all costs by creating terror in someone else. When such grim feelings are overwhelming and can't be adequately contained, understood, or coped with, the person feels compelled to act them out. The fear of loss of self is successfully managed by cruel projection onto another person, a central defense mechanism in perversion (see Freud, 1905 for the introduction of the concept of perversion).

Ogden additionally observes that these damaged people perpetrate evil not only to rid themselves of the menacing feeling of annihilation dread by creating it in others, but also in an attempt to access a feeling of vitality and meaning. Revealingly, one inmate in Alford's interviews is quoted as explaining that "stomping for intimacy" by committing a brutal assault is the only way to get really close to that person (Alford, 1997, p. 13). This is a perfect example of perverse psychology; in order to relieve annihilation anxiety, the abuser distorts, or perverts, the means for obtaining closeness. Alford quotes the psychoanalyst Otto Rank who noted that there are "a thousand ways evil aims to sacrifice the soul of another" (p. 10). Like Ogden, Rank observes that if a person's own soul feels lifeless, an attack on another feels like a way to gain access to a feeling of aliveness for themselves. Such a disturbed person developed the defense mechanism of dissociation and internal deadening, so as not to feel terrified when he or she was being abused as a child. But the internal dead feeling, once incorporated as part of the self, feels intolerable. Alford writes,

> Evil, I argue, is best seen as a response to what Ogden describes as . . . the dread that the self is leaking away. Everyone experiences this dread in one form or another. Whether we do evil depends . . . upon whether we can find and use abstract symbolic forms to express and contain our dread. If we cannot, we are more likely to inflict this dread on others in the form of violence, or more subtle acts of sadism.
>
> *(p. 39)*

The dread is rooted in a menacing sense of internal lifelessness and a fear of death. Feeling alive can't be fully experienced by those individuals. The depraved excitement created to avoid inner deadness is another central aspect of perversion.

Looking to the concept of perversion, specifically a sadistic perversion, can be helpful in understanding these vivid descriptions of how a feeling of dread can lead to evil acts. The psychoanalytic definition of sadistic perversion is that it has a psychologically dynamic function: it is defined as the response to intolerable anxiety evoked by a dreaded feeling of emptiness by projecting, or getting rid of, the feeling of dread by doing something terrible to another person; and by the creation of intense, often sexualized excitement by hurting another person in order to avoid a feeling of inner deadness. Both of these aspects of sadism include the idea that to pervert something is to distort its true meaning in order to avoid confronting an unwelcome truth, for instance harming someone in a desperate, misguided attempt to feel a sense of the other person's aliveness, while evading the realization that you can't actually get close to someone this way. Psychic reality is distorted, and the lens through which external reality and relationships are perceived is warped (Stein, 2005; Kaplan, 1991).

How does this twisting of experience play out in *Tosca*? Perverse relatedness often manifests itself as a sexualized enactment with another person of an unconscious story in ways such that feelings of hatred and destructiveness are disguised by excitement.

> Sadomasochistic object relations are a way of loving (and hating) others and oneself, and are especially concerned with intense ways of engaging another so as to mitigate dangers of separateness, loss, loneliness, hurt, destruction, and guilt. Aggression and sexuality are adapted to this end of intense connectedness with another person. When one feels unloved

and unloving, illusions of intense, excited involvement with another are substituted.

(Coen, 1991, p. 191)

These terrible feelings are managed and projected in the excitement of sado-masochistic acts, and there we have Scarpia, start to finish. In these sexual acts, there's a lack of real interest in the other, who is not seen as a person to be related to, but rather an object to be used for one's own purpose. Many things, not just sex, can be perversely distorted and used. For instance, Scarpia misuses the church to maintain personal and political power. In doing so, he achieves his objective: an excited feeling of dominance. His relationship with the church is clearly a distortion and perversion of the church's intended meaning. When sexual excitement is perversely distorted, the erotic becomes a narrow, exclusive requirement, and sexual expression is rigidly held to this one thing in a compulsive, repetitive way. Scarpia has to be a serial predator in order to keep the excitement going, excitement that protects him from the experience of a precarious sense of self, a fragile, unstable self that feels dead, not alive.

In a sadistic perversion, the sadist's aggression is sexualized as a means to exert control and power over another. Without a secure sense of identity, the ecstatic letting go and mutuality of adult sexuality can feel threatening, raising the fear that the vastly insecure person will cease to exist if he or she surrenders to even temporary ecstasy where boundaries are felt to dissolve. The sadist needs to avoid this dreaded experience of self-dissolving or dying. To gain an experience of self, he doesn't simply want to cause pain. Rather, his desire is to humiliate the other in order to take pleasure in knowing he's forced someone to have torturous feelings. Coen writes, "It is exciting to feel able to induce intense emotional responses in another person, to overcome the other's barriers, to feel in control and dominant, able to make the other feel bad, guilty, weak, inferior, defective" (Coen, 1991, p. 191). Weakness and fear are thus projected onto someone else through sexualizing acts of dominating, hurting, and psychologically manipulating another.

What creates such a need? The origin of this terrifying feeling in early child-hood often involved an experience and a fear of being intruded upon, trauma-tized, and controlled or abandoned by a more powerful figure. The sadist needs to feel that it is no longer he, but rather his victim, who is little, helpless, and powerless (Pulver and Akhtar, 1991). We see Scarpia aiming to take over Tosca's free will, her soul, and we can surmise that by controlling her, he wants to feel powerful and gain access to her vitality for himself, if only for a moment. She's not a separate person to him, but is a source of life-giving sustenance. Political and sexual dominance make him feel he's the powerful one and other people are weak. In these ways he perfectly demonstrates sadistic perversion and the need to commit evil acts.

Consider why Scarpia is shown as such a starkly evil character, without nuance or ambivalence. He's truly a caricature of powerful masculinity. The brutal reality of his sexual dominance is hyperbolic. In male sadism, it's been hypothesized that a man defensively uses a phallic exaggeration of masculinity to prove he's living up to the prevalent social stereotype of masculinity – he's strong, not weak. But sexual violence against women is a perversion of sexual mutuality between two full human beings. The sadist's aggressive ideal of male virility must be exaggerated to defend against his unconscious fear of humiliation if his insecure identity is exposed, even to himself. He may, in fact, experience his vulnerable identity as forbidden and dangerously effeminate. As Scarpia senses his political power slipping away, he feels increasingly powerless and empty, but he disguises his insecurity as excitement. When the opera's dramatic tension barrels toward its climactic apex, Scarpia's perverse defensive strategy of sadistic control begins to look desperate; he can't hold his grip on his political power, on the escaped prisoner, on Mario or on Tosca. He dies by being stabbed, penetrated by Tosca, right at the moment of his attempt at perverse climax in rape. This irony is aptly symbolic of a failed perverse strategy; he can't maintain the excited frenzy that makes him feel powerful, and when it collapses, he can't survive. As if this weren't retribution enough for such a villain, Scarpia's essential, depraved fragility gets exposed to the audience night after night.

Let's look at how the words of the opera illustrate the sadistically perverse character. Early in Act I we learn that Tosca is prone to feeling jealous whenever she worries that Mario may be interested in another woman. She sees his painting of a blond Madonna resting on a scaffold in the church, and she worries that the model is having a rendezvous with her lover. Mario reassures her, and Tosca easily feels reconnected to him. They sing a loving aria together in the church, and both express genuine love and passion. But later in Act I, when Scarpia appears in the church where Mario had been painting, he discovers a woman's fan near the easel; he's delighted, realizing he can use the fan as a tool to incite Tosca's suspicions. He sings, "Iago had a handkerchief, and I a fan to drive a jealous lover to distraction!" Beyond his obvious identification with a villain whose name has become a synonym for evil, note the telling exclamation point: wicked manipulation is thrilling! When Tosca enters the church searching for Mario, Scarpia turns up the heat by showing her the fan left by the Marchesa. He cunningly claims he found it "there on the scaffold. Obviously somebody surprised the lovers, and she lost her feathers in her flight!" Distressed, Tosca sings sadly about how much this hurts her, and the delighted Scarpia sings to himself: "I've hit the mark! . . . The poison hits home already." His psychological manipulation of Tosca begins by creating jealousy that will isolate her from Mario and make her vulnerable. He reveals his motivation, singing excitedly to himself:

> Scarpia now sets loose the soaring falcon of your jealousy! How great a promise in your quick suspicions! Now Scarpia digs a nest within your heart!
> *(Libretto, p. 14)*

Scarpia's moves are those of a parasite; he'll bore inside, nest and feed off Tosca's pain.

He's manipulated her into jealous anger to get her to voluntarily give him information to locate both the escaped political prisoner Angelotti and her lover Mario, so he can kill them and then force her to submit sexually to him. He whips up his own excitement as he does this.

Scarpia uses anything he can to further his desire to rape, dominate, and control. He misuses and perverts the power of the church to legitimize his political dominance as well as his power over women. Puccini shows this clearly at the end of Act I, when the religious chant of the church's Te Deum is sung as a duet with Scarpia who sings of his lust and intention to murder:

The worshipers sing (in Latin): "We acknowledge thee to be the Lord; all the earth doth worship thee," while Scarpia sings: "Ah, to see the flame of those imperious eyes grow faint and languid with passion. For him, the rope, and for her, my arms . . . Tosca, you make me forget God!" He doesn't want the inconvenience of remembering God, which might cause him to feel guilt. Inability to bear guilt is another hallmark of perversion; perverts evade facing the reality of hurting another person. Instead, Scarpia pumps himself up into a grandiose state and the Te Deum intertwined with his words implies that he uses the church to bolster his feeling of omnipotence. An intact self is strong enough to face reality, bear guilt, and make reparations. Scarpia, though, is empty, and needs to fill himself with guilt-free excitement. He misuses the church to inflate himself.

When Tosca comes to the palace that evening to perform, Scarpia summons her to his rooms. While waiting for her, he sings with eager anticipation, revealing unabashedly that he views her as an object to be manipulated, used in a violent sexual conquest, then discarded, so he can move on with his habit of serial predation. These are the most telling lines revealing his character:

> For myself the violent conquest
> has stronger relish than the soft surrender,
> I take no delight in sighs or vows
> exchanged at misty lunar dawn.
> I know not how to draw
> harmony from guitars, or horoscopes
> from flowers, nor am I apt at dalliance,
> or cooing like the turtle dove. I crave,
> I pursue the craved thing, sate myself and cast it by,
> and seek new bait. God made diverse beauties
> as he made diverse wines, and of these
> God-like works I mean to taste my fill.
>
> *(Libretto, p. 12)*

He has no resource for inner comfort, such as the symbolic use of beauty and music, or verbal expressions of love in a relationship, that could help him process his feelings; he must feed on the life energy of another. Desperate emptiness like Scarpia's indicates that he has been abandoned by his inner objects, his inner parents, and must figure out how to survive on his own. Lacking empathy even for his early self in such dire, abandoned, straits, he instead feels enraged by his condition of lack. Now his only way to connect with another is by use of perverse sexual excitement and violence; other ways of connecting, such as "soft surrender," are not strong enough to inflate him. He needs to fill himself with perverse rapes of women, and then dismiss his guilt by claiming God gives him permission.

Meanwhile, he has captured Mario, who refuses to reveal where the political fugitive Angelotti is hidden. When Tosca arrives, Scarpia shows her he's captured Mario, who in turn tells her to reveal nothing. Scarpia then sends Mario out to be tortured, and goads Tosca in an effort to make her turn on her lover by reminding her of her jealousy. Defiant, she refuses. But when she hears Mario's tortured screams, Scarpia further manipulates her by telling her she is killing him and can only stop the torture by revealing where Angelotti hides. In anguish she finally complies. The sadist's next layer of torture comes when Mario is brought back in and, discovering Tosca's capitulation, becomes furious at her. The villain has achieved his aim of causing a rift between the lovers, further psychologically torturing Tosca. He's driven to destroy anything good, such as love.

Unfortunately for Scarpia, his pleasure is immediately interrupted by news that Napoleon has just defeated his troops; Mario cries out triumphantly:

> Victory!
> The avenging dawn now rises
> to make the wicked tremble!
> And liberty returns,
> the scourge of tyrants!
> *(Libretto, p. 15)*

Since sadists fear takeover by more powerful figures, Scarpia's sadism crescendos with Napoleon's approach, augmented by Mario's powerful cry of victory. At this moment both Mario and Napoleon outdo Scarpia when it comes to power and vitality. What's left for a threatened sadist to do but send Mario out to die and trap Tosca in the room with him. In a chilling moment, he further reveals his lack of empathy by smiling coldly, complaining that his supper was interrupted. Scarpia is cold, not fully alive, filled with a terrible feeling of internal lifelessness. He defends against his inner deadness with perverse excitement and revels at now gaining access to Tosca's aliveness, whose expression of passion for Mario only increases his excitement. Listen for his parasitic feeding on her vitality as he sings,

> Already in the past I burned
> with passion for the Diva.
> But tonight I have beheld you
> in a new role I had not seen before.
> Those tears of yours were lava
> to my senses and that fierce hatred
> which your eyes shot at me only fanned

the fire in my blood.
Supple as a leopard
you enwrapped your lover.
In that instant
I vowed you would be mine!
Yes, I will have you. . .

     (Libretto, p. 15)

When he tells her she must now submit sexually to him or he will kill Mario, the more she expresses hatred of him, the more excited he is at taking her against her will.

Tosca cries out to him: "Don't touch me, devil! I hate you, hate you! Fiend, base villain!"

But Scarpia replies: "What does it matter? Spasms of wrath or spasms of passion . . ."

She hates him more, calling him "foul villain!" Tosca's suffering, hatred, and energy thrill him. He directly conveys that this is what makes him feel more alive: wrath and passion are the same to him. Again, we see how the sadist doesn't care how he gets excited; he just needs constant frantic excitement, and gets it mostly by sexualized wrath which he equates, in a perverse distortion, with passion.

Tosca realizes her dire predicament and so agrees to submit, but only after Scarpia has agreed to instruct his servant to have a sham execution staged, in which Mario will be shot with fake bullets. She has the presence of mind to demand that Scarpia first write a safe passage letter for her and Mario to flee the city the next day. Neither a masochist who enjoys suffering, nor a woman completely helpless and devoid of any aggression, Tosca demonstrates that she's not just a malleable object performing in Scarpia's fantasy; she has agency. She is able to think about survival and get what she needs. As she becomes more real and more powerful, we see the onset of the collapse of Scarpia's fantasy, the one that has shored him up against his terror of inner emptiness and death.

Tosca then sings the hauntingly beautiful aria "Vissi D'arte," lamenting, "I lived for art, I lived for love, never have I harmed a living thing." In her innocence and love for Mario, and in her capacity to forgive, Tosca represents goodness. The perverse mind hates goodness, itself lacking the psychic qualities it takes to be able to love and to forgive. Hatred of the good is another central facet of perversion, stemming from the lack of capacity to feel the empathy required to love and forgive. Scarpia is compelled to destroy anything good.

However, as he writes Tosca's requested letter, she discovers a knife in a fruit bowl. It turns out she does in fact have the capacity to murder Scarpia, and as he approaches to rape her, she stabs him in the chest. Unlike her abuser, Tosca has never caused harm maliciously, but she's able to be aggressive in defense of herself and her lover. As she stabs him to death, she sings,

Is your blood choking you?
And killed by a woman!
Did you torment me enough?
Can you still hear me? Speak!
Look at me! I am Tosca!
Die accursed!
He is dead! And now I pardon him.
All Rome trembled before him!
(Libretto, p. 17)

Here Tosca allows herself a moment of sadistic pleasure; her words humiliate Scarpia before he dies, making him suffer psychologically as well as physically. Thus she puts an end to the rape, and to the terror and humiliation he's inflicted on her. Asserting that she is a full person, she sings, "Look at me! I am Tosca!" As Scarpia dies, she demeans and emasculates him by making him feel subservient to a woman. By letting him know he can no longer insert himself into her mind, or "nest" inside her to control her, Tosca makes him feel powerless. In a masterful reversal, she penetrates his mind, demanding he see and hear her for the real person she is. She voices her valid aggression with a note of legitimate victory, spiced with a measure of sadistic affect, gloating at her success and his demise, and making sure he knows it. Her words demonstrate that sadism is an aspect of even healthy personalities when expressing aggression; she acknowledges her enjoyment of her triumph over her tormenter, and of his suffering. His death represents what he feared most: confronted by the reality of another's separateness and abandonment of him, he is to be left with a terrifying feeling of inner emptiness and dissolution.

Despite drawing on her aggressive and sadistic capacity out of necessity, Tosca is able to return to her empathic self once Scarpia is dead and she is safe. She isn't rigid or perverse; in her expression of triumph, she acknowledges his humanity by forgiving him, and this makes her a more multidimensional being than he was. Asserting the power to kill and the power to forgive, Tosca can love and absolve, the capacities the sadist lacks. By placing candles and a crucifix near his body, she also reclaims the power of the church's symbols, objects used throughout history to dominate and ignore the personhood of women. Rather than pervert the power of the church for her own ends as Scarpia did, Tosca subtly sidesteps the dominating male institution by claiming a personal connection with a just and fair God. Her last words before leaping to her death are that she will see him before God, because she trusts that God sees her as a full person (Tosca, Act 3). Just as evading God represented Scarpia's inability to feel guilt or empathy, Tosca trusts God, since God represents her superego, that part of herself that can be kind and forgiving and help her know right from wrong. Unlike Scarpia, Tosca can draw on an internal good parent. She doesn't allow her sense of self to be diminished by either the church or a powerful man, both of whom would claim that a woman is less than human. In contrast, she embraces the true spiritual meaning of the church as representing a just and kind parent.

Tosca is an object in Scarpia's rigid perverse fantasy. His depraved requirement of her is that she takes the part of a desired object who hates him but
acquiesces because she has no choice. It excites him when she calls him "a
monster" while agreeing to give in. However, he cannot survive if she refuses
to be used in this way. If we view survival as psychic survival, the sadist fears
internal death if unable to repeatedly enact the interminable quest for exciting
aliveness via the sadistic control of another. And so it's precisely at the height of
Scarpia's excitement that Tosca evades his fantasy of her as an object he dominates; she survives his hatred by becoming a subject. She reclaims her subjectivity by taunting him as he dies, insisting that he experience her as a real person,
one with authentic agency.

As I've discussed, Scarpia's sadism is evident. In order to be aroused, he ruth-
lessly tortures Mario, intertwined with his attempt to compel Tosca to consent
to forced sex. But isn't there a masochistic side to a story of sadism? It isn't
evident in Tosca; she does neither invite nor enjoy being dominated. Rather,
Scarpia appears to harbor masochistic yearnings behind his sadism. "Much of
Scarpia's character may be read within a masochistic framework, which casts
Tosca in the dominant role" (Englund, 2020, p. 136). I have described how
Scarpia's sadism operates in the service of excitement and a feeling of aliveness.
Another component is required for his arousal. He requires Tosca's revulsion,
he wants to be hated; revealed as he cries, "How you hate me; that is how
I want you!" He doesn't imagine her compliant gaze, rather he longs for her
to shoot "piercing darts" of hatred into him in order to inflame his desire.
He wants her penetration, foreshadowing the moment when she enters his
body with a knife. The masochist can be coercive, controlling, and directing
the scene that excites him while pretending to be submissive (Panken, 1993).
Scarpia calls the shots in order to be hated by a powerful woman.

Scarpia allows Tosca to hear Mario's screams, and when she rushes to Mario
he sees her as a fierce panther, which makes him want her even more. Scarpia
the masochist forces Tosca to look at his desire, which she finds repellent, while
pretending he is giving in to her demands. When she has no way out, he sings
"Cedo," "I yield . . . you ask of me a life, I of you an instant." He wants to foster
her contempt while he kneels at her feet. The fetishes of feet, shoes, and furs
have been highlighted in some stagings of the opera (Englund, 2020, p. 138).
The purpose of the fetish object for the masochist is to represent the penis so he
can believe the woman doesn't lack a penis, and the masochist can deny the fear
of castration. He gives the woman phallic power with the fetish object, such as
shoes, and furs, which then become erotic objects. Scarpia fears emasculation,
but with the fantasy of the phallic woman, castration is no longer a possibility.

Scarpia desires and fetishizes Tosca's voice in vocal penetration; "if fetishism
is understood as the disavowal of lack, the soprano voice is the ultimate maternal phallus . . . it pours into the body of the listener" (Englund, 2020, p. 141).
Since Scarpia must pursue repeatedly to achieve excitement, relief can only be
achieved in death. Hence

the heart of an interpretation of Scarpia as a masochist would have to be the moment when Tosca thrusts the dagger into his body . . . does he not, in some sense, actually want to expire in Tosca's arms? Is his death not the climax toward which his mise-en-scene has been directed all along?

(Englund, 2020, p. 143)

As the sadist he forces others into humiliated submission, as the masochist he forces others to become the instruments of his excited humiliation. It appears that he wants Tosca to feel revulsion and hatred, and ultimately to penetrate him. She piles on the humiliation as he dies, but he forced her to do this to him. As she stabs him she cries, "This is the kiss of Tosca!," which is perhaps the kiss of death he has been longing for. It is what he deserves, yet he also wants it. She fulfills his desire. She sings as she stabs him, penetrating him vocally as well as literally.

This may be Scarpia's most remarkably deviant desire: he perverts the operatic norm – to be spiritually penetrated by a gradually immaterialized vocal object – by turning it into its opposite, the longing to be physically penetrated by a voice that has taken the material form of a sharp object.

(Englund, 2020, p. 146)

The border between playing safely with the "little death" of orgasm and the lethality of "the big death" disappears, and this boundary violation becomes the ultimate means of achieving ecstasy.

Puccini is a master at using leitmotifs for his characters, which deepen the emotional power of the opera. Scarpia's theme has three chords, B-flat, A-flat, and E. These chords are not harmonically related, signaling Scarpia's unpredictable quality. The orchestra blares out these menacing chords to open the opera, and we feel the foreboding of something terrible about to happen. His theme repeats throughout; one of the more intriguing moments is when in Act II he proposes to Tosca that if she gives in to him sexually he will free Mario. Two of his three chords play, but the music remains suspended while she hesitates. When she agrees, the third chord finally sounds, low and ominous; perhaps it foreshadows her death? Or his? The music is what moves us in opera, and Scarpia's dark theme unequivocally signals evil.

In the third and final act, the story ends with the sorrow of Tosca and Mario's deaths such that love cannot triumph in the face of evil. Does Tosca's death imply that she's being punished for her defiance of a powerful man, and by inference, for defying powerful societal structures? One wonders if perhaps now, as portrayed in a contemporary dramatic work, an abused woman can exact revenge without dying or being deemed insane. Has the calculus changed over time? Perhaps modern artists are more likely to imagine an ending to a drama that allows the woman to have agency, survive, and triumph in love. If the movie were made today, perhaps Thelma and Louise would go to court and mount a legitimate defense. Maybe, maybe not. Art is not meant to be prescriptive or to represent only pure and just ideals or outcomes. But ideas have a context, and social change affects both psychology and artistic expression.

Perhaps there is another symbolic meaning in the deaths of Tosca and Mario. They bravely stood up to perverse sadistic attacks with their goodness and love, but could not survive. Ominously, the perverse attacks continued even after Scarpia's death. It's noteworthy to see how pervasive over time evil characters have been, and disturbing to interpret this opera's ending as implying the enduring nature of such pathology. The ambiguity is sobering; opera is not so far removed from real life. Indeed, Puccini's character of Scarpia, examined from a psychoanalytic perspective, remains a very convincing, timelessly evil perverse sexual predator. The brilliant libretto and incandescent music illuminate the essence of a person who preys on women. We can understand Scarpia's predatory character as perversely organized, both sadistic and masochistic, tormented by terrifying anxieties that overwhelm him and can't be adequately contained. The opera vividly dramatizes how he's compelled to act out his dread by projecting his fear onto others, by sexualizing his aggression, and by trying to suck a feeling of life out of others by being violent towards them, and by compelling his own violent death.

Tosca moves us with its drama and music, and pushes us to feel deeply unsettled by the disturbingly evil character of Scarpia. But uncomfortably we, the audience, become implicated as fantasy becomes reality. We cheer at Scarpia's death. Perhaps we are too uneasy to be aware of our participation in the sadomasochistic excitement as Scarpia is humiliated and Tosca dominates and triumphs. As Ogden noted, containing dread involves finding and using abstract symbolic forms; this opera exemplifies how art can express dread symbolically, helping the audience experience, process, and contain its own.

References

Alford, F. C. (1997). *What evil means to us*. Ithaca: Cornell U. Press.

Balas, A. (2019). Psychoanalytic perspectives on the empowerment of women. *Journal of the American Psychoanalytic Association Review of Books*, 67, 533–544.

Baron-Cohen, S. (2011). *The science of evil: On empathy and the origins of cruelty*. New York: Basic Books.

Calder, T. (2020). The concept of evil. In *The Stanford encyclopedia of philosophy*. Edward N. Zalta (ed.), plato.stanford.edu/archives/sum2020/entries/concept-evil, 1.1–4.6.

Cleckley, H. (1964). *The mask of sanity*. Saint Louis: The C.V. Mosby Company.

Coen, S. J. (1991). The excitement of sadomasochism. In *The misuse of persons*. Hillsdale: The Analytic Press.

Cordingly, J. (2015). *Disordered heroes in opera; A psychiatric report*. London: Plumbago Books and Arts.

Englund, A. (2020). *Deviant opera; Sex, power, and perversion on stage*. Oakland: University of California Press.

Freud, S. (1905). Three essays on the theory of sexuality. In J. Strachey (Ed. and Trans.) *The standard edition of the complete psychological works of Sigmund Freud* (Vol. 7, pp. 125–245). London: The Hogarth Press.

Kaplan, L. (1991). *Female perversions*. New York: Doubleday.

Kerman, J. (1988). *Opera as drama*. Oakland: University of California Press.

Maloy, R. J. (2002). The polymorphously perverse psychopath: Understanding a strong empirical relationship. *Bulletin of the Menninger Clinic*, 66(3), 273–289.

Ogden, T. H. (1989a). On the concept of an autistic-contiguous position. *International Journal of Psychoanalysis*, 70, 127–140.

Ogden, T. H. (1989b). *The primitive edge of experience*. Northdale: Jason Aronson. *Psychoanalysis*, 70, 127–140.

Panken, S. (1993). *The joy of suffering*. Northvale: Jason Aronson.

Plotkin, F. (1994). *Opera 101: A complete guide to learning and loving opera*. New York: Hyperion.

Puccini, G. (Composer), Giacosa, G., and Illica, L. (Librettists) (1900/1953). *Tosca*. W. Burdett (Trans.), V. de Sabata (Conductor). Milan: Angel Records 3508 B (35060–1).

Pulver, S. E. and Akhtar, S. (1991). Sadomasochism in the perversions. *Journal of the American Psychoanalytic Association*, 39, 741–755.

Sorrentino, R., Miussleman, M., and Broderick, L. (2019). Battered woman syndrome; Is it enough for a not guilty by reason of insanity plea? *Psychiatric Times*, 36(1), 24.

Stein, R. (2005). Why perversion? 'False love' and the perverse pact. *International Journal of Psychoanalysis*, 86, 775–799.

Zarrucchi, J. M. (2000). Review of images of rape: The "Heroic" tradition and its alternatives. by Diane Wolfthal (1999). *Woman's Art Journal*, 21(2), 58–60.

9 Sliding Walls and Glimpses of the Other in Puccini's *Madama Butterfly*

Steven H. Goldberg

Pinkerton: " . . . and the walls . . ."
Goro: "They come and go at will, as the mood takes you . . ."
Puccini, Madama Butterfly, Act 1

(Libretto, p. 47)

Japan's borders were opened by force to the West in 1853, and Puccini's *Madama Butterfly* (1904) is in part a result of European interest in all things Japanese. In the opening lines of this opera, the sliding walls of traditional Japanese design, which have sustained Japanese life for many centuries, are viewed by the westerner as "fragile as a puff of wind" (Libretto, p. 49). Walls, and the complicated ways in which they open and close, are built up and taken down, and are employed flexibly or rigidly, constitute a central psychological metaphor in this opera, referring to barriers between cultures, genders, and social classes. Walls as explored in this opera also refer to internal barriers of defensive repressions, splits, projections, and dissociations, as well as areas of psychic blindness that result from what is not yet, or what is only weakly, represented in the mind.

From another vantage point, walls constitute healthy and necessary boundaries that allow for the development and maintenance of a cohesive sense of self. And it is the sliding open of walls, tenuous as that often is, that affords a glimpse of an other, and provides testimony to the connectivity and porousness potentially present in all human relationships. Music itself – and nowhere more than in opera, with its synergy of libretto and music – often serves this latter function of connectivity in that its essentially embodied nature and privileged access to emotional life allows us more fully "to feel" our way into contact with self and other. "Because the forms of human feeling are much more congruent with musical forms than with the forms of language, music can *reveal* the nature of feelings with a detail and truth that language cannot approach" (Langer, 1996, italics in original). In its capacity to reveal and explore emotional life, music serves to bridge defensive disconnections between mind and body, idea and feeling. This bridging function exerts an impact on the audience experiencing this opera; though the events depicted occurred over a century ago, the psychological/emotional issues involving barriers to understanding of self and

DOI: 10.4324/9781032271408-9

other may be seen as a mirror in which we see our own ongoing struggles with these basic human dilemmas.[1]

Recognizing the Subjectivity of the Other

As the opera begins,[2] Pinkerton, a handsome, testosterone-driven young naval officer, self-confident to the point of being intoxicated with himself and the virtues of his culture, is posted to Nagasaki. Japan has recently opened its walls to visitors from the West, and the West is fascinated by its exotic art, clothing, and women. The young man rents a house, whose walls, in the Japanese style, are easily movable so that the rooms and open spaces can be re-configured at will. Along with the house comes a beautiful fifteen-year-old geisha, Cio-Cio-San, better known as Butterfly, with whom he becomes increasingly enamored. He admits that he doesn't know the proportions of love or lust that fuel his romantic desire, but he is not too concerned about this, nor does he fret about the opening and closing of walls, both internal and external, because he knows that their marriage is not for real, and that soon enough he will have a "real" marriage to a suitable American woman.

The young Japanese woman is from an impoverished though honorable samurai background; her father was ordered to commit ritual suicide by the emperor, and her mother ekes out a life as best she can. For this young woman, this is the man with whom she will spend the rest of her life. She converts to his religion and embarks upon learning about his culture; her family disowns her for doing so. As the marriage ceremony is about to begin, we hear in the orchestra the death/suicide theme that will resound with devastating effect at the conclusion of the opera. The germ of this tragic tale of insensitivity and misunderstanding is foretold in its opening minutes.

Stepping back from the specifics of misrecognition between American naval officer and Japanese geisha, and viewing the opera from a more broadly psychological perspective, we might ask a number of questions. How well can we know another person or the other in ourselves? How much do we want to know about ourselves and others, especially when such knowing disrupts precious illusions and undermines firmly held projections? Is our understanding of self and other like the walls of the Japanese house that we consciously and unconsciously open and close as we wish, alternately promoting and foreclosing psychological growth? Finally, which questions can we not even register as questions, because they have not yet achieved sufficient representation in our minds? While on the one hand there is much that we don't want to know, there is at the same time a fear of not knowing, which leads to oversimplified and misleading solutions, often in the nature of projections and stereotypes. These are questions that are at the emotional heart of this opera, a tragedy in which there are no full-fledged villains, and which holds up a mirror to our own capacities for misunderstanding, abuse of power, and self-serving constructions (and constrictions) of ourselves and others.

Madama Butterfly explores grievous and eventually tragic misunderstandings based upon barriers of culture, gender, wealth, and social status. The clash of cultures between the United States and Japan conveyed in both the drama and the music brings into bold relief the unavoidable differences between people and the inevitability of misunderstanding. The cruel misunderstanding and mistreatment suffered by Butterfly from within her own family and culture deepen the universality of these themes. To consistently experience the subjectivity, the individuality of the other person is one of the most difficult psychological attainments, even under the best of circumstances. And yet, as the literary critic Lionel Trilling famously wrote, "The essence of moral life is making a willing suspension of disbelief in the selfhood of someone else" (quoted in Shengold, 1995, p. 61). In this formulation, disbelief in the selfhood of the other is the default position, and psychological work and emotional growth are required to suspend it. Often it requires the presence of another mind to offer a third perspective. The extreme failure of suspending such disbelief is captured in Erik Erikson's notion of "pseudospeciation," in which the fundamental humanity of the other is radically denied and denigrated (Erikson, 1966). At our best, in our relations with others, we are like Sharpless, the seasoned American consul in Nagasaki, at least raising questions about how the other person experiences the world, and relating with a certain empathy and concern for the hurt our misunderstanding might cause. At our worst, we are like Pinkerton, or in certain ways like Butterfly, either not wishing to ask or not able to raise the questions that would matter, because they are potentially too disruptive and painful.

Pinkerton

For Pinkerton, Butterfly is all too much a product of his own fantasies and imagination, not yet a fully conceived other. She is a beautiful and alluring woman in a Japanese painting, who flutters out of the painting and into his life, only to be possessed and enjoyed by him in the present moment. The walls that foreclose Pinkerton's understanding of the other are shut tight. For Butterfly, Pinkerton is a dream come true, a powerful and wealthy young man who can rescue her from the poverty of her childhood and the humiliations of her work. He is to be her new family, a combined father-mother-husband. Her internal barriers to understanding cloud a realistic view of her situation, while at the same time her boundaries are insufficiently stable, rendering her vulnerable to exploitation and loss of a stable sense of self.

Each character sees the reality that he/she wishes to see, and is incapable of seeing, even when confronted with the wisdom of the fatherly and in many ways psychoanalyst-like Sharpless. There is an asymmetry here in that Pinkerton is involved in deliberate deception regarding his motives, while Butterfly's intentions are transparent and without artifice. And yet each is lost in his/her own subjectivity, unaware of and misunderstanding the subjectivity of the other.

Pinkerton is recognizable – both in his words and perhaps even more so in his music – as a self-confident but not entirely unlikable, somewhat immature, and oblivious young man. Though not at all reflective or self-aware, he has a romantic side, as he is truly "taken" by Butterfly, whom he weaves into his fantasies of love and erotic pleasure. He is not so oblivious, however, as to be unaware, on some level, that he is exploiting her. "He does what he pleases wherever he goes" (Pinkerton, Libretto, p. 61). A collector of women, he is drawn to Butterfly's mystery and difference, and wants to possess it and her. Her cultural and physical difference from the women of his culture is part of her allure; such difference renders her especially suitable for stereotyping and projections of erotic fantasy. The implicit power differential fuels his sexually charged fantasies as well.

What eventually renders Pinkerton a more interesting and three-dimensional character is some opening up of insight and psychological transformation at the end of the opera. This is manifest in his genuine guilt, remorse, and increased self-understanding, reflected both in the text and in the emotional tone of the music, which takes on an unmistakably more weighty and tormented quality. Unlike the brash and extroverted quality of his music earlier in the opera, much of his music in the final act is in a minor mode, with a plaintive quality that at times seems to border on weeping. For example, in his final aria, he sings, "Addio fiorito asil/ Farewell flowery refuge" (Libretto, p. 221). The final vocal notes of the opera are Pinkerton sobbing "Butterfly! Butterfly! Butterfly!" (Libretto, p. 235). These qualities of both music and text depict him as less emotionally walled off both from himself and from Butterfly. He is tormented by his past behavior and recognizes that its consequences will be permanent.

> Yes, all at once I see my mistake, and I feel that I shall never be free from this torment . . . Farewell, flowery refuge of joy and of love! I shall be tortured forever by the sight of her sweet face.
>
> *(Libretto, pp. 220–221)*

The wrenchingly sad resonance of Pinkerton's music in these final moments lends weight to the genuineness of his contrition and self-awareness of the damage he has wrought.

No sliding of walls can hide the damage or the inter-generational suffering set in motion by Pinkerton's actions. Though his comprehension of Butterfly remains limited, he now shows some understanding of what Sharpless had told him at the outset, that the marriage meant something entirely different to Butterfly than it did to him. "And if you think the marriage contract and her trust are only a mockery, think what you're doing. She trusts you" (Libretto, pp. 105–107). A tragic "confusion of tongues" (Ferenczi, 1933) has occurred, in which Pinkerton and Butterfly have spoken vastly different languages of love and commitment. Pinkerton has crushed Butterfly's wings, and he will never be quite the same for knowing this.

A further sense of loss for Pinkerton is an intimation, at least in some productions, that the intense pleasure and excitement he experienced in his youthful affair with Butterfly is something he will never again experience in his marriage to Kate, his new American wife. From this point of view, whatever happiness he experiences in his marriage to this seemingly loving and sensitive woman will be tinged with his loss of innocence and the unhappiness connected to Butterfly's betrayal and suicide. His son will be a reminder of both what he has gained and what he has lost.

On the other hand, there is much that has not changed for Pinkerton. It is only when he learns that they have a child that he decides to see Butterfly again. There is a terrible callousness in his willingness to take their child from her, even if he is convinced that it is best for the child. (Interestingly, the fatherly Sharpless and the maternal Kate collude with him in this. While their internal walls seem more flexible, even they go only so far in their suspension of disbelief in Butterfly's full status as a mother and as a person). And even at the end, Pinkerton does not see clearly enough what seems inevitable – that his abandonment of Butterfly and his taking their child would not only clip her wings but would also leave her without honor and reason to live.

Butterfly

Early in the opera, Butterfly is characterized as both sweetly innocent and vulnerable, and as mysterious and exotic. All of these qualities are conveyed musically in her use of both real and invented Japanese folk melodies, which rely on pentatonic and modal harmonies that sound exotic to western ears. Although immensely likable and deserving of our sympathy, she is childlike (and only fifteen years old!) and naïve in many respects, and seems an easy target for exploitation. Like Pinkerton, she has a way of avoiding certain realities, swayed as she is by her immense longing and the power of her wishes, dreams, and fantasies.

There is a merger-like quality to Butterfly's love, as she seeks to re-find the parents she has lost and to repair the trauma she has suffered. She wishes for a relationship without walls, essentially without boundaries or separation, a quality captured in Balint's concept of "primary love" (Balint, 1960, 1979). She idealizes and makes efforts to adopt Pinkerton's culture, but she has no real understanding of it below the surface. Those walls are not easily shifted, constituted as they are by the almost sacred nature of the transitional space of the culture into which we are born (Winnicott, 1967). For several years, Butterfly is unable to face the reality of her loss, as she holds to a tenacious but fragile wait for her husband to return; "fragile" because there are a few brief and terrifying moments when reality threatens to break through her defensive barriers. She experiences herself as powerless and abandoned, and it is only the quasi-delusional belief that Pinkerton will return that sustains her. Butterfly, like Pinkerton, cannot tolerate anyone doubting the truth of her convictions, and she determinedly silences anyone who would try.

If Butterfly's difficulty in facing reality is reinforced by the ways in which her culture has limited and derogated her, Pinkerton's difficulty with reality is enhanced by the ways in which his culture has elevated and aggrandized him. Neither deserves the treatment he/she has received (Harasemovich, 2017). Each is both defined and, in some sense, imprisoned by the culture that they inhabit and which inhabits them.

For Butterfly, without acceptance of the reality of her loss, there is little possibility of mourning or psychological change, though she does seem to develop a certain depth through suffering, as well as fortitude in her motherly devotion to her son and her steely conviction that Pinkerton will return. It is only in the very last moments of the opera that Butterfly can no longer avoid what is real and imminent. It is the jolt of encountering Kate that leads to a deeper understanding of her situation. These are moments of genuine psychological insight and growth, involving shifting of her internal boundaries, in which she finally opens her eyes to what she could not allow herself to see earlier. She then acts with resolve and dignity, simultaneously expressing her deep love for her son and her wish for him to have a better life, her recognition that her own life is over, and both her love and her hate for Pinkerton. Her farewell to her son is one of the most heart-wrenching moments in music theater, embodying the primal intensity of a mother's love for her child. And perhaps in fantasy she is also saying goodbye to her own infantile self, which now has no way of surviving in her own body and culture, but can live on vicariously in the beloved son who carries a part of her.

As was the case with Pinkerton, the deepening of Butterfly's character is reflected in her music, which now has a greater dimensionality, emotional range, and conviction, moving among confusion, despair, fury, tenderness, and resignation, to name only a few of the many affective shadings conveyed in her singing. (In her second act aria "Un bel di vedremo" ["one fine day we will see"] (Libretto, p. 155) the shifting nuances of emotional experience are almost too numerous to count). This is no longer the music of a vulnerable fifteen-year-old. An abandoned wife and mother, she now accepts what is, and resolves to take her fate into her own hands. Her suicide is her last remaining remnant of power, honor, and self-determination, reflecting the development of needed internal walls that demarcate a sense of self and feeling of agency. Her turning her sword against herself embodies a phallic quality that belies her submissiveness earlier in the opera and challenges the boundaries of fixed gender stereotypes.

Why does Butterfly give up her son without more of a fight? Here, one hundred plus years after this story takes place and in an entirely different cultural milieu, we strain our own capacities for empathy in our attempts to understand. Perhaps we can't really understand – those walls let in too little light. Perhaps that is reflected in the way in which the opera ends on an unresolved chord – that is, a chord which leaves the music, and us, hanging. Is it something like the emperor's order to her father to kill himself, an authority which must be obeyed within the hierarchical and cultural rules of that society?: "So be it. I have to obey him" Libretto, p. 229). As a woman of that time and place, does she feel that she has any rights at all? Does her new identity as an "American" wife obligate her to ensure that her son will become a proper American boy? Or at a deeper psychological level, is it an act of maternal devotion and sense of agency, agreeing (perhaps without sufficient questioning) that she has little to offer her son, while Pinkerton and Kate offer the prospect of a better life? She wants her son to remember her as a proud wife and mother, and not as a dishonored and humiliated woman singing and dancing for her supper. Perhaps submitting to

Pinkerton's will is less malignant and less dishonoring than submitting to the harsh fate of her own culture and its treatment of a husbandless mother and young boy, without financial resources and disowned by her own family.

Sharpless

Sharpless is the third major character in this opera, representing a voice of maturity and compassion. His particular interest in the drama is that, unlike the other characters (except to some extent Suzuki, Butterfly's beloved maid) he is reflective enough to ask the difficult questions that others would not, and could not, raise. In the questions and quasi-interpretations with which he challenges Pinkerton, and in his resigned acceptance that he can only partially penetrate Pinkerton's walls, he displays a psychoanalyst-like manner. He also conveys a quasi-analytic attitude in his agonizing attempts to confront Butterfly with truths that she is unready to face.

But his walls, too, place limits on the questions he is willing to ask, the assumptions that he is willing to jeopardize or displace. Wise and experienced as he is, he retains a certain attitude of unexamined cultural hegemony, especially in accepting uncritically the idea that the boy should return to America. Partly this is a function of defensive repressions and internal splitting operations that keep at bay the problems to which he might otherwise have access. And partly it is a matter of what Steiner (1985, p. 161) has termed "turning a blind eye," in which reality is partly or potentially known, but turned away from and ignored. But perhaps because of his very thoughtfulness, Sharpless displays even more clearly than Pinkerton or Butterfly yet another kind of barrier in which potential questions are not yet represented, and so are unavailable for conscious reflection for reasons other than those involving internal defensive moves. These not yet represented thoughts/feelings have not yet been submitted to mental processes that would render them suitable for thinking, dreaming, and other forms of psychological work (Ogden, 2004.) In this state of mind, Sharpless is reminiscent of the fish in the celebrated David Foster Wallace's (2005) speech who, when asked how is the water, responds "what the hell is water?" Empathy requires awareness of both what one does and doesn't know. "Empathy means acknowledging a horizon of context that extends perpetually beyond what you can see . . ." (Jamison, 2014, p. 5). Such dilemmas characterize every human relationship, not least the analyst's struggle with each patient. For patient and analyst alike, lifelong character defenses and turning a blind eye obscure what we might otherwise know, while entrenched cultural attitudes make it difficult to notice the very water in which we psychologically swim.

Sharpless takes a fatherly interest in Butterfly; he is the only one who tries to protect her in a non-self-interested way. Does he have an erotic interest in Butterfly? He does seem taken by her beauty and her vulnerable and sweetly innocent manner, but he seems respectful of the generational and cultural boundaries (another constructive sense in which walls function), and by what he recognizes as her continued devotion to Pinkerton. He may be somewhat overwhelmed by the intensity of her suffering, and while he wants to help, he may have reinforced his internal walls of self-protection that keep him at a certain distance: "This is unbearable" (Libretto, p. 211). In his evident anger at Pinkerton for the harm Pinkerton has done to Butterfly (three times in the final act he says to Pinkerton, "Didn't I tell you"), it seems likely that he is deflecting a current of self-blame – justified or not – for not having done more to protect her. Whatever range of feelings he has seems both sublimated and responsible. And yet he, along with Pinkerton and Butterfly, is likely to be changed permanently by his immersion in the tragic unfolding of events.

Walls That Divide and Walls That Connect

The configuration of walls both divides and connects – in architecture, in interpersonal relationships, and in internal relations with oneself. Having emphasized some of the barriers, which separate and lead to misrecognition and misunderstanding, I want now to underscore a theme of connectivity – porousness and opening of walls – that I believe also pervades this opera, and which is in dynamic tension, both in text and in music, with the barriers that divide. The marriage, betrayal, and eventual suicide at the center of this opera radiate outward with a centrifugal force that deeply affects the lives of each character going forward. Even events in the more remote past have this effect: in a chilling repetition, the emperor's order that Butterfly's father commit ritual suicide affects her life in powerful ways, playing a potent role in her own suicide. For how many generations will these events continue to live on in the conscious and even more so in the unconscious minds of those that follow? This notion of connectivity is reminiscent of another "butterfly" story, this time from the annals of chaos theory: a butterfly flaps its wings in the east and a hurricane is stirred in the west. While there is much to divide the characters from each other's emotional lives, there is also a powerful interpenetration that connects the characters far beyond their conscious awareness.

Musically, the theme of walls that do or do not move, that both divide and connect, is explored in this opera in relation to the shifting boundaries that are represented in the musical rendering of time. *Madama Butterfly* has a particularly complicated relation to time, in which chronological time and psychological time are constantly juxtaposed and played with. Puccini exploits the unparalleled ability of music to represent linear as well as recursive time, and to layer simultaneously past, present, and future. In subtle but compelling ways, early musical events prefigure later ones, while later developments repeat, reflect upon, and transform the past, lending a particular richness and texture to the present. This attenuation of boundaries is true to one's lived experience of psychological time and renders particularly noticeable its non-linear and at times uncanny aspects.

The boundaries between present, past, and future are both maintained and dissolved in Puccini's use of leitmotivs, or recurring musical phrases identified with a psychological experience or material event, to convey aspects of the inner worlds of his characters. This technique, derived from Wagner, allows Puccini to capture at once both the movement and evolution in time of their inner lives in the continuous musical transformations of the motivic material, as well as the recursive nature of character and the force of one's personal and familial history reflected in the musical continuities and repetitions (Goldberg, 2011). Like narrative motives that appear and re-appear in clinical psychoanalysis, Puccini's musical leitmotivs "take time to disclose their full potential" (Budden, 2002, p. 272), and adopt different colorations depending upon context, vicissitudes of interpersonal relationship, and degree of access to previously unconscious or unrepresented material.[3]

Further musical examples of the shifting of time boundaries abound in this opera. In the Act 1 love duet, time both expands and contracts as boundaries involving person (sharing the same melodic phrases, at times singing in perfect unison) and time (the boundlessness of romantic bliss, the telescoping of Butterfly's development from childlike beauty to sexual bride) seem to dissolve. And even in the midst of this sensual and transporting duet, Puccini has a way of insinuating a passage of darker and more disturbing music that anticipates future suffering. This appears in a disturbing moment when Butterfly confronts Pinkerton with "They say that in other countries if a butterfly is caught by a man, she is transfixed with a pin and fastened to a board" (Libretto, p. 141). Here, in both text and music, Butterfly is foreshadowing the determined steeliness and separateness that characterize her final moments before her suicide. Similarly, for Pinkerton, a poignant moment of foreshadowing of his later contrition occurs in Act 1, when he attempts, in a moment of unexpected verbal and musical tenderness, to console Butterfly after her renunciation by her family: "My child, do not weep because of the croaking of these frogs" (Libretto, p. 129). Events disconnected from each other in chronological time take on meaningful interconnections and layerings in such musical rendering of non-linear time.

In the overnight vigil scene in Act 2, one has a sense in the music of time slowing down almost to a standstill, with Butterfly waiting, longing, and hoping. Musical themes from the Act 1 love duet come and go, as Butterfly recalls the past, and in some sense re-lives the past and longs for the future in the present of her waking dream. And in her suicide, which echoes her father's suicide many years before, there is a sense of time as recursive and non-linear. Music from the same love duet also returns for Pinkerton in the closing moments of the opera, but now with a darker and more somber cast. Musical transformation of the earlier material reflects, both for Pinkerton and Butterfly, a new and more integrated understanding of what occurred between them, an instance of musical *après coup*.

Themes of connectivity and the tension between what connects and what divides are also conveyed musically in the use of pentatonic scales and melodies from Japanese folk songs, mostly heard in Butterfly's music, and which inflect the essentially western character of the musical exposition. Again quoting Budden:

> The Japanese folk-element adds a fresh colour to the Puccinian spectrum. [Connection] Be it noted, however, that the native melodies are heard

strictly through Western ears and their expressive possibilities exploited accordingly. [Division] The character of the original texts bears no relation to the use Puccini makes of them. In this way they become fully integrated into the language of the score instead of remaining extraneous patches on it.

(2002, p. 243)

The notion of "hearing through Western ears" resonates with the opera's theme of the other seen and experienced through the only sometimes movable barriers of one's own eyes and ears. This is a musical version of what Edward Said (1978) has termed "Orientalism." One might also say that this is a musical version of perhaps the most challenging problem faced by the psychoanalyst in trying to achieve optimal receptivity to the patient's unique language.[4]

The orchestral writing throughout the opera provides far more than an evocative accompaniment for the voices. Rather, particularly in its use of recurring musical phrases, it constitutes an "orchestral register of experience" (Goldberg, 2011) that amplifies, comments upon, and adds layering and associations to the unfolding of both character and story. As previously mentioned, the use of these Wagnerian leitmotives looks both backward and forward in time, as well as inward into shadings of emotions and ideas of which the characters may not be consciously aware. An additional quality of the orchestral writing is the way in which it moves back and forth between more harmonic and contrapuntal accompaniment of the singers, and instrumental doubling of the vocal line in which two (or more) separate sonorities double the same note. At times there is a sense of a near merger between singers and orchestra; at other times, which are not infrequent, the orchestra plays either extended passages alone, or all but stops as we hear one voice alone, in its utter emotional nakedness.

In the final moments of *Madama Butterfly*, there are several occasions when the sung music, at least in some performances,[5] becomes close to a human scream or sob, in which the power of the primal emotion seems to burst the boundaries of what can be contained in music. Two examples are Butterfly's goodbye to her son, and Pinkerton's cry of "Butterfly, Butterfly, Butterfly" in the final moments. Just as words, in their organizing function, often lose contact with the actual qualities of lived experience, which are better conveyed in music, these are moments when we become aware that music, too, has its own organizing quality that struggles at times to convey the disordered and primal quality of certain emotional experiences. When melody shades into a scream or a cry, we are made aware of this boundary.

A final tension that I wish to discuss between what connects and what divides is reflected in the complicated relationship between words and music in this (or any) opera. The overall relationship is one of synergy, each modality going beyond what the other alone is capable of conveying. And yet that very synergy also demarcates some of the essential differences between words and music: "Where words leave off, music begins" (Attributed to the German poet Heinrich Heine, 2021). Or as famously expressed by Wagner

Wait until you hear the work with the music; that will make everything plain to you, in terms, however, not of words, which are a clumsy tool created by human reflection, but of feeling; for music, which comes from the foundations, not the surface, of man and things, is capable of a thousand shades of suggestion that are beyond the capacity of words.

(Newman, p. 231)

For the characters in the opera as for the audience, the emotionally evocative quality of the music facilitates connection, or re-connection between mind/idea and body/feeling. Understanding of self, like understanding of other, is based on an embodied quality of experience, in which one feels oneself into another (or another aspect of self). Such experience is an important element of Trilling's willing suspension of disbelief in the reality of the other. When Pinkerton describes Butterfly as a figure in a painting, he has lost contact with her as an embodied, and hence real, person. Tragically it is only when he witnesses her suicide that she is more fully returned to her embodied form as a full human being. Music, in its intrinsically embodied nature, serves to re-connect some of those defensive separations of mind and body that lead to grievous misunderstandings of self and other that underlie untold human suffering.

Notes

1 Though many implications for the psychoanalytic situation, not to mention contemporary political issues, will undoubtedly occur to the reader, I have chosen in this contribution to leave most of these connections to the experience and imagination of the reader.
2 A synopsis of the opera is attached as an appendix for readers insufficiently familiar with the outlines of the story.
3 Budden provides a cogent example.

> The second fragment of "The Lion of Echigo" [Japanese folk tune] first appears as mere descriptive *japonnerie*. Only when harmonized unequivocally in a minor key does it convey Butterfly's regret at life's tempests and the consul's despair at her credulity.
>
> *(2002, p. 272, italics in original)*

4 Puccini may be lauded for studying Japanese musical idioms and making a serious effort to question ethnic and cultural differences in his work as a musician. Like Sharpless, he is willing to ask at least certain questions. On the other hand, I by no means assume that Puccini was at all times consciously representing these themes in his music, much of which would have been unconscious. In addition, Puccini had other, more purely musical reasons for his interest in Asian music in that, like other composers of his time, he was searching for unfamiliar harmonies and novel sounds to broaden his musical palette.
5 While the musical score of the opera is constant, the realization of the music by the individual artist makes a great deal of difference in the impact and effects on the listener. In an additional manifestation of the interrelationship between walls that divide and walls that open, the musician must interpret and perform the music in his/her own way, rendering it his/her own, depending upon abilities, training, individuality of voice quality, etc. At the same time, the performer must re-dream or re-compose Puccini's musical dream in the moment of performance, all the while interacting with the other musicians in their own re-dreaming of the music, in what amounts to a highly complex artistic co-creation.

References

Balint, M. (1960). Primary narcissism and primary love. *Psychoanalytic Quarterly* 29: 6–43.

Balint, M. (1979). *The basic fault: Therapeutic aspects of regression*. London: Tavistock Publications.

Budden, J. (2002). *Puccini: His life and works*. Oxford: Oxford University Press.

Erikson, E. (1966) Pseudospeciation. https://en.wikipedia.org/wiki/Pseudospeciation.

Ferenczi, S. (1955 [1933]). The confusion of tongues between child and adult. In *Final contributions to the problems and methods of psychoanalysis*. New York: Basic Books, 156–167.

Goldberg, S. (2011). Love, loss, and transformation in Wagner's *Die Walkure*. *Fort Da* 17: 53–60.

Harasemovich, J. (2017). Personal communication.

Heine, H. (2021). https://www.goodreads.com/author/show/16071.Heinrich_Heine.

Jamison, L. (2014). *The empathy exams*. Minneapolis: Grey Wolf Press.

Langer, S. (1996). *Philosophy in a new key: A study in the symbolism of reason, rite, and art*. Cambridge, MA: The Belknap Press/Harvard University.

Newman, E. (1949). *The Wagner operas*. Princeton, NJ: Princeton University Press.

Ogden, T. H. (2004). This art of psychoanalysis: Dreaming undreamt dreams and interrupted cries. *International Journal of Psychoanalysis* 85: 857–877.

Puccini, G. (1904). Madama butterfly. *London Records* 411: 634–2 (Tullio Serafin, Conductor).

Said, E. W. (1978). *Orientalism*. New York: Random House.

Shengold, L. (1995). *Delusions of everyday life*. New Haven, CT: Yale University Press.

Steiner, J. (1985). Turning a blind eye: The cover up for Oedipus. *International Review of Psychoanalysis* 12: 161–172.

Wallace, D. F. (2005). Kenyon college commencement Address. https:web.ics.purdue.edu/~drkelly/DFWKenyonAddress2005.pdf

Winnicott, D. W. (1967). The location of cultural experience. *International Journal of Psychoanalysis* 48: 368–372.

10 Elektra

Traumatic Loss and the Impossibility of Mourning

Catherine Mallouh

> But it is not so easy to decide what it is that gives these cries of Electra in her anguish their power to cut and wound and excite.
>
> *(Woolf, 1925, p. 43)*

The opera *Elektra* delves into a world of tragedy, vengeance, violence, and murder, and the figure of Elektra stands at its center with her unwavering drive to avenge the death of her father. Filled with narrative dramatic tension and unrelenting emotional intensity, the opera moves forcefully to its tragic conclusion. The dramatic themes in the music, marked by its distinctive dissonance and atonality, create and heighten this tension.

What is behind the tragedy and emotional intensity? A psychoanalytic lens brings into focus the motivations and inner states of the characters, evoking ideas such as identification, repetition, pathologic mourning, and melancholia. What is seen clearly in this opera are the effects of trauma on the individual and across generations. I will discuss and elaborate how Elektra has experienced traumatic losses that foreclose mourning, profoundly affect her states of mind, and lead to a desire for vengeance that distorts her sense of herself, her relationships, and, ultimately, sacrifices her life. I will also explore how the other members of her family contend with these traumas, their difficulties with loss and mourning, and living out the repercussions of the past.

The History and Context of the Opera

The opera premiered in 1909 in Dresden. It was one of Strauss's early operas and his first collaboration with the Austrian writer, Hugo von Hofmannsthal. Hofmannsthal's play, *Elektra*, based on the Sophocles tragedy, inspired Strauss when he saw it performed around 1905. He and Hofmannsthal adapted the text of the play for the opera. The opera's narrative elaborates the repercussions of the brutal murder of Elektra's father, Agamemnon, by her mother, Clytemnestra, and her lover, now husband, Aegisthus, with whom Clytemnestra now rules Mycenae. Miserable, abject, and badly treated by her mother and Aegisthus, Elektra is consumed by her father's murder and a seething desire for revenge.

DOI: 10.4324/9781032271408-10

At the same time, her sister, Chrysothemis, resides compliantly with her mother and step-father, but still keeps an allegiance to Elektra. Elektra awaits the return of her brother Orestes, who will carry out the vengeful murders of Clytemnestra and Aegisthus. At a young age, Orestes had been sent into exile by his mother, and has now been called upon by the gods to avenge his father's death. Elektra also has called for her brother's return but despairs he will never come. When the sisters and their mother are told that he is dead, she asks her sister to commit the murders with her. But Chrysothemis does not agree, running away in horror. As Elektra then contemplates murdering them herself, she is encountered by Orestes. They do not recognize each other at first, as Orestes is in disguise and has constructed the ruse of his death to steal back into Mycenae. He sees Elektra's broken state, and they have an emotional and bittersweet reunion. The murders then ensue: Orestes first kills Clytemnestra while Electra listens outside the palace, and then Aegisthus, after Elektra coaxes Aegisthus to enter the palace despite his misgivings. After a final exchange with her sister, Chrysothemis, Elektra dances a triumphal dance, and falls to the ground dead.

The opera shifts away from the moral complexity and focus on justice of the Sophocles play, with its more restrained emotion and references to the gods as powerfully influential on the actions of men. Instead, Strauss and Hofmannsthal created an opera that is deeply psychological, exploring the subjective motivations and feelings of anguish, dread, hope, and fear – primarily of Elektra, Chrysothemis, and Clytemnestra in the long aftermath of Agamemnon's murder. Freud's contemporaneous development of psychoanalysis and his understanding that Greek myths reflect interior psychological conflict reverberates throughout Strauss and Hofmannsthal's expressionistically aesthetic elaboration of the inner turmoil of these characters. The dynamics that play out in this complex family structure are born of their own individual inner conflicts and feelings, and the profound effects they have on each other. Structured around a series of conversations, entreaties, disclosures, and arguments, filled with harrowing, raw emotion – between Elektra and her dead father, her sister, her mother, and her brother – the action of the opera is driven forward by Elektra's single-minded desire for revenge, and the music powerfully expresses their emotional states.

The Sophocles play refers directly to the earlier death of Iphigenia, the older sister of Elektra, whom Agamemnon sacrificed in order to appease the goddess Artemis and gain her sanction to set sail for Troy. In the contentious scene between Clytemnestra and Elektra in the play, Clytemnestra asserts that Iphigenia was needlessly and wrongly sacrificed, while Elektra defends her father's actions as a necessary response to the gods, pointing out that, even so, Clytemnestra should not have taken justice into her own hands. It is noteworthy that this important history is left out of the opera. The viewers, however, know of this history, implicitly making it part of the opera, even though it is not discussed or ever referred to.

The tragedy of the house of Atreus and the history preceding the action of this opera also live in memory – again, a history that is known but not explicitly named. From a psychoanalytic perspective, the questions arise: How does the sacrifice of Iphigenia and the preceding generations of trauma and violence, which are not openly acknowledged, have expression in this work? How does this history of loss live on in the psyches of these characters? How do the more immediate traumas shape their emotional lives and relationships?

In the discussion of the opera that follows, a psychoanalytic perspective will be interwoven with an in-depth description of each scene and the characters with whom Elektra is in conversation. Each of these conversations further elucidates Elektra's inner world as well as that of the family member she is engaging. The richness and complexity of the exchanges between Elektra and her family, what is revealed of their inner lives, and the dynamics between them brings us inside the emotional experience of the opera as it unfolds.

Traumatic Loss and Identification with the Dead Object[1]

The opening scenes of the opera focus on Elektra and her relationship with her murdered father, and her wish for revenge. What becomes apparent is that the loss of her father is a trauma that she has never recovered from, and has become the driving force of her existence, distorting her sense of self, confusing their identities, and creating an unnatural bond with his actual death.

The maidservants of the house describe how Elektra has become an outcast, living as a prisoner, and suffering brutal treatment by her mother and Aegisthus because of her refusal to give up her indictment of their betrayal and murder of Agamemnon. Unstoppable, Elektra will not let anyone forget, especially the murderers themselves, who disavow the heinous nature of their actions, and make her the repository of their hatred and aggression. The maids also describe her as speaking of the stains of murder and blood tainting the palace, declaring Elektra's preoccupation with the horror of the events that have transpired not only in the palace but also in the house of Atreus.

Elektra takes the stage, expressing her utter aloneness, calling out to her father, Agamemnon, at the hour of his death, an hour she feels they share as sacred. Driven, as if in a spell, she recounts in detail his gruesome murder in the bath, and the dragging of his body: "Thine eyes with thy red blood were deluged. From the bath the steam of blood arose" (Hofmannsthal and Strauss, 1908/1943, p. 11). The compelling image of blood indelibly stains her mind, strongly punctuating this memory and permeating her expressions throughout this scene. Quasi-dissociated, she relives the events, as if drawn to this painful remembrance. This is not a memory that has faded with time. In fact, time stands still, as the present collapses into the past. These are the markings of trauma: a shock to the mind, overwhelming in intensity, relived in the present, with long-lasting effects. The witnessing of her father's murder lives in her as a traumatic memory, recalled in detail, frozen in time, repetitive in its recitation. Her brutal remembering of the murder is a reliving of it. As she continues to speak to her father, the image of blood recurs as Elektra describes a vision of blood raining down on his tomb from sacrificial victims. She promises her father a bloody, gruesome revenge to be committed by those who are of his blood, his children, followed by a dance of victory. This is not simply a call for justice. These images of blood are further evidence of the traumatic experience of his murder, and the shock of its raw physicality.

The trauma of this loss distorts Elektra's sense of self. In her recounting of Agamemnon's death, the sacrifice of her own self and personhood are evident. In fact, over the course of the opera, it is clear that her life has devolved into a repeated experience of calling up her father's death, either through recollection or a call for revenge, resulting in her very being becoming a memorial to him. She gives offerings at the shrine she has created within herself, the offering of her life, vitality, and growth. She is infused with the nature of his death as if his death was poured into her. Her fate, intertwined with his, annihilates any sense of her own life. She is in a miserable physical and psychical state, like that of a decomposing body with her flesh eaten by vultures, so she tells the maidservants. She has come to unconsciously identify with Agamemnon's actual dead body.

As seen so vividly with Elektra, a traumatic loss pulls for a sustained identification with the lost object. There is confusion between self and other, a breakdown of separateness, resulting in a loss of identity. What is also striking is that her father, the lost object, is taken in and identified with as a dead object, rather than an identification with the valued parts of him and their relationship, as would happen over time with mourning. This morbid identification is a result of the trauma of his death – a murder. In this breakdown of separateness between Elektra and her murdered father, the only identity left to her is that of a daughter who must avenge her father.

Her state of mind and body is at odds with the usual description of the "Electra complex." Carl Jung used the term to describe a girl's passionate attachment to her father, and the wish to possess him, with rivalrous and hostile feelings toward her mother, analogous or parallel to the Oedipus complex in boys (Jung, 1914, p. 177). Traditionally, as part of development, the resolution of the complex results in identification with the same-sex parent and an acceptance of the parental relationship with a wish to find new love objects in place of the original attachment. Freud was not in favor of the idea of the Electra complex, as his understanding of these phases was not exactly analogous or parallel for boys and girls (Freud, 1931, p. 229). Furthermore, Elektra's pull to her father is not in this register, although there may be remnants of the Oedipal situation and even a previous, strong attachment to her father, but she has now become intertwined with him from a different emotional source, her identification with him through the trauma of his death.

Elektra is attached to a dead father – moreover, a father murdered by her mother. While this point is not the central focus in the classical idea of the Electra complex, it is central to both the opera and the Sophocles drama. This is a daughter fixated on the death of her father, and the nature of that death, not a living father whom she wishes to possess, with hostile feelings toward a mother she wants out of the way, ultimately coming to accept their relationship and going on to form new attachments. Her mother betrayed Elektra's father, first by the affair with Aegisthus and, ultimately, by his murder. In turn, she also betrayed Elektra, in effect, abandoning her. This heightens and distorts Elektra's attachment to her father. Besides a father, Elektra has also lost a mother, and moreover, a good mother to hold inside of her, to identify with and be protected by (assuming her mother may have been this good object at one time). The murder of her father by her mother distorts her relationship to both her parents, overtaking her emotional life and inciting her hostility against a mother who has abused and abandoned her, not a mother who is a rival. This is a complex born of horrific trauma and betrayal.

Trauma and Psychic Fragmentation

In this same scene in which Elektra speaks to her father, Elektra is (unconsciously) in a conversation with herself that reveals the fragmentation of her mind in the wake of the trauma of her father's murder. Psychic trauma overwhelms – it is too much for the mind to hold and alters the mind's functioning: "Trauma is a brute fact that cannot be integrated into a context of meaning at the time it is experienced because it tears the fabric of the psyche" (Bohleber, 2007, p. 335). For Elektra, this is an extreme psychic tear. As we see her loneliness and sorrow, as she calls out to Agamemnon for a visitation, for brief moments – she is a daughter who has lost her father, and is longing for him, wanting to be near him. These vulnerable moments are transient. Her intense anger, and her wish for revenge, take over, which is true for her throughout most of the opera, showing us that more vulnerable feelings of sorrow and loss are unbearable for her, and threaten her mind's stability. She also suggests that she has already had such ghost-like visitations from him: "Let me behold thee, leave me not this day alone! But as thy wont is, like a shadow, from the wall's recesses come to greet thy child!" (Hofmannsthal and Strauss, 1908/1943, p. 13). These near hallucinatory experiences show how her mind is fragmented, with a tenuous hold on reality. In Elektra's call for blood and a dance of victory, in her fantasies of violence and vengeance, an omnipotent, manic, near- delusional quality emotionally shifts her away from her vulnerability and helplessness.

What is notable is how Electra is driven to recount the murder of her father. She conjures up the memory of her father's death, holding it steadily before her, seeming even enthralled by it, drawn to her violent images despite their traumatic nature. This is much more than simple recollection; nor is this an unbidden memory that suddenly intrudes as in posttraumatic states. In recounting the memory of his death and her need for vengeance, she is attempting to hold her mind together. Even her hallucinations of her father and her manic visions of revenge are paradoxical attempts to salvage her mind. The delusions and hallucinations of psychosis, while they are pathologic, serve an important purpose: an attempt to repair a catastrophic internal state (Steiner, 1993, p. 65). Her sustained sense of grievance against her mother and Aegisthus, while it has very real origins, also serves a deeper psychological necessity. Given the nature of her father's death, a murder, she can maintain that his death should never have happened: "when such injuries are felt to be unfair, they give rise to a wish for revenge that is accompanied by extreme hatred and destructiveness" (Steiner, 1996, p. 433). However, this grievance also serves to prevent her from further collapsing into a psychotic or even suicidal state. Hers is a mind that faces an abyss, and, in attempting to avoid utter madness, she conjures up his presence and his murder and her call for vengeance in an endless repetition.

Pathologic Mourning, Melancholia, and an Unlived Life

The scene between the sisters brings forward the difficulty of mourning in the face of traumatic loss. True mourning is a letting go of the lost person, integrating the loss emotionally, allowing for growth, and a choice to go on living fully and with vitality (Ogden, 2002, p. 779). When mourning is distorted or pathologic, growth is not possible and there is a deadening of existence. This is seen in both sisters to varying degrees. For Elektra, trauma causes a significant distortion in the process of mourning, and Freud's idea of melancholia lends itself to an understanding of her state of mind.

It is evident that Chrysothemis has a different relationship to the death of her father. She is able to express her wish for a full experience of life and generativity with a husband and motherhood. Although she has experienced the same terrible losses, she appears to have accepted the reality of the situation and the loss of their father, despite the brutality of his death, stating simply, "Our father he is dead. Our brother comes not home" (Hofmannsthal and Strauss, 1908/1943, p. 17) – statements plainly showing that she has come to terms with the loss of her father in a way that Elektra has not. To the extent that she has mourned these losses, she is freed up to at least imagine reengaging with life and the future, and find other love relationships, rather than remaining in a stagnant existence. Here, the music holds beauty and vitality with a more sustained melody, in contrast to many of the musical motifs and compositional style for Elektra. This reflects Chrysothemis' more integrated state and the emotion of her longings.

Chrysothemis cannot fully mourn, however, and suffers as a result of the trauma of her father's death in her own way. She recognizes that they are imprisoned by Elektra's hatred and "untamed soul," which has created oppressive fear in their mother: "We surely had long since been free, had fled this dungeon" (Hofmannsthal and Strauss, 1908/1943, p. 17). Chrysothemis speaks of her own madness and tormented existence, wandering restlessly in the palace, hearing "strange voices," and living in fear. She exhorts Elektra to give up her desire for revenge and free them both, seeing the deadness in both of them, ultimately saying, "Far better dead, than live a living death" (Hoffmannsthal and Strauss, p. 19).

Chrysothemis cannot bring herself to leave Elektra and actually free herself in order to create her own life. Despite her protests, she keeps herself imprisoned with Elektra. Later, when they are under the illusion that Orestes is dead, she pleads with Electra to "help us to freedom!" (Hofmannsthal and Strauss, 1908/1943, p. 43). She waits to be freed by Elektra, as Elektra awaits Orestes to free her. Here, the effects of the trauma of Agamemnon's death on Chrysothemis are revealed. Both sisters have suffered, and she cannot leave Elektra, out of a sense of guilt about her sister's suffering, and, perhaps, guilt for Elektra's acceptance of the role of avenger on their father's behalf. Chrysothemis' ability to fully mourn and enter the world of the living is constrained. Trauma is the tie that binds.

Despite her palpable sense of misery, Elektra cannot even approach mourning, come to terms with the loss of her father, and imagine a life for herself. What is preoccupying for Elektra are the circumstances of Agamemnon's death: her mother is the murderer, and the violence is inhuman, leaving Elektra with a psychic trauma, rather than a person to be mourned. Freud defined a particular form of pathologic mourning – melancholia – which not only shares some features of normal mourning but also holds an intense, heightened ambivalence toward the lost person, and a strong identification with them (Freud, 1917). Elektra's condition is partially mirrored in Freud's description of melancholia.

> The distinguishing mental features of melancholia are a profoundly painful dejection, cessation of interest in the outside world, loss of the capacity to love, inhibition of all activity and a lowering of the self regarding feelings to a degree that finds utterances in self reproaches and self revilings, and culminates in a delusional experience of punishment.
>
> *(Freud, 1917, p. 244)*

Elektra has unconsciously taken on this abject state, with its punishing qualities, submitting to the position in which her mother and Aegisthus have placed her. She differs from the melancholic as nothing in her even indirectly or unconsciously suggests ambivalence toward her father. Given the absolute necessity of her sense of grievance and desire for vengeance, ambivalence would be unbearable for her, threatening her fragile state of mind. Indeed, traumatic loss may foreclose the possibility of ambivalence. What Electra does share with the melancholic is an identification *with* the lost object, rather than working through the feelings *toward* the object.

> The painful experience of loss is short-circuited by the melancholic's identification with the object, thus denying the separateness of the object; the object is me and I am the object.
>
> *(Ogden, 2002, p. 773)*

Here, the connection between the effects of traumatic loss and melancholia takes hold, where the loss of boundaries inhibits the process of mourning and the experience of loss.

Haunted by the Past and the Unmourned Dead

In the scene between Clytemnestra and Elektra, the effects of the murder of Agamemnon on Clytemnestra are brutally evident. Furthermore, the profound effects of the murder of Iphigenia on both of them can be seen: they are haunted by a ghost whose presence they are not aware of and whose loss they have not mourned.

After the conversation with her sister Chrysothemis, and with the approach of Clytemnestra, Elektra determines to speak with her mother as never before (Hofmannsthal and Strauss, 1908/1943, p. 19). In spite of her intense wish for vengeance, Elektra does not commit the murders of her mother and Aegisthus, herself, over the course of the years after her father's death. She cannot bring herself to kill her mother, her only surviving parent, and what might be a fear of actually committing violence leads to an "endless revenge in which there is a very intense tie to the object which must be kept alive in order that the process may continue" (Steiner, 1993, p. 76). Elektra's complex attachment to Clytemnestra is one of endless suffering as well as grievance, and she keeps her mother alive in a relationship of mutual torment.

Clytemnestra approaches her daughter Elektra with horror and disdain while simultaneously beseeching her for some solace and an answer to her suffering. Mother and daughter face each other, seeming to search for mutual understanding. It is ironic that Clytemnestra would seek her help, revealing how truly desperate she is. With Aegisthus, she has betrayed and murdered her husband and keeps her son in exile, all of which is not without psychological repercussions for her. She acutely fears retribution upon the return of her son. She has refused to speak of him, and later in the scene, Elektra accuses Clytemnestra of hoping to have her exiled son killed under the pretense of sending gold to support his upbringing. The mother has also betrayed her son.

Like Chrysothemis, Clytemnestra invokes the metaphor of the living dead in speaking of the desert of her existence and her physical deterioration. She asks Elektra, "Can one rot, living, like a tainted corpse?" (Hofmannsthal and Strauss, 1908/1943, p. 25). She cannot sleep in peace, and describes the torment of her nights of horrible dreams and a strange crawling feeling over her body, as if she were possessed. These endless nights, in which time stands still, are relentless in their torment. The music particularly reflects the disturbance deep within her: "Clytemnestra's report of her dreams . . . is conveyed with a high degree of dissonance, an atomized or fragmented musical discourse, and stark declamatory naturalism. . . . This part of *Elektra* is virtually atonal" (Frisch, 2005, p. 86). Strauss's musical style expresses the depths of these fractured psyches, and, here, the dissonance in the music reflects the fragmentation of Clytemnestra's internal experience.

Clytemnestra's dream of Orestes' return, which she fears is a portent, has another emotional meaning. In the way that dreams express unconscious feelings and wishes, Clytemnestra's dream reveals an intense feeling of guilt and culpability, and a wish for punishment. Elektra's accusations are a relentless reminder of, if not a punishment for, the betrayal and murder of her husband. She would lock Elektra and her accusations and indictments away, but she cannot escape from her own mind. Clytemnestra desperately seeks relief, through a ritual, or a blood sacrifice, and looks to guidance from Elektra. Elektra takes up her questions and gives mysterious and duplicitous answers. Here, like Elektra, Clytemnestra refers to blood repeatedly, and more specifically: "bid me rise in steam of blood" (Hofmannsthal and Strauss, 1908/1943, p. 27), unconsciously alluding to the murder of her husband that still haunts her. She may have willingly killed Agamemnon, but this does not mean she has evaded unconscious guilt or trauma in committing murder. For mother and daughter, blood becomes a symbol and a lingering trace of the horror of that experience.

Clytemnestra persists in the idea of a sacrifice to banish her nighttime torments and asks about the victim, which Elektra answers is a woman. Clytemnestra asks further: "a child? a pure maid, still unwed? A wife? A mother, duly wedded?" (Hofmannsthal and Strauss, 1908/1943, p. 27). Here is a signal, pointing to the past, a trace of the death of her daughter Iphigenia. Given the nature of her daughter's death, through a sacrifice, it seems uncanny that she would consider this to expiate her guilt, and the text suggests earlier that she has already practiced the ritual of sacrifice under the sway of her advisors. Here is the expression of the unconscious, like a dream or a slip of the tongue, seen in oblique references, providing a clue to an aspect of the past that has not been really considered or understood. Clytemnestra has not been able to mourn the loss of her daughter.

Clytemnestra's inability to mourn the loss of Iphigenia is also seen in her longstanding grievance against Agamemnon. For her, grievance is a powerful means to circumvent the emotional experience of loss, foreclosing the possibility of mourning. But, killing Agamemnon, the ultimate revenge, has not assuaged her. Nor has her brutality toward Elektra, another means of expressing her hatred for Agamemnon and a projection of her own guilt and need for punishment, making Elektra the criminal. Ultimately, she has not come to terms with the loss of her daughter, Iphigenia, or the nature of this loss, a killing. She may not have been able to prevent it, but unconsciously, as a mother, she feels that she failed to protect her daughter from being sacrificed for the sake of war, due to her either real or imagined powerlessness. She cannot face this directly – it would no doubt undo her in her already fragile state. In asking about the sacrifice of a wife and mother is Clytemnestra not speaking of herself? What solace is she ultimately seeking, except that of her own death?

So, what can't be mourned, what can't be thought about, is repeated, as in Clytemnestra's compulsive sacrifices. She has suffered the traumas of her daughter's murder and her own act of killing. In the aftermath of a traumatic experience, there is repetition and action rather than painful reflection and mourning. This is also true of Elektra's repeatedly conjuring up the traumatic memory of her father's murder, which is more of a psychic action than real reflection. As a trauma is re-experienced again and again, a kind of remembering that goes beyond recollection, it becomes a living legacy of the past. Freud saw this as an aspect of mental life, a repetition that is unconsciously driven despite the disturbing nature of what is repeated (Freud, 1920).[2] He thought that this was one outcome of traumatic experiences. Iphigenia's death is a shadow that falls upon Clytemnestra and exerts a hold over her – in effect, all of them, inciting further violence.

Where does the death of Iphigenia reside in Elektra's psyche? Is she able to fully realize the extent of her feelings about this loss? This is another powerful reason for her inability to mourn the loss of her father, as she would have to acknowledge and confront his murder of her sister as part of who he was and what he was capable of. This is an unconscious aspect of her grievance against Clytemnestra onto whom she has shifted the blame. Elektra was unable to prevent the death of her sister and, unconsciously, feels guilty, but she also would have expected her mother to protect Iphigenia. Elektra and Clytemnestra cannot share their sorrows, and mourn together, so they remain unconsciously tied through their suffering and guilt. Painfully, despite her wish, Elektra cannot have a different conversation with her mother. The scene devolves into mutual hatred, as Elektra, with chilling satisfaction, tells her mother that she will be the sacrificial victim, describing in terrifying detail how she will be unable to escape her assassin.

The House of Atreus and Violence Across Generations

After Elektra tries to entice Chrysothemis to commit the murders with her, and her sister flees, Elektra is moved to the act of murder herself, having kept the axe used to kill her father. Orestes's arrival relieves her of this. He sees her broken state, which helps him go forward with the murders, although he also references having come at the bidding of the gods (Hofmannsthal and Strauss, 1908/1943, p. 55). In committing the murders, Orestes continues the legacy of ongoing violence and hatred that has been part of his family background for several generations. Revenge and murder are not unknown to this family into which Clytemnestra has married. She and in turn her children have become entangled in this web of killing and vengeance.

This legacy of violence involves the relationship between Agamemnon and his uncle, Thyestes. Agamemnon is the son of Atreus, and Aegisthus is the son of Atreus's brother, Thyestes. These cousins have a tragic background. Thyestes seduced Atreus's wife, and, in revenge, Atreus had Thyestes feast on the dead flesh of his own children at a banquet. Aegisthus, born later, is no stranger to murder, having then killed Atreus, his uncle, and restored his father, Thyestes, to the throne of Mycenae. Agamemnon drove Thyestes from the throne, becoming the king himself. Restoring the honor of the father was a primary motivation for Agamemnon, as well as for Aegisthus and, now, Orestes. Aegisthus saw Agamemnon as his enemy and no doubt had a great interest in drawing Clytemnestra into betrayal, allowing him to murder Agamemnon with her, to avenge his father. These are only the more immediate murders. In fact, there are several generations of murders motivated by a wish for power or vengeance, along with curses rendered by some of the victims or the gods. Orestes has inherited the consequences of his father's actions, as his father did from Atreus. He and Aegisthus are locked into this tragic replaying, and Orestes carries the burden of killing his mother as well. Later in the opera, in Electra's enticement of Aegisthus to enter the palace to meet his death, there is an echo of Clytemnestra's luring of Agamemnon into the palace upon his return from Troy, and Elektra seems to replay this aspect of her mother's murderousness.

One generation can live out the history and the effects of the violence of previous generations, with a wish for retribution and vengeance: "The conscious aim of the revenge may then be to clear the good name of the injured object and to restore the family honor" (Steiner, 1993, p. 85). This aspect of revenge is related to a wish for justice. While each killing is avenging the one immediately preceding, this is also part of a larger history of murderous revenge, which continues to exert influence. While Elektra and Orestes are acting on their own behalf, they are, at the same time, part of a family legacy of hatred and vengeance, which are the ultimate source of their actions. The opera and the Greek tragedy show the human capacity for violence born of vengeance, on a personal, familial, and societal level.

Identification with Death and Psychic Collapse

In the exchange with Orestes, Elektra's loss of separateness with her father is powerfully seen and another view of her identification with him is brought into focus. She tells Orestes, as he begins to discern who she is, that rather than "kindred" blood, "I am that blood. I am the blood so foully by vile curse shed of great King Agamemnon. Elektra am I" (Hofmannsthal and Strauss, 1908/1943, p. 51). In her psyche, they are literally one, forever tied together, through his actual blood. Here, the reference to blood is not a signifier or symbol of the trauma, but an actual experience of a dissolution of boundaries, giving it a psychotic quality.

She will not let Orestes touch her and, here, at her most vulnerable and open, Elektra reveals her innermost feelings and sorrows. She feels ashamed, and declares herself to be a corpse (Hofmannsthal and Strauss, 1908/1943, p. 53). She painfully recalls the loss of her beauty and youth, and laments that instead of coming into her own as a woman, she was haunted by her father, as he sought "expiation" through her (p. 55). Expiation for her father death – and unconsciously Iphigenia's – she takes on as her own burden. Rather than desiring children and a husband as her sister does, Electra says:

> he sent to me from Hell, Grim hate, hate hollow-eyed, my spouse to be . . . And nothing e'er came forth from me, but curses without end, and fierce despair and frenzy.
>
> *(p. 55)*

She is the bride of hatred and death, giving birth to darkness. She has been taken over and emptied out by her identification with her dead father and his corpse. Any life in her is sacrificed, as her father has become a tormentor who demands her allegiance. This brings an added dimension to Elektra's relationship with her dead father. She not only identifies with him but also relates to him as a persecuting object, living inside of her, with a fierce hold over her.

When Elektra tells Orestes that "the deed is a couch on which the soul reposes, as a bed of healing, on which the soul can take its rest . . ." (Hofmannsthal and Strauss, 1908/1943, p. 55), she mistakenly believes that she can be healed through these murders and finally be at peace. She seeks her own solace through vengeance and murder, as Clytemnestra would through ritual sacrifice, through the murder of Agamemnon, as solace for the death of Iphigenia, which only brought them torment. While her mother is being stabbed, Elektra cries out, "Stab again!" – an expression of her hatred of her mother, but also, a hope for freedom.

In the final exchange between Elektra and Chrysothemis, after the grisly murders, we see that Elektra has no chance for freedom. As Chrysothemis rejoices in joining Orestes and a life that begins anew, she also reflects upon the sorrow of their existence – "Who ever loved us?" (p. 67) – possibly beginning a process of mourning. Elektra's responses to her are manic, omnipotent, and psychotic. She describes the thousands on the earth who await her, as she will lead the dance, but cannot as she is weighed down by the Ocean that holds her limbs captive, and says further:

> The seeds of darkness did I sow and reap, Joy upon joy. A blackened corpse once was I, Among the living and this glad hour, The flame of life hath made me, And my fierce flame consumeth, the gloom of all the world . . . And who so beholds me, Must unto death be stricken, Or be lost in pain of joy.
> *(Hofmannsthal and Strauss, 1908/1943, pp. 65–67)*

While Chrysothemis speaks of love, Elektra replies that "Love destroys, but none can go the appointed way, That knows not love" (Hofmannsthal and Strauss, 1908/1943, p. 67). She has been destroyed by a distorted love for her dead father, love and death twisted together. As the attempt to hold her fragile, broken psyche together through grievance and seeking vengeance comes undone, she finally collapses psychically. She has no way forward, to be freed, to be restored to life or transformed. Finally, after she calls out to others to join her in "the sacred dance," she falls to the ground dead (p. 67).

Conclusion

Complex forces come to bear on this doomed family as the result of the traumatic deaths of Iphigenia and Agamemnon, and the longer history of family violence. Traumatic loss leads to complicated identifications and troubled relationships. In addition, this kind of loss can foreclose or distort the process of mourning, and, as in this opera, the unmourned dead have a psychic hold over those they have left. The inability to mourn precludes an engagement in life and any sense of a real future, leading to a deadened existence. Chrysothemis' desire for life is also inhibited by her attachment to Elektra, based on their shared traumas. Clytemnestra is doomed to repeat the sacrifice of her unmourned daughter, Iphigenia, reliving the trauma of her killing, in the murder of her husband and in her ensuing psychic torment.

Elektra, the most profoundly affected, is caught in a tragic relationship with her dead father and his murder. In her, the effects of traumatic loss are seen most powerfully, as her mind verges on collapse. Elektra is haunted by the immediacy of traumatic memory, untouched by time, and lived experience. It is also these memories and the call for vengeance that keeps her from that collapse.

What is compelling in thinking about *Elektra* is how the unacknowledged murder of Iphigenia reflects an important aspect of psychoanalytic thinking about experience, memory, and the mind's capacity to deal with loss. That which is repressed and kept in the unconscious and cannot be called to memory is a powerful source of motivation, internal conflict, and deep emotion. Freud saw this as central to a psychological understanding of the mind. The murder of Iphigenia entangled both Elektra and Clytemnestra, and its influence as a powerful motive and the feelings in connection with it – feelings of anger, outrage, fear, grief, and sorrow – were kept out of their conscious awareness. These unresolved feelings catapulted Clytemnestra into an affair with Agamemnon's cousin, and then, the vengeful murder of her husband, leaving her with a tormented and scarred psyche, under the sway of repeating the trauma. Elektra reacts in turn to her mother's actions and neither of them is capable of the mourning that would free them.

Ultimately, the death of Iphigenia stands behind the death of Agamemnon. This leads back to the scene in the Sophocles play, in which Elektra and Clytemnestra argue over Clytemnestra's actions motivated by the murder of Iphigenia. While the scene has its share of acrimony and accusation, it stands in stark contrast to the scene between them in the opera, filled with excoriating inner torment and a deadly relationship, unconsciously driven by feelings about Iphigenia's death. The gods' influence has been overthrown by the influence of inner unconscious conflict. Traumatic, repressed, and unmourned experience lives on, shaping actions and emotion. This is how the narrative of the opera itself, with its repression of Iphigenia's death, reflects the workings of the mind and the nature of the unconscious. In its compelling retelling of the myth, the opera has a truly modern sensibility, both in the music and in its psychoanalytic view of the existence of a powerful inner life unknown to us.

Notes

1 Psychoanalytically, one way the term object is used is to refer to a person, who exists in reality or phantasy, and is usually the subject of strong feelings, for example, love, hate, ambivalence (Laplanche and Pontalis, 1973, p. 273).

2 Freud also applied this idea further which speaks to the experience of the opera itself:

> Finally, a reminder may be added that the artistic play and artistic imitation carried out by adults, which, unlike children's are aimed at an audience, do not spare the spectators (for instance, in tragedy) the most painful experiences and can yet be felt by them as highly enjoyable. Under the dominance of the pleasure principle, there are ways and means enough of making what is in itself unpleasurable into a subject to be recollected and worked over in the mind.
>
> *(1920, p. 17)*

References

Bohleber, W. (2007). Remembrance, trauma and collective memory. *International Journal of Psychoanalysis*, 88, 329–352.

Freud, S. (1917). Mourning and melancholia. In J. Strachey (Ed. and Trans.), *The standard edition of the complete psychological works of Sigmund Freud* (Vol. 14, pp. 243–258). London: Hogarth Press.

Freud, S. (1920). Beyond the pleasure principle. In *The standard edition of the complete psychological works of Sigmund Freud* (Vol. 18, pp. 1–64). London: Hogarth Press.

Freud, S. (1931). Female sexuality. In *The standard edition of the complete psychological works of Sigmund Freud* (Vol. 21, pp. 225–243). London: Hogarth Press.

Frisch, W. (2005). *German modernism*. Oakland: University of California Press.

Hofmannsthal, H. and Strauss, R. (1908/1943) *Elektra*. Translated by A Kalisch. London: Boosey & Hawkes Ltd.

Jung, C.G. (1914). The theory of psychoanalysis. *Psychoanalytic Review*, 1, 153–177.

Laplanche, J. and Pontalis, J.-B. (1973) *The language of psycho-analysis*. Translated by D. Nicolson-Smith. New York: W. W. Norton and Company.

Ogden, T. (2002). A new reading of the origins of object-relations theory. *International Journal of Psychoanalysis*, 83, 767–782.

Steiner, J. (1993). *Psychic retreats: Pathologic organizations in psychotic, neurotic and borderline patients*. London: Routledge.

Steiner, J. (1996). Revenge and resentment in the Oedipus situation. *International Journal of Psychoanalysis*, 77, 433–443.

Woolf, V. (1925). *The common reader*. New York: Harcourt, Brace and Company.

11 Yearning for Intimacy

Bela Bartók's *Duke Bluebeard's Castle*

Anna Balas

Duke Bluebeard's Castle, the sole opera of Béla Bartók (1881–1945), written in 1911 with librettist Béla Balázs (1884–1949), is a one-act portrayal of the eponymous nobleman's saga of hope and despair. More often performed in concert than in full production, *Duke Bluebeard's Castle* is considered one of the masterpieces of 20th-century opera.

As prolific as Bartók was, and although he was intrigued with Hungarian language and folk music, he wrote no other opera. Apparently, Balázs' version of the Duke's macabre story uniquely captured his imagination. My essay seeks to explain how the composer's personal psychology attracted Bartók to this story, this libretto, and thus to compose this opera. I contend that the opera reveals Bartók's interior self in a way no memoir ever could.

A prisoner of illness-imposed insecurities and obsessions, Bartók suffered from a fear of abandonment that compelled him to pursue unattainable young women, whose rejection reinforced his anxieties and drove him more deeply into himself, into the castle of his mind. Balázs' version of Bluebeard's tale echoed the composer's personal preoccupations, which present themselves in the music into which Bartók wove the tale.

> I can conceive of a work of art solely as a medium in which unlimited enthusiasm, despair, sorrow, anger, revenge, burning scorn, and sarcasm of its creator finds expression. . . . I found out myself that the works of an individual imparted more precisely than his biography the most portentous events and defining passions of his life.
>
> *(Béla Bartók, written in 1909 and quoted in Botstein, 1995, p. 49)*

A synopsis follows to provide a scaffold for the analysis. (Lyrics quoted from the opera are from the libretto (Bartok, 1966).

Opera Synopsis

Prologue

Often omitted in translation, the prologue is delivered without musical accompaniment in the style of an ancient ballad. The bard invites us to

DOI: 10.4324/9781032271408-11

open the curtain of our eyelids to see our inner selves reflected in the story.

Opening

Bluebeard and Judith enter the gloomy, darkened castle and stand facing seven locked doors. Bluebeard offers to let her leave, but she demurs. She notes that the castle looks so dreary, it even "silences the rumors." Judith requests that he open the seven doors; reluctantly, he gives her the first key.

Door 1 – The Torture Chamber

Judith opens the first door, and we hear a sigh as a bright red beam of light emanates from within the chamber. She recoils in horror and explains that she sees shackles, daggers, racks, and pincers covered in blood. Judith demands more keys.

Door 2 – The Armory

As she unlocks the second door, a yellowish light pervades, and martial music plays. She describes arms and armor, cruel battle weapons. She is undeterred and wants more keys. "It no longer matters," he says as he hands her the next three keys.

Door 3 – The Treasury

Opening the third door reveals the golden glow of Bluebeard's treasury. Gold, jewels, and crowns lie within, but Judith is alarmed by the blood she sees dripping from the loveliest crown. Bluebeard hurries her on to Door 4.

Door 4 – The Secret Garden

The fourth door opens to a bluish-green light. Blossom-laden branches lean from within. "My castle's secret garden," Bluebeard explains. Judith is enchanted but once again repulsed by the blood seeping from the flowers' roots.

Door 5 – Bluebeard's Realm

In this musically climactic scene, Judith opens the fifth door to find a brilliant white light illuminating Bluebeard's vast domains. She is impressed, but she notes that the clouds are bloody. Bluebeard presses her to put her hands on his heart and kiss him. But her only interest lies in unlocking the next door.

Door 6 – The Lake of Tears

The sixth door releases a woeful sigh. The darkness deepens as she spies a silvery-white, motionless lake. It is "a lake of tears," Bluebeard tells her. He wants to kiss her, wants her to leave the last door closed. Judith exclaims that his murdered wives must be behind Door 7.

Door 7 – The Wives

The castle sighs as Door 7 opens. "See my former wives." Bluebeard announces. Three beautifully clothed, bejeweled, and crowned women emerge slowly. They are alive but strangely unreal. Bluebeard introduces the three wives in turn, and moves to crown and adorn Judith. She protests, "I am your poor living wife!" Realizing she is already in his past, solidified in his mind, Judith steps into place next to the three wives. The door slams shut with all the women locked inside.

Bluebeard is left alone, consigned to an eternity of darkness.

Brief History of the Opera

Duke Bluebeard's Castle originated as a play by poet and dramatist Béla Balázs. Balázs' college roommate and friend, Zoltán Kodály, had turned down the opportunity to collaborate on an operatic adaptation of the play, but Kodály's friend, Béla Bartók, agreed to create the music.

Balázs' Bluebeard is a symbolist play with an unusual protagonist. It was inspired by the title character of *La Barbe Bleue*, a popular French fairy tale by Charles Perrault (1607), in which Bluebeard is a villain whose latest victim is rescued by her brothers (Tatar, 1998, 2004). Balázs' adaptation differs from many versions of the tale, as it has neither a hero nor a villain. This Bluebeard and his wife are one another's lovers, victims, and torturers. Balázs transmuted the tale into a modern, interior, symbolist drama. Further, he wrote it in a Hungarian ethnic idiom, in the form of a Székely (a subgroup of Hungarians, from a remote area in Transylvania) ballad – an ancient peasant style of narrating in simple language set to verse.

Balázs was heavily influenced by the German philosopher Hebbel's romantic theories about the conflict between individual and universal wills, and by Maeterlinck's symbolist theories. In *Duke Bluebeard's Castle*, Balázs integrated Wagner's "*das ewig Weibliche*" (the eternal – and, according to Wagner, eternally devoted, loving – woman). He integrates the romantic notion that a man's hope of salvation lies in the love of a woman with the static model of interiority that Maeterlinck espoused. Maeterlinck's symbolist theories served this interiority by emphasizing the imagination, poetic fancy, and especially submission to the inevitability of one's destiny (Leafstedt, 1999).

The simple language and interiority of Balázs' account of the gloomy tale resonated for Béla Bartók, who already had a great admiration for Balázs' work. As Balázs wrote of Bartók's response to his play,

> The poetry was addressed to Bartók in the same way as when a weary, parched wanderer strikes up a tune to induce his still more exhausted companion to sing because a melody will carry you along for a while when

your legs are at a point of giving way. And I contrived to trick him into music. Bartók broke into such singing as has not been heard in Europe since Beethoven.

More image than plot, the opera had a difficult beginning. Unconventional and disturbing, it had no familiar story line and none of the action usually found in operas. It is fashioned as a series of poetic vignettes, and its vocal manner is faithful to spoken rhythms. The end is one of the bleakest in all opera, in which the castle and its inhabitant return to their original state, untransformed. Interior and sad, the work lacks relief of any kind. Opera-goers accustomed to melodic vocal lines and self-contained numbers found the pentatonic idiom of the music, its conformity to speech rhythms, and its through-composed twists and turns difficult to absorb.

So cold was Bluebeard's reception that the discouraged Bartók limited his composing for some time afterwards and turned to collecting folk music. In his letters he admitted that he doubted he would ever see Bluebeard performed (Demény, 1971).

It was Balázs' persistence that saved the opera from obscurity. He paired it with *The Wooden Prince*, a more accessible ballet that Bartók created for one of Balázs' stories. The writer ultimately convinced director Dezsö Zádor to present it at the Hungarian State Opera in 1918. The conductor, Ernesto Tango, understood the music and the premiere succeeded. *Duke Bluebeard's Castle* was published in 1922 and subsequently translated into several other languages; it has become part of the 20th-century opera repertory.

After Balázs' political exile in 1919, the opera was not performed again in Hungary until the 1930s. The law mandated that the work of an exiled artist could only be performed without attribution, and Bartók categorically refused to show the work without crediting Balázs (Leafstedt, 1999).

Biographical Information

Connections to the opera begin with Bartok's early childhood. When he was three months old, Bartók had a reaction to a smallpox vaccine, which caused a severe allergic rash to erupt all over his face and body (Bartók, 1981 and Cooper, 2015). His mother isolated him from other children. She was afraid that an irrational fear of contagion might cause others to cruelly avoid him, and she feared as well that he might be stigmatized by the rash's repellent disfigurement of his countenance. Young Béla suffered from torturous pain and itching. True to his mother's fears, he likely experienced negative mirroring as he encountered people who reacted to his repulsive face. The rash finally cleared after he received arsenic treatment at the age of five.

Though young Béla was late to speak, by age four he could sound out over 40 melodies at the piano. Recognizing a remarkable affinity for music, his mother undertook to teach him to play and became his first teacher.

The absence of peers, the delay in speaking, and the shared language of music fostered an unusually close bond between the mother and the son. In addition, she aimed to fashion her son into a paragon of good behavior by comparing him to an impossibly saintly child (Cooper, 2015). This parental method was bound to make Béla feel inadequate.

Sickness, loss, and closeness to his mother attached him further to music. When the boy was six, his father and aunt took him to a spa. There he was subjected to the Priessnitz cure, a harsh hydrotherapy invented by a sheep farmer, which alleviated symptoms of bronchitis and pneumonia, which might have rendered him more lonely. Soon after, at age 7, Béla lost his father rather suddenly. His mother sought jobs in places where her son would have access to the best musical education. With ambitions for Béla, she obtained jobs and moved the family to new locations as the boy's musical accomplishments progressed. Béla had his first public recital at age 11.

After the initial concert, the Bartóks, including his four-years younger sister Erzsi, moved to Bratislava (Pozsony, in Hungarian) for a time. There, Bartók gained access to his first serious teacher László Erkel, son of the famous Hungarian composer, Ferenc Erkel. Another move necessitated that his mother Paula send the boy to live with her sister in Nagyvárad until they returned to Bratislava and lessons with Erkel. Erkel remained Bartók's principal teacher until he died unexpectedly when Béla was 15. The bereft boy, disillusioned with the teachings of the Catholic Church, became an avowed atheist and remained so until he became Unitarian near the end of his life.

From adolescence onward, Bartók's love life was affected by his childhood suffering. In adulthood, he developed intense crushes on younger women, especially on those who did not reciprocate, probably because he was more comfortable with fantasy relationships. When he became infatuated with well-known violin prodigy Stefi Geyer, Bartók dedicated his first Violin Concerto to her. He awkwardly courted her and alienated her by criticizing her religious faith, calling it childish. Not surprisingly, Geyer disengaged from Bartók. In 1907, in the wake of the rejection, Bartók inscribed his dedication of the concerto with desolate lines, "No two stars are as far apart as two human souls," from a poem by Balázs (Cooper, 2015).

In 1909, at the age of 28, Bartók abruptly married Martha Ziegler, aged 16, one of his students, whom he loved less ardently. Their son Béla Bartók III was born in 1910. Béla Bartók dedicated *Duke Bluebeard's Castle* (1911) to Martha, with gratitude for her help with practical matters, such as transcribing his opera.

In 1916, when he was 35, Bartók became infatuated with his 15-year-old assistant Klara Gombossy. When he offered to divorce Martha and marry her, Klara wisely refused. He remained married to Martha but spent stretches of time traveling, collecting folk music and concertizing abroad.

Bartók divorced Martha and married for the second time in 1923, when he was 42 years old. His wife Ditta Pásztory (1903–1982), aged 19 at the time, was an accomplished pianist. Bartók's manner of proposing was to give Ditta a three-day ultimatum to decide about tying her life to his, and they were married within 10 days. They had a son Péter, born in 1924. Ditta later became a recognized interpreter of her husband's music.

It is worth noting that Bartók's pursuit of women much younger than himself was due, at least in part, to his need to mold and control his companions. This pattern fits in with his social awkwardness and his lack of capacity for reciprocal intimacy, which led to rejections and subsequent feelings of perpetual loneliness. In a letter to the composer Frederick Delius, dated June 7, 1910, Bartók wrote, "I am very much alone here and apart from one friend Kodály, I have nobody to talk to, and I have never met anyone to whom from the very first I could feel so close." (Demény, 1971).

The early loss of his father weighed heavily on Bartók, contributing to his abandonment issues, and causing the composer to seek father substitutes. Like Richard Wagner, who also lost his father at a young age, Bartók turned to the Fatherland as surrogate (Botstein, 1995). Unlike Wagner, however, Bartók was flexible in his nationalism and later became a pan-nationalist (Laki, 1995). Even so, in the early years of the 20th century, he became part of a group of artists in Hungary who turned to folk art for inspiration.

Bartók, an ethnomusicologist as well as a pianist, teacher, and composer, had a passion for collecting folk music and other cultural artifacts, such as hand-carved and painted furniture. He also collected beetles, butterflies, and stones. Though ordinarily quite austere, he treasured his collections, which reflected his personal esthetic. Eventually, in addition to Hungarian music and memorabilia, Bartók amassed a vast collection of Romanian, Serbian, Bulgarian, Turkish, and even Arabian folk music.

In fact, Bartók's biographer David Cooper suggests that the composer had a variant of Asperger's, a hypothesis based on reports of Bartók's aloofness, as well as on his propensity for collecting and organizing. Certainly, like many creative individuals, Bartók had a predilection for self-imposed aloneness (Cooper, 2015).

Unable to tolerate hypocrisy or superficiality, Bartók's talent was most compatible with the "artlessness" of folk-inspired music. This passion for folk art, which he shared with Kodály and Balázs, also fits into a popular artistic trend of the era. However, while Bartók was nourished by the folk music itself, he maintained a sense of isolation from the artistic community. Others described him as melancholic: a lonely, pathologically sad person (Pethö, 1981).

Bartók's early trauma of isolation likely exacerbated his separation anxiety, a phenomenon typical of young children, the kind of anxiety that often leads to serious trust issues. Any potential abandonment generates feelings of helplessness, which in turn give rise to underlying rage. The fear of repressed rage in turn intensifies fears of further abandonment. Bartók coped with this vulnerability by building a protective "castle" of self-sufficiency that made him seem aloof to those who knew him.

Analysis of the Opera as a Reflection of Bartók's Personal Dynamics

I first met Bartók when I was two and a half years old. At the time, my father had been arrested and was being held in solitary confinement as a political prisoner. My mother enrolled me in a school for young children that taught music by way of Hungarian folk songs, using a pedagogic method introduced by Bartók and Kodály some years before. To this day, the loneliness and longing, the sense of isolation, and the anxiety that accompanies great loss, resonate with me when I listen to or see *Duke Bluebeard's Castle*. Similarly, I feel deeply the powerful language of the libretto, into which the cadences of Bartók's music naturally weave themselves.

At the same time, the fairy-tale simplicity of *Duke Bluebeard's Castle* still appeals to the child in me: the mysterious hidden chambers – the terrifying torture instruments in one room, another laden with precious jewels. These are the fantasies of young children, who are fascinated by what might lie hidden in forbidden places. Such images stir intense anxiety and excitement all at once.

In the world of the opera, Bluebeard's own castle embodies a fortress of self-protection like the impenetrable emotional walls that Bartók built around himself. This imaginary castle represented Bartók's own body, which became both a defense and a prison that subjected him to the interminable pain and itching of severe eczema.

Bluebeard's bride Judith is a new kind of female protagonist, who intrigued me from the first. She is both a welcome guest at Bluebeard's castle and an aggressive intruder, as she pushes to discover the secrets of the locked rooms. In a more propitious context, the secrets she unearths might lead to a joyful reunion after so perilous an adventure. But in Bartók's personal story, as in our opera, there is little room for joy.

Judith is both Bluebeard's captive and his captor. As such, Judith's character exemplifies aspects both of Bartók and of his mother, the captor of his early childhood. She especially represents the confusing dichotomy in the character of Bartók's mother: Doting and nurturing, she was also controlling and smothering. The same mother who fostered his discovery of music isolated him and impeded his social skills. The one person who should have understood his need for human companionship imposed a protective solitude around him and tethered him to a lifelong vulnerability to rejection.

Further, in Judith's character, Bartók may have recognized an amalgam of two types: his own steadfast wives, who devoted themselves to his welfare and willingly submitted to his commands, and the young women the composer idolized and courted unsuccessfully. Judith both acquiesces to Bluebeard's demands and resists them. Despite her avowals of everlasting love, she refuses to withdraw her questions, thwarting his bid for unconditional acceptance.

Bartók's was driven to pursue women who, like Judith, spurned his demands. For Bartók, control was the expression of love, and submission was proof that his love was requited. We see a reenactment of the power struggle with the mother of his earliest years: the roles are reversed, with Bartók, the controlling suitor, identifying with his mother. Each rejection caused him to re-experience the torment of his infancy. Bartók reacted by forming romantic attachments with even younger women.

Like Bluebeard's women, many of Bartók's loves were idealized but out of reach. At the same time, he perceived them as guilty of the unforgivable transgression of rejecting him, so he gets to reenact this rejection. Those women became his muses, inspiring compositions.[1] By contrast, Martha, his first wife, was submissive and apparently taken for granted, no longer able to feed his need for rejection to inspire his creativity.

Bartók's immense loneliness (Chipman, 2004, Moricz, 2016 and O'Brien, 1984) and isolation shaped the music he would compose for *Duke Bluebeard's Castle*. One can perceive the tortures in Bluebeard's castle chamber as equivalent to the tortures that Bartók's rash-ravaged skin inflicted on the boy. Bluebeard's armory, like the walls of his castle, can be seen as his way of protecting himself from perceived danger. Bluebeard's treasury represents, for Bartók, the wonderful array of folk songs and folk artifacts in the musicologist's collection. With his gifted aural sensitivity, Bartók managed to find salvation and solace in assembling, ordering, and gathering up sound. As Bluebeard finds reassurance in his riches and his vast domain, so Bartók found comfort in his music and the things he gathered.

What are the other signs that Bartók and Bluebeard can be interpretively aligned? There is ample evidence of Bluebeard's dogmatism in Bartók's courtship rituals. In one of his letters to violinist Stefi Geyer in 1906, Bartók encouraged her to abandon her religion and become a freethinker like himself (Demény, 1971). The tone in his letter resembles the one with which Bluebeard speaks at Judith, alternating between affectionate language and controlling demands. Geyer was respectful and deferential where their musical lives intersected, but she was adamant in declining Bartók as romantic partner. Similarly, while Judith appears to submit to her husband, she actually defies him by resisting his pleas until he relents.

In her zealous quest to conquer Bluebeard, Judith also personifies Bartók himself as a domineering suitor. Judith exerts continual pressure on her Bluebeard to convert, to become a lover of light, and to change his ways. She insists that he must open up to her and keep no secrets, that he maintain no privacy. There is a sadomasochistic tenor to their power struggle, where each one attempts to control the other. Both inflict pain to define their relationship boundaries. Judith tries to mold Bluebeard to her expectations of happiness, disregarding his need for privacy and separateness. The duke inflicts pain by asking her to accept his unrelenting gloom and by attempting to terrorize her by showing her the torture chamber and armory first, exposing the murderous side of his personality. How she responds to the ordeals will show her mettle.

Bluebeard, like Bartók, presents as depressed, and his personality has led to a failure in love. He mistreats and demeans his women even as he idolizes them. Like Wagner's *fliegende Holländer*, he is a very interior sad person with great longing to be understood and loved, but he maintains a skepticism that any woman could understand or love him.

Scene-by-Scene Analysis

Throughout the opera, we encounter freely changing rhythms, in the style of *parlando rubato*, which are reminiscent of the "natural" sounds of the Hungarian language's declamatory cadence. At times, the speech-singing is separate from the orchestra, or minimally accompanied. At other times, the music underlines and expands the emotional content of the words. The music of the recitatives so closely follows the inflections of spoken Hungarian that even when the opera is translated into other languages, it sounds Hungarian.

Opening Scene

A somber, pentatonic melody, accompanied by a brief, shrill, and menacing half-trill of a trumpet, slowly emerges as the curtain rises to reveal Bluebeard and Judith entering the darkened castle through an exterior entrance, which remains ajar. Bluebeard speaks first. "We have arrived," he says.[2] "Bluebeard's castle does not glisten like your home. Will you follow me?" Judith replies, "I am coming!" To the emphatic sound of a low, ominous drumroll, he persists. "Your mother has donned mourning clothes, your father sharpened his sword. Do you want to go back?"

In cadences echoing Bluebeard's entreaties, Judith affirms that to follow him, she has left behind her parents, brother, and fiancé. She has nowhere to go. In a swell of wind instruments and strings, the full orchestra expresses her intense desire to love him. Then, suddenly alarmed by the wet walls, with an abrupt dissonance in the music, she wonders aloud, "Is your castle weeping?" Low woodwinds accompany her voice.

She observes that the castle looks so dark and gloomy that it "silences the rumors." "So, you have heard the rumors," he asserts menacingly. Judith begs him not to hurt her and reiterates her wish to stay with him. She came, she says, to rescue him from his sadness, and she is determined to do so. While her words are cheerful – she plans to bring light and air into his castle – the orchestra sounds strident, showing her agitation. As Bluebeard wryly repeats that his castle does not shine, Judith reassures him that she does not mind. Accompanied by the sound of a solo oboe, she gently asks him to show her everything. In response to her reassurances, Bluebeard decisively closes the front entrance, trapping the two of them within.

Mutual entrapment and a dogged commitment to a joint future bind the two. Judith wants Bluebeard to believe in her, to trust her; Bluebeard wants Judith not only to fear him but also to protect him. In sudden shifts from large orchestra to unaccompanied voice, from harmonious melody to sinister warning sounds, the music builds suspense and keeps the drama off balance. In its juxtaposition of ominous warnings and sweet promises, we hear the two taking one another's measure.

Balázs constructed the specific order of the doors so that the dramatic tension between the protagonists builds to the fifth-door climax. At first, Bluebeard tries to intimidate Judith. When she does not succumb, he attempts to seduce her with his wealth and power. The story and the order of events are Balázs', but the rising tension, the ever-increasing sense of foreboding, and the emotional bleakness find their way to the audience through Bartók's music. As each of the seven doors opens, the orchestra informs the audience of the emotional tone of the contents of each chamber. Behind every new door, a miniature orchestral tone poem awaits, as if a special chamber orchestra were lurking there among the horrors (Abbate and Parker, 2012).

As Judith inquires "Why are the doors locked?" Bluebeard answers, "So nobody can see inside." With *forte* orchestral accompaniment, Judith demands that Bluebeard open all the doors. Undeterred by reminders of the rumors, she insists. He reluctantly gives her the key, and she moves to unlock the first door.

Door 1

As Judith opens the first door, we hear a sigh and see a bright red beam of light emanating from the chamber. Judith exclaims in horror at the sight. Woodwinds along with the shrill, high sound of a xylophone create an ominous atmosphere accentuated by the blood motif: a grating trill that will repeat each time Judith opens a door and sees blood. She reports that she sees shackles, daggers, racks, pincers, and branding irons. The orchestra reintroduces the blood motif as Bluebeard informs her that "this is the torture chamber."

Bluebeard asks Judith if she is frightened, wanting her to be. He then communicates his own fear, saying that his castle is "shaking at the roots" and bleeding from open wounds. He begs her to protect them both. A lilting melody, a lullaby of sorts, plays softly as Judith promises to be gentle in rescuing his poor castle. She firmly demands more keys.

Already we see that the protagonists are intertwined in their conflicting needs: she wants open doors and light, he wants acceptance of his secrets and gentle tolerance of the darkness. Bluebeard has stepped out of his lonely isolation with the dim hope of finding new intimacy.

Door 2

As Judith unlocks the second door, a yellowish light pervades. We hear a muted brass fanfare – martial music – then high trills, shrill xylophone runs, a trumpet, woodwinds. The blood theme rises once again as Judith describes arms and armor, cruel battle weapons. She admires Bluebeard's valor and notes blood on the arsenal. Bluebeard reiterates his demand to know whether she is frightened, and he warns her, "you don't know what the doors are hiding!"

Judith ignores him, engrossed in a beautiful brook that she imagines. The idyll passes as the music abruptly turns ear-piercingly harsh, while she insists again that she came for love and demands more keys with full orchestral back-up.

Accompanied by a harp, when Bluebeard sings tenderly that his castle is bleeding from open wounds, the personification confirms his identification with the castle, his alter ego. He seeks, he says, to protect himself and his castle from further pain. He pleads gently. Judith is not sufficiently frightened by the instruments of torture and the mighty weapons. Although she notices the blood, she remains detached from the horrors and oblivious to danger. She is focused on her mission to change Bluebeard.

He reluctantly agrees to give Judith more keys, asking that in exchange she pose no further questions. Helpless to resist her pressure, he says, "it matters no more" and hands her the next three keys. The audience understands that both his and Judith's fates are already sealed.

Door 3

Judith opens the third door, revealing the glow of Bluebeard's treasury, filled with great heaps of gold, jewels, and crowns. She is awed by their beauty. We hear the "sob of the violin rhapsodizing in the treasury, the horn arpeggios" (Abbate and Parker, 2012, p. 447). An *ostinato* from a celesta combines with woodwinds to create the light, transparent texture of precious jewels shimmering. Judith soon becomes alarmed by the blood she notices staining the loveliest crown. Bluebeard, though generous with his possessions, refuses to be questioned about his secrets. He hurries her on to the next door.

Door 4

The fourth door opens to a bluish-green light, with blossom-laden branches leaning through. The music here is lyrical and sensual, suggesting a growing intimacy. Horn calls emanate from within, followed by sharper trills from the flute. The sound of the harp and celesta accompany a small, harmonious musical poem. "My castle's secret garden," says Bluebeard. He willingly shares his tenderest side. Judith is enchanted by fragrant flowers the size of persons. For a moment, Bluebeard and Judith sing in harmony. "You have the power to make the garden grow or wilt," he tells her. Harmony turns to dissonance. Judith is alarmed that blood seeps from the flowers' roots and nourishes the plants. "Never ask me questions," Bluebeard threatens.

The blood, the sighs, the growing suspense are intriguing. Who suffers so? Whose blood was shed to feed these amazing flowers?

Door 5

In this climactic scene of the opera, the fifth door opens to brilliant white light. A C-Major *Tutti*, with organ accompaniment, resounds as Bluebeard reveals to Judith the full glory of his secret realm, hoping to win her over. He wants to share his wealth and to deter her from further inquisition. The grand orchestration alternates with Judith's small solo voice as she admires the expanse of Bluebeard's domains. Bluebeard describes them to her – "Hills and valleys, forests and rivers, mountains in the distance" – and sings his promise that all this vast domain is hers. The sun, the moon, and the stars will be her playmates. His voice is grandiloquent and lonely.

"Your land is beautiful and grand!" She notes with concern. "But the clouds are bloody." The musical blood motif returns. Bluebeard sings tenderly to her that he wants her to touch his heart and to kiss him. Judith protests. "Two doors are still closed. By my life or death, no locked doors for me!"

Bluebeard tries to stall, to enjoy with her the beauty of his realm. He warns her that it will not get brighter anymore! She is unmoved and insists on the next key. Shrill music returns to accompany her demands. The rhythm quickens, hastened by a threatening drum roll, as she prepares to open the sixth door. The music grows to a quarrelsome *agitato* with drum rolls.

The two protagonists are locked in an intense power struggle. He expects her to enjoy his domains and to be intimate with him. He begs her not to open any more doors. She is obdurate.

Door 6

A deep sigh greets the opening of the sixth door. Darkness deepens. Judith sees a silvery-white, motionless lake, as the oboe and other woodwinds play a fluttering trill motif, suggestive of water. "It's a lake of tears," Bluebeard admits. Are these his own tears? Or are they those of the former wives? He wants a kiss, to prevent her opening the last door. Judith asks about his past loves to a lyrical melody. She now assumes that there is "Blood everywhere. . . . Are the murdered wives behind the last door? I want to know everything!"

The orchestra creates a crescendo of accusation. Judith says, "I know now the whispered rumors are true!" The audience shares her suspicions. But Bluebeard conveys only profound sadness. He longs for her to comfort him. He seeks to prevent the inevitable tragedy that unfolds before him. Though we don't yet know what is to be, forebodings of gloom are everywhere. Bluebeard hands Judith the last key.

Judith's alarmed curiosity is expressed musically in a manner reminiscent of Salome's hysterical demand for John the Baptist's head in Strauss' 1905 opera. Even as her demands will surely destroy both of them, she intends to save Bluebeard with her abiding love, like Wagner's Elsa in *Lohengrin* (1850), (Moricz, 2016) or Senta in *Der fliegende Holländer* (1843). Judith's dual roles are reflected in Balázs' choice of name, with allusion to the "femme fatale" representations of the Biblical Judith/Salome in *fin-de-siècle* 19th-century art (Leafstedt, 1999).

Door 7

We hear a sigh, and Bluebeard sings: "You will see my former wives." During a brief orchestral interlude, three women emerge slowly from behind the seventh door. They move as dream creatures, strangely unreal but bejeweled and crowned, looking magnificent. Judith is shocked to see them alive. Bluebeard falls to his knees and recounts that having met the first one at dawn, all dawns are hers. The second wife he met at noon, and she reigns over middays. Evenings belong to the third wife, whom he met at dusk. To each wife, Bartók has assigned an individual musical key. Finding them all more beautiful than herself, Judith is overwhelmed.

Then Bluebeard sings, "The fourth I met at night," and he attempts to crown Judith and adorn her with jewels. She protests in counterpoint, "I am your poor living wife!" He rejoins that she is the most beautiful one of all, and she alone now owns all nights. Woodwinds, strings, and cymbals clamor in a sudden dissonance that pronounces Judith's recognition: she already exists in the past. He has entombed her in his mind.

To the sound of a lyrical melody in the full orchestra, Judith meekly, soundlessly takes her place among the other wives. The door closes, shutting the women inside. "There will be night forever," sings Bluebeard. The pentatonic melody from the first scene of the opera repeats, but as the accented trills slowly fade, Judith descends into his memory, the dungeon of his mind. Bluebeard utters the last words, "Darkness. Night." The lights fade, and he stands alone, resigned to his fate.

Resisting Judith's prying the doors open are his vain attempts at relief. As each door inevitably opens, Bluebeard's resignation and awareness of loss bring forth new lyricism that had heretofore been impossible. Earlier in the opera, we expect a brutish Duke Bluebeard rumored to kill his wives. We discovered instead a sad, desolate man trying to break out of his longstanding loneliness. Having failed in his last attempt at intimacy, he is thrust back into his former state, mired in feelings of damnation. Unlike his counterpart from Wagner's *Der fliegende Holländer* (*The Flying Dutchman*, 1843), whose centuries of loneliness and damnation were redeemed by the wifely sacrifice of Senta, Duke Bluebeard returns to his prior stasis. The return to the opening bars conveys the message of utter defeat for Bluebeard.

This catastrophic defeat reflects the composer's own inner state of "eternal loneliness." In a letter to his mother in 1905, Bartók wrote:

> As for myself . . . I am a lonely man . . . yet there are times that I suddenly become aware of the fact that I am absolutely alone! And I prophesy, I have the foreknowledge that this spiritual loneliness is to be my destiny. I look about me in search of the ideal companion, and yet I am fully aware that it is a vain quest. Even if I should ever succeed in finding someone, I am sure I would soon be disappointed.
>
> *(Demény, 1971)*

Just so, Bluebeard feels compelled to emotionally kill Judith, to consign her to the others' fate, and is left desolate.

The layers of emotion in *Duke Bluebeard's Castle* reside in the finely shaded tonal colors of its orchestration. At times it is as transparent as chamber music, with a quality reminiscent of Debussy's *Pelléas et Mélisande (1902)*. At other times the music explodes in sensuousness and shrillness. *Salome* and *Elektra* (1909) echo in *Duke Bluebeard's Castle*: all three are musically dark and unrelentingly intense. Bluebeard also mirrors the relative stasis of Debussy's opera: Mélisande is an equally bleak and lonely protagonist who fails to escape her desolation.

Conclusion

That Balázs' libretto captured Bartók's sensibilities manifests in the music. Throughout the opera, the interplay between singers and orchestra carries the fluctuating emotional dynamic of the drama. The orchestra magnifies the sentiment of the characters and expresses all that is left unsaid between Judith and Bluebeard. The music divulges her excitement, his despondency, and their mutual desperation. Judith's initial hesitancy gives way to an increasingly demanding manner, while Bluebeard's gloomy restraint and icy demeanor gradually reveal a vulnerable, tender interior. The lyricism of his singing expresses that transformation. Yet, the two are unable to meet each other's urgent needs; the opera, just like Bartók's passionate love affairs, ends in tragedy.

From a frightened, isolated, pockmarked infant – a fatherless youth searching for belonging – Bartók grew into a man yearning for the ideal woman to rescue him from loneliness. As Bluebeard reveals his vulnerability to Judith through his desperate imprecations, Bartók revealed himself to Stefi Geyer in his uncharacteristically ardent letters. At the same time, Bartók's controlling manner and unrealistic demands resemble Judith's insistence on opening all the doors. In the end, both character and composer were left alone, worshipping their women as a memory. Bluebeard holds on to his wives by locking them in his dungeon, while Bartók immortalized and bejeweled them in his compositions.

For us psychoanalysts, the music and story of *Duke Bluebeard's Castle* are about more than a tragic love affair: they are reminiscent of the desolation experienced in a case of failed treatment. Judith, akin to an ambitious psychoanalyst in the throes of a rescue fantasy, tries to save the Duke. She risks everything to rescue him from his loneliness; however, she is unable to register the depth of his despair. The more he seeks to express his need for privacy and solitude, the more she becomes caught up in her own mission.

In the chapter "Witnessing: Its Essentialness in Psychoanalytic Treatment" (Kaufman and Kaufman, 2013), the contributing therapists grapple with the challenge of a patient who feels deeply lonely and misunderstood, hiding the depth of his despair to comply with the unspoken agenda of his analyst. The analyst may inadvertently pressure the patient to present as more cheerful than he feels, maintaining a "false self" (Winnicott, 1965). The only way to save such a failing treatment is for the analyst to unsparingly tolerate and witness the unadorned depth of despair of the patient.

Some analysts are incapable of such an effort. Just like a bad analyst, Judith insists on bringing "light and air" into the castle, disregarding the depth of Bluebeard's despair. As in a failed treatment, the protagonists are unable to communicate and sing and talk past each other. While Judith is deaf to his pleas, Bluebeard's suffering resonates with the audience. We, the audience, become the witnesses to Duke Bluebeard expressing his loneliness and suffering, through both his words and the music that conveys his sentiment. He does not cover it up with a "false self:" his authenticity gives power to the opera. Perhaps Bluebeard's longing to be understood is impossible to fulfill. Similar failures have compelled him to metaphorically kill off all his loves, one by one.

Bartók revealed his innermost suffering through his opera. However, unlike the lonely Duke Bluebeard, who sank into darkness, Bartók carried on with his projects of musical collecting, composing, and publishing, performing and teaching, raising two families, emigrating when necessary. By remaining true to himself, to his own idiosyncrasies, without compromising any of his iconoclasm, he was able to eschew all external political, societal, musical, and cultural pressures (Cooper, 2015). While Bluebeard and the castle represent his innermost self, Bartók lived a full and productive life: he continued to work on new compositions until the time of his death.

Duke Bluebeard's Castle is a highly personal work: it embodies the universal conflict between our yearning for intimacy and need to maintain autonomy. When intimacy fails, we may each temporarily become Duke Bluebeard, feeling alone and abandoned, fortifying our castles.

Notes

1 Adele Tutter (2015) discusses the role of fantasy in musical creativity in the life of Janacek, who had his muse, Kamila.
2 All quotations from the libretto are the author's translations from the original Hungarian.

References

Abbate, C. and Parker, R. (2012). *A history of opera*. New York: Norton.

Bartok, B. (1966). *Duke Bluebeard's Castle*. István Kertész conducting the London Symphony. Decca Record Company, E4663772-CD. (Original Work 1911).

Bartók, B., Jr. (1981). *Béla Bartók's diseases. Studia Musicologica Academiae Scientiarum Hungaricae. Centenario Belae Bartók Sacrum*. Budapest: Academia Kiado.

Botstein, L. (1995). Out of Hungary: Bartók, modernism, and the cultural politics of the XX century. In *Bartók and his World* (Peter Laki, ed.). Princeton: Princeton University Press.

Chipman, A. (2004). Loneliness and liberation in the life and stage works of Béla Bartók. *The Psychoanalytic Review*, Vol. 91, 663–681.

Cooper, D. (2015). *Béla Bartók*. New Haven: Yale University Press.

Demény, J. (ed.). (1971). *Béla Bartók's letters*. New York: St. Martin's Press.

Kaufman, J. K. and Kaufman, P. (2013). Witnessing: Its essentialness in psychoanalytic treatment." In Richards, A., Spira, L., and Lynch, A. (eds.). *Encounters with loneliness: Only the lonely*. New York: IPBooks, pp. 139–158.

Laki, P. (1995). The gallows and the altar: Poetic criticism and critical poetry about Bartok in Hungary. In Laki, P. (ed.), *Bartók and his world*. Princeton: Princeton University Press, pp. 79–101.

Leafstedt, C. (1999). Bluebeard's theater: The influence of Maeterlinck and Hebbel on Balázs's Bluebeard Drama. In Laki, P. (ed.) *Bartók and his world*. Princeton: Princeton University Press.

Moricz, K. (2016). Cosmic loneliness in Bartók's Duke Bluebeard's castle. In Bergam, R. and Smith, M. (eds.), *Modernism and opera*. Annapolis: Johns Hopkins University Press.

O'Brien, J. D. (1984). Alienation as expressed in three twentieth-century operas. *Journal of the American Academy of Psychoanalysis*, Vol. 12, 441–450.

Petho, B. (1981). Bela Bartók's personality. In *Studia Musicologia Academiae Scientiarum Hungaricae*. Budapest: Akadémia Kiadó, pp. 443–458.

Tatar, M. (1998) *Classic fairy tales: A Norton critical edition*. New York: Norton.

Tatar, M. (2004) *Secrets beyond the door: The story of bluebeard and his wives*. Princeton: Princeton University Press.

Tutter, A. (2015). Text as muse, muse as text: Janáček, Kamila, and the role of fantasy in musical creativity. *American Imago*, Vol. 72, 407–450.

Winnicott, D. W. (1965). Ego distortions in terms of true and false self. In Winnicott, D.W. (ed.), *The maturational process and the facilitating environment*. New York: International University Press, pp. 140–152.

12 Reflections on Applied Analysis and a Secret Program in Alban Berg's *Wozzeck*

Ralph H. Beaumont

Early on in my efforts to shed light on operas from a psychoanalytic perspective, I was confronted from both within and without with the question, what exactly does a psychoanalyst have to contribute here? It seemed uncomplicated enough early on to raise certain questions about less than obvious motivations. Why did Don Giovanni invite the Stone Guest to dinner, and why did he answer his questions about repenting honestly? Why did a seemingly empowered Carmen go back to her vengeful former lover, only to meet her death? These, by the way, were two of the few operas Freud (1900, 1905, 1911, 1928) acknowledged liking.

The method of applied analysis might be schematically compared with our clinical method in terms of the minimal number of steps involved in the process. When I was writing up my cases for certification, and trying to think of how to show a psychoanalytic process, I found, amidst all the confusion in the literature, a helpful pointer in a paper by Arlow and Brenner (1990). They said that psychoanalytic process contains a minimum of three steps: the patient says something, the analyst says something, and the patient says something further. In short, evidence, hypothesis, and confirmation or refutation or modification. In applied analysis we have only the first two steps. We are left, however plausibly or not, to imagine step number three. The work of art, or the long-deceased composer, does not offer a reply to our hypotheses.

These sorts of problems sufficed to get me started, but, over time, I have felt prompted to try to go further into the matter of what I think I, along with other practitioners of applied analysis, think we are up to. So I will start with some comments on this issue, before proceeding to Alban Berg and his first opera, *Wozzeck* (Berg, 2011) and the rich opportunity the composer and his work offer for applied analysis.

I. Reflections on Applied Analysis

For many, Freud's greatest contribution was the clinical method of psychoanalysis. Beyond that, on matters of theory, the controversy begins. The search for common ground has been a complex matter. Applied analysis, sometimes now called multidisciplinary analysis, would not be high on most lists ranking

DOI: 10.4324/9781032271408-12

Freud's contributions. There is, I think, some irony in this state of affairs. Freud, after all, devoted considerable attention to this pursuit. His results, we know, have not infrequently been found to be problematic. Clinical psychoanalysts understandably might have doubts about the hypotheses of applied analysis, which are not worked through with repeated spontaneous confirmations in a clinical dialogue. This situation might suggest Jonathan Lear's Kierkegaardian version of irony, with the question: among all works of applied psychoanalysis, are there any works of applied analysis (Lear, 2014)?

But Freud persisted in this direction. We have his analyses not only of Oedipus Rex and Hamlet but also of Leonardo da Vinci and his childhood, Michelangelo and his Moses, Dostoevsky and his fiction, *Civilization and Its Discontents*, and *Moses and Monotheism*. Beyond those, there are his ventures into the study of anthropology and religion, exemplified not only in his study of Moses, but also in *Totem and Taboo* and *The Future of an Illusion*. When his anthropological speculations in *Totem and Taboo* were questioned, he was ready to concede that they may be "Just So Stories," along the lines of Kipling's fantastic tales of origin. Some have found contemporary anthropological relevance in this work (see, e.g., Paul, 1996). Freud also commented in his paper on Dostoevsky that, before the work of art "analysis must, alas, lay down its arms" (Freud, 1928, p. 178). But none of this seems to have been much of a deterrent. I think Freud's commitment to his applied analytic work can be seen in a letter from Ernest Jones to Freud, written in 1923. There Jones comments on the publication of two recent papers by Freud: *The Ego and the Id*, and *A Seventeenth Century Demonological Neurosis*. The former, of course, remains a foundation stone in our field. The latter, a powerful work of applied analysis and object relations theory, which takes up the psychotic dynamics of a well-documented case of demonic possession, is largely neglected today. Jones in his letter to Freud makes passing reference to *The Ego and the Id*, before writing, "The Teufelneurose was charming and obviously aroused your personal interest. It was a happy idea to seek yet another field for confirmation of your theories, like observation of children and study of anthropology" (Jones, 1923, p. 524).

Freud's followers also seem to have been little deterred by qualms about applied analysis. Peter Gay, a biographer of Freud and a notable practitioner of applied analysis, has commented on the widespread inclination of analytic writers on art and literature to have boldly rushed in where Freud feared to tread (Gay, 1988). This has indeed proceeded so far that in recent years meetings of the American Psychoanalytic Association have introduced a new format, designed to emphasize the clinical, and diminish the distracting uproar of the analysis appliers.

Why, then, when we have the clinical method of psychoanalysis, would we, and why did Freud, occupy himself with these "Just So Stories?" Juxtaposing Freud's work on applied analytic issues and his clinical work may perhaps shed some light. While a number of these comparisons might be found, I think an especially vivid example involves the theories of *The Interpretation of Dreams* (Freud, 1900) on the one hand and the Dora case (Freud, 1905) on the other. In his clinical account of the case of the adolescent young woman Dora, Freud hoped to demonstrate in a clinical context the validity and clinical value of the theories about dreams he had developed in his earlier work on their interpretation. He wanted to show that his clinical work with Dora on her dreams would confirm his theory of dreams as disguised wish fulfillments. The demonstration did not go as smoothly as Freud hoped. His attempts to analyze Dora's dreams according to his theory were soon followed by his young patient's increasing discomfort with the treatment and eventual flight from it. Before publishing the Dora case, he added his "Postscript" with its reflective reconsideration of Dora's negative responses to his interpretations. He went on to offer innovative methodological reflections on matters such as the clinical management of transference and acting out. There the speculative theories of Chapter 7 of *The Interpretation of Dreams* encountered the rigors of the clinical situation, yielding, in a synthetic creative leap, enduring advances in our understanding of method and its relation to theory.

Freud found that he had to consider that Dora's view of his contributions to the clinical process with her was sometimes decisively different from his perspective on the meaning of his contributions. He saw that his method had to accommodate the former, no matter how compelling he found his theoretical insights to be. His theoretical formulations required validation within the clinical method, and this validation required that a careful distinction be made between the inner psychic reality of the patient and the hypotheses of the analyst.

I do not think we would want to do without the contributions of *The Interpretation of Dreams*, however much they may have been filled with multidisciplinary speculations and applied analytic ideas not fully validated in clinical work. What I would like to suggest is that the rigorous inner-outer, fantasy-reality order of distinction required for clinical verification does not apply in the same way in the realm of hypothesis generation and creative theory building. It is also not relevant in the same way in applied analysis, where the dialogic process of validation is not generally available.

In essence I am suggesting that before we can bring our hypotheses and theories into the testing ground of the two-person clinical process, where they might be confirmed or disconfirmed, we must engage in representing our notions about unconscious activities within others. Our inferences must take some shape before they can be verified. This process of representation, which I think has much to do with applied analysis, contains elements of what Winnicott describes as the paradoxical qualities of transitional phenomena. A provisional, speculative quality prevails in relation to our applied analytic formulations. This quality, I think, is akin to what Winnicott called the "essential paradox" of "the conception-perception gap" in transitional phenomena (Winnicott, 1953, p. 95). In Winnicott's definition of this territory, validation and falsification of hypotheses do not have a place. He wrote in 1953 that in the transitional area we must accept that "We will never ask the question, 'Did you conceive of this, or was it presented to you from without?'" In this area we proceed with a certain freedom to pursue connections and meanings unconfined by the constraints of verification, but not without, I would suggest, some memory of our foothold in veridical reality.

What is the point of this? I suggest, as I think Winnicott also did, that it has to do with symbolization, and the elaboration of mental representations. Freud engaged this area, sometimes quite subtly, and sometimes directly. In *The Interpretation of Dreams* (Freud, 1900) his concept of "considerations of representability" in relation to what appears in the manifest content of the dream seems apropos in this regard. These matters also bear on the paradoxes that emerge from efforts to articulate the relation between our inner experiences and mental contents, on the one hand, and the words that we use to express and describe them on the other (see Wittgenstein, 1953). How are our inner mental lives represented with the symbolic means available to us, and, in the process of such representation, what is left out and what is added on? As Fred Busch has pointed out in his recent book (2013), many European analysts have explored the analytic significance of symbolization and representation. This obviously has far-reaching significance for our understanding of our patients in relation to their inner lives, conflicts, and development. I want to suggest that this area may be of importance for us not just as analysts of our patients' intrapsychic lives, but also as analysts in relation to our own thinking about what we might possibly understand and represent to ourselves in our hypotheses about unconscious mental contents and processes. We develop these hypotheses, of course, not only as clinical analysts but also as applied analysts in response to our sometimes-ineffable experiences of works of art. Must we decide whether the hypotheses that we represent to ourselves and others in these contexts are conceptions or perceptions?

Applied analysis is certainly not an example of transitional experience in its primary developmental sense. It involves more a reaching back into the ferment of representation and representability, into a territory where Winnicott's "essential paradox" about conceptions and perceptions is preserved. Winnicott describes this in his paper, "The Fate of the Transitional Object." He wrote:

> I think we really do find a third area, an area of living which corresponds to the infant's transitional phenomena and which actually derives from them. No doubt you easily see what I mean. Put rather crudely: we go to a concert and I hear a late Beethoven string quartet. (you see I am high-brow). The quartet is not just an external fact produced by Beethoven and played by the musicians; yet it is not my dream, which as a matter of fact would not have been so good. The experience, coupled with my preparation of myself for it, enables me to create a glorious fact. I enjoy it because I say I created it, I have assimilated real and would have been there even if I had neither conceived of it nor been conceived.
>
> *(Winnicott, 1959, p. 58)*

On the other hand, when we reach toward the verification of hypotheses about questions of what is inner reality and what is outer, we have returned to a place where considerations not only of representability but also of method and confirmation by the analysand must be brought to bear.

While Jones suggested that Freud's Demonological Neurosis paper was offered simply as further confirmation of his theories, I think Freud was also using the case of demonically possessed Christoph Haizmann to play with object relations ideas. This paper constituted not only more evidence for established theories, but also a sort of transitional step to something new and as yet untested.

II.   Alban Berg and *Wozzeck*

Alban Berg, who lived in Vienna from 1885 to 1935, was a prominent composer and member of the so-called second Viennese school, which was founded by his teacher Arnold Schoenberg. Berg is remembered for his two operas, *Wozzeck* and *Lulu*, and a number of vocal and instrumental works.

Shortly before completing the score of *Wozzeck* in May, 1922, Berg wrote to his wife, Helene, "To whom, other than yourself, am I indebted for Wozzeck!" (Perle, 1980, p. 192). He goes on to show that this question was not merely rhetorical, mentioning the dear Lord, his mother, and Schoenberg, "even though he tried to discourage me from doing it". I shall suggest that the answer to his question includes individuals left unmentioned in his letter, whose impacts on Berg's psyche reach into the heart of his creative process.

Musicological sleuthing has yielded some psychologically fascinating results about well-disguised emotionally meaningful secret programs in many of Berg's compositions. This is perhaps most notoriously the case in Berg's Lyric Suite for string quartet, composed from 1925 to 1926. In 1976 George Perle discovered an annotated score, which demonstrated the work's long suspected secret meaning. It showed how, hidden and encoded within the mostly instrumental music, there is the story of a love affair between purportedly devoted husband Berg and the also married Hanna Fuchs. The quartet presents the affair, according to one commentator, "from its innocent beginnings (first movement), to their declaration of love (third movement) and finally, in the last movement, to the recognition of the impossibility of its ever developing into anything more permanent" (Jarman, 1997, p. 167). Subsequent investigations have revealed a combination of hidden and overtly acknowledged programs in all of Berg's compositions subsequent to the one that we will be considering here, opus 7, *Wozzeck*, composed from 1914 through 1922. While in the case of the Lyric Suite, the secret is clearly a consciously intended one for Berg, the program that I shall suggest in *Wozzeck* seems likely to have been hidden, at least in part, from Berg himself.

There have been speculations in the literature about programmatic and autobiographical elements in *Wozzeck* too. A number of writers have emphasized Berg's experiences of the war years as relevant to the interpersonal horrors of the opera. Indeed, he wrote to his wife, Helene, in 1918 about his character, Wozzeck, "There is a bit of me in his character, since I have been spending these war years just as dependent on people I hate, have been in chains, sick, captive, resigned, in fact humiliated" (Ross, 2007, p. 74).

While *Wozzeck* as a sort of dark, expressionistic Catch 22 opera has a certain appeal, I think that there is compelling evidence that points in other directions.

On the most concrete level, we have a vivid account of the pre-war moment when Berg's interest apparently became riveted to Georg Büchner's play, **Woyzeck,** as a subject for an opera. In a memoir in 1981, Paul Elbogen wrote of a performance of Büchner's newly revived play in Vienna on May 5, 1914,

> Four rows behind me sat Alban Berg, whom I greeted as I came in because I had known him very well for many years. They played the drama for three hours without the smallest interruption in complete darkness. Indescribably excited and enthusiastic I stood up amidst wild applause, met Alban Berg a few steps behind me. He was deathly pale and perspiring profusely. "What do you say?" he gasped, beside himself. "Isn't it fantastic, incredible?" Then, already taking his leave, "Someone must set it to music."
> *(Quoted in Jarman, 1989, p. 1)*

Now, Elbogen's memory may seem far from incontrovertible. It would be easy to think of it in connection with a sort of *après coup* induced by his friend's and the opera's later fame. Nevertheless the facts that Berg attended and read current versions of the revived and long unknown play, and was moved to use much of its text as the libretto of his first opera, are beyond question. I suggest that, as a hypothetical supposition, we consider the moment Elbogen describes of the powerful affective impression that Büchner's play made on Berg as a nodal point. From this experience and its affective resonance we might orient ourselves in considering how to reconstruct the secret program of *Wozzeck* in relation to its meanings for Berg, both conscious and unconscious. Gauguin titled his late painting, "Where did I come from? What am I now? Where am I going?" It seems to me that we might usefully consider Berg's response to the play as the "What am I now?" moment in investigating the program of the opera.

Operating on the assumption that this moment proved crucial in stimulating the intrapsychic representations within Berg that ultimately led to the composition of the opera, I will now consider the "where did I come from?" part of Gauguin's questions for Berg.

He was the third of four children in a middle-class Viennese family. He resembled his father in appearance, and as an adult was tall and thin, with a nervous, tired, melancholy expression. His mother was robust and energetic, and notably unsentimental. His father worked as a salesman in the export trade. His mother appreciated music and other arts. His brothers were 13 and three years older and his sister, his closest sibling, two years younger. He was not a prodigy, but by age 14 had begun to show a strong interest in music, perhaps abetted by his next older brother's singing and his sister's piano playing. He began to play piano, and became deeply fascinated with everything musical.

Shortly after he turned 15, his father died suddenly of a heart attack, and the family finances became strained. His love for music increased and he was deeply affected by a performance of *Fidelio*. Teaching himself, he began to compose songs in the style of Wolf and Brahms. His brother and sister performed them for the family.

Soon after his father died he had his first asthma attack. This ailment burdened him for the rest of his life. He also showed some familiarity with depressive affect at this time. He wrote to a friend, "You left on Thursday. Melancholy – as it is unfortunately always the case with me followed on the heels of gaiety! I was attacked again by that old life-pain which clings to me like some old inherited ill" (quoted in Reich, 1974, p. 15).

He failed an important school examination at 17 and felt depressed again. The following spring and summer at the family summer residence, he had a romantic involvement with a Corinthian peasant servant girl named Marie Scheuchl. In December, 1902, an illegitimate daughter, Albine, was born. This was a scandal for the family, and her existence was kept secret. During the following year, Berg made a suicide attempt. Little is known of the circumstances.

After managing to pass his exam, he returned to school. During the summer of 1904, he wrote to a friend:

> I am sitting alone in my room – father's bust in front of me in the corner – further on my favorite portrait of Beethoven, then the statue of Brahms – to the left and right of that, portraits of Mahler and Ibsen, my living ideals. On the night table is Beethoven again and over him my favorite painting. . . . by Correggio. There – that is my surroundings – a little child of man set amongst gods and heroes.
>
> *(quoted in Reich, 1974, pp. 16–17)*

The next chapter for Berg was a six-year tenure as a student of Arnold Schoenberg, extending from 1904 to 1910. His sister saw an ad for lessons placed by Schoenberg, and arranged to have his brother secretly bring the teacher some of his songs. Schoenberg was impressed, and took him on, at first at no fee. Berg quickly became a devoted student, along with others, notably including Anton Webern. A biographer writes,

> Schoenberg seems to have exerted an almost hypnotic power on his pupils, and perhaps on no one more strongly than on the highly sensitive and impressionable Berg, for whom – fatherless as he had been since the age of 15 – his master seems to have become a towering father figure. . . . Both Berg and Webern held Schoenberg in awe, even after they had finished their studies with him.
>
> *(Carner, 1983, p. 11)*

Berg's mood seems to have improved under Schoenberg's tutelage. Another biographer writes,

> Berg made rapid progress under Schoenberg's direction, not only in music, but in his whole spiritual development. He worked with inflexible industry, relentlessly harnessing all his strength to his work. His great teacher's instructions brought him the greatest happiness, which was reflected in his

whole appearance and in everything he did (all agree who knew him at the time).

(Reich, 1974, p. 19)

He composed, and began to have his music performed, usually along with that of Schoenberg and Webern.

In 1910, Schoenberg moved to Berlin, and Berg's studies with him came to an end. He had completed his piano sonata, his first string quartet, and a number of songs.

In May 1911, Berg married Helene Nahowski, an aspiring opera singer he had known since 1906. Their courtship had been complicated by strong objections to the match on the part of her father. Mr. Nahowski saw Berg as compromised in health, and lacking a profession.

His relationship with Schoenberg continued to be strong. He was pleased at Schoenberg's positive response to his first orchestral composition, the Altenberg Songs. His uneasiness about how Schoenberg would respond to his new composition comes through in a letter from January 1913.

> I now have a greater understanding of the new sounds created by the new means. I hear them even where one could do without them and employ them because I cannot help it. The way I express myself resembles perhaps that of a child who hears at home so many foreign words that it constantly employs them, even when it cannot yet speak German properly. But I hope that this child knows at least how to use foreign words correctly. – Or does here the saying apply: "don't use new means." You never know how they will sound.
>
> (quoted in Carner, 1983, p. 26)

The performance of parts of this work, along with others by Schoenberg and Webern, in March 1913 led to a riot. Two months later, Stravinsky's *Rite of Spring* led to a similar response in Paris.

In June 1913, Berg and Helene visited the Schoenbergs in Berlin for a week. While most of the visit is reported to have gone quite well, on the last day Schoenberg criticized Berg severely over his new, post-student compositions. Shortly after the visit Berg wrote to Schoenberg,

> You will surely understand, my dear Mr. Schoenberg, that together with the loveliest memories of unclouded enjoyment, there is also the memory of that last afternoon with its depressing home-truths. Yet I have to thank you for your reproof as for everything I have received from you, knowing well that it was meant for my own good. I don't need to tell you that the great pain it has caused me, is proof of the fact that I have heeded your criticism. And, should I succeed in this intention for which I hope with an anxious heart (for the doubt of myself is always very strong and the slightest reproof from you robs me of almost all hope) – should I succeed in my

good intention, then this pain will lose its bitterness. – I hope to show you by deeds that I am hardly able to express in words. As soon as I am in the country, I want to begin with the suite. Perhaps one day I shall succeed in writing something cheerful.

(quoted in Carner, 1983, p. 29)

This appears to have been the beginning of an estrangement between the two men that continued until 1916.

Less than a year after visiting Schoenberg in Berlin, in the context of continuing strain in their relationship, in May 1914, Berg attended a performance of *Woyzeck*, Georg Büchner's recently revived play. We have an idea of how he responded.

Georg Büchner, the son of a physician, was a German revolutionary of Utopian socialist sympathies, and shortly before his death at age 23 in 1837, a physician and professor. He is now remembered for several literary works produced during his final two years, the last of which to survive was a series of fragments which together constitute the drama *Woyzeck*. His works were lost until the 1870s, when they were collected and published. They became influential in the Expressionist movement. Arnold Zweig described *Lenz*, a work of prose fiction, as the beginning of modern European prose. Some passages from Lenz may serve to illustrate Büchner's defiance of the heroic romanticism of his day.

They are supposed to want idealist figures, but they have produced nothing to my knowledge but wooden puppets. This "idealism" displays the most shameful contempt for human nature. People should try it sometime, they should enter completely into the life of the meanest of men and then reproduce it with every twitch of eyebrows, every wink and nod, the whole subtle, hardly perceptible play of facial expression.

(Büchner, 1993, p. 149)

Again from *Lenz*, "You need to love mankind to be able to reach the essential being of each individual, you must consider no one too lowly, no one too ugly, only then can you understand them" (Büchner, 1993, p. 150).

Woyzeck was based on an actual person and real events. The historical Woyzeck, a soldier, murdered his mistress in 1821. After a failed insanity plea, he was executed in 1824. His medical examination, which defeated the insanity plea, was published in a medical journal in 1825. Much in Büchner, play is taken from that account.

The surviving play was in fragments of uncertain order, and has been arranged and published in different sequences. For his libretto Berg used one published sequence, and omitted a number of scenes. Otherwise the libretto is taken directly from the play. It tells the story of a humble, beaten-down soldier who is tormented by various authority figures, including a Captain and a Doctor. He has an illegitimate child with Marie. The Captain tells him he lacks morality because he has the child. The Doctor uses him for medical experiments, and ignores his blossoming psychosis. Marie is unfaithful to him with a Drum Major. All of this drives an already fragile Woyzeck further into psychosis, to the murder of Marie, and to his own drowning while searching for the murder weapon, as the Captain and Doctor look on. Whether his end is a consciously intended suicide or an unconsciously driven one is left ambiguous. As the opera concludes, the orphaned son of Woyzeck and Marie plays, oblivious to children who tell him that his mother is dead.-

Now let us return again to the moments of Berg's encounter with Büchner's play in May 1914. I want to consider, given what we know of Berg's history prior to this moment, how the first scene of the play might have registered in his psyche. Consider the following segment of the first scene, where the Captain pronounces on Wozzeck's lack of morality:

CAPTAIN: *Very dignified.* Morality: that's behaving morally! . . . You have a child
   is not blessed by the clergy! . . .
WOZZECK: Yes, sir. . . *He stops.*
CAPTAIN: . . . as our reverend regimental chaplain says to us when he preaches:
   "which is not blessed by the clergy." – (The words are not my own.)
WOZZECK: But Captain, the good Lord God will not spurn the poor little mite
   just because the Amen was not spoken before a child was made. The Lord
   spake: 'Suffer the children to come to me!'
CAPTAIN: What does he mean? And what sort of curious answer is that? You
   make me quite confused! When I say "he," then I mean "you," "you" . . .
WOZZECK: Poor folk like us! Money, you see, Sir, money! With no money . . .
   Let one of us try to bring his own kind into the world, in a good moral way!
                                    (Berg, A, Nicholas, J. ed., pp. 62–3)

It seems to me not so difficult to imagine the impact of this scene on Berg, still conflicted about his own illegitimate child and the scandal of his late teens, and still struggling with feelings of oppression by externalized superego figures, such as Schoenberg. Here it seems worth noting that Berg is reported to have sent a ticket for the Vienna premiere of the opera to his illegitimate daughter, Albine. The musical form of the scene is a suite, a form Berg mentioned in his letter to Schoenberg, quoted above. The Captain is given some music with Baroque allusions, suggesting his archaism in other than musical modes.

This is about as far as most commentators have gone in suggesting a hidden program in *Wozzeck*. While I find the Marie/illegitimate child connection compelling, it seems to me that as psychoanalysts, we may be able to usefully imagine more that went into creating Berg's agitated creative state of mind after the play. By way of analogy, it seems to me relevant to listen to the second scene of Act one. After his encounter with the Captain, Wozzeck is cutting wood in a field with his friend, Andres. Agitated, he begins to unravel, experiencing ominous end-of-the-world visions, somewhat like those described by Freud (1911) in his analysis of the autobiography of the psychotically disturbed Judge Schreber.[1]

ANDRES: *rather uneasy, in order to calm Wozzeck and himself, speaking* Sing it with me!

> *exuberantly* [Two hares were sitting there,] Eating off the greeny [greeny] grass.

> *Wozzeck stamps on the ground.*

> Down –

> *He stops.*

WOZZECK: [Do you hear, Andres, there's something moving?] Hollow! All quite hollow!

ANDRES: – -to the roots.

WOZZECK: A gulf! It quakes. . .

> *He staggers.*

> Listen, there's something moving with us down there! *In mounting fear, he shouts.*

> Away!

ANDRES: *Holding Wozzeck back, speaking*

> Hey! Are you mad?

> *He stands still.*

WOZZECK: It's strangely still and close. So close that your breathing seems to stop. [Andres!]

> *He stares into the distance. The sun is just setting. The last rays make the horizon appear flooded with sunlight.*

ANDRES: *Almost spoken*

> What?

WOZZECK: [Say something. Andres! How bright!] A fire! A fire! It rises from earth to heaven and with a deafening clamour,

> *Rather suddenly, twilight sets in, to which the eye gradually becomes accustomed.* Just like trumpets.

> *Shouting*

> It gets closer!

ANDRES: *Feigning calmness*

> The sun has set, hear the drummers.

> *He puts his sticks together.*

WOZZECK: Still [again], all is still, as if all the world's dead.

> (Berg, A, Nicholas, J. ed., pp. 64–66)

What, we might ask, within Berg, beyond his Marie and their daughter, might have found in Büchner's drama a pathway for creative representation, almost as if it were a pre-formed dream? How might analytic concepts of overdetermination and representability relate to his creative process?

From the few biographical facts I have mentioned, I want to venture some speculative inferences on Berg's intrapsychic life at the time he attended *Woyzeck* in May 1914:

1   Berg knew something of the experience of the loss of and longing to refind a father.

2   Berg had had some experience of regression into a pathological state in which sado-masochistic transformations of feelings made suicidal impulses and their enactment possible.

3   Berg's depression seems likely to have been connected to intolerable feelings of guilt and shame, and their regressive transformations, including externalizations.

4   Berg's relations with women seem to have been characterized by a conflictual split object choice[2] between the acceptable and idealizable woman, and the secret, shamefully unacceptable woman.

5   Events that occurred shortly before Berg encountered Büchner's play included the ending of his student-teacher relationship with Schoenberg, his marriage, and his subsequent estrangement from Schoenberg. It seems possible that their combined effect may have revived memories of the loss of his father, of conflicted feelings that may have driven him to behave as a Don Giovanni-like Lord of the Manor with Marie Scheuchl, and of Albine, the fatherless child who was the product of that behavior.

My hypotheses about Berg's inner life at the time of his encounter with the Büchner play, then, include feelings of loss, sado-masochistic dynamics, and memories of self-destructive impulses coupled with guilt and shame about his abandonment of his lover, Marie, and their child. In the light of these inferences, consider the dark, obsessive interiority of Act three, Scene two, where Marie meets her end at Wozzeck's hand. The music is in the form of an "Invention on a Note." It continually returns, like an irresistible impulse, to the note E natural.

WOZZECK: All heaven I would give and eternal bliss, if I could always kiss you. But no, I cannot! You shiver?

MARIE: The night dew falls.

WOZZECK: When cold, we don't shiver! You'll freeze no more in the morning dew. [But what about me? It has to be!]

MARIE: What are you saying?

WOZZECK: Nothing. *Long silence. The moon rises.*

MARIE: How the moon rises red!

WOZZECK: Like blood-red steel! *He draws a knife.*

MARIE: You're shivering [like that?]! *She jumps up.* What now?

WOZZECK: No one, Marie! If not me, no one!! *Wozzeck seizes her and plunges the knife into her throat.*

MARIE: Help! *She sinks down. Wozzeck bends over he., Marie dies.*

WOZZECK: Dead! [Dead! Murderer! Murderer!] (*He rises to his feet anxiously and then rushes silently away.*

(Berg & Nicholas, 2011, p. 105)

Now I think I am ready to offer a few conjectures about how in an unconsciously overdetermined way Büchner's *Woyzeck* may have been suitable to represent a secret program for Berg.

1   Like Berg, Wozzeck has a Marie, and an illegitimate child with her.
2   Like Berg, Wozzeck goes into a pathologically regressed state connected to conflicts over his Marie and their child.
3   Like Berg, Wozzeck feels oppressed and shamed by paternalistic authorities.
4   Like Berg, Wozzeck uses defenses of superficial submissive compliance to hide resentment and defiance.
5   Like Berg, Wozzeck is driven to act on destructive and suicidal impulses by regressively heightened and externalized feelings of guilt and shame.
6   Like Berg, Wozzeck manifests highly ambivalent and dynamically split attitudes toward the women in his life.
7   Like Berg, Marie's son searches with childhood feelings of longing and aloneness for a lost parent.

This last element is poignantly conveyed in the last scene and in the instrumental music that precedes it. This music is more harmonic and less dissonant than much of what comes before. It well represents the sad searching and longing of the child for his lost mother, Berg's idealizing longing for his own lost father, and the tenderness of Berg's feelings for his lost daughter. Interestingly this music may owe more to Mahler's influence than to that of Schoenberg. Schoenberg, after all, often chided Berg about his music being too sad and not cheerful enough.

In front of Marie's house. Bright morning sunshine. Marie's boy is riding a hobby horse. Children are playing and shouting.

CHILDREN: Ring-a-ring-a-roses, all fall down!
          Ring-a-ring-a-roses, all. . . . *They stop as other children come rushing in.*
ONE OF THE CHILDREN: *Spoken* Hey, you, Kathe! D'you know about Marie?
SECOND CHILD: What is it?
FIRST CHILD: Don't you know? They've all gone over there.
THIRD CHILD: *To Marie's boy.* Hey, you! Your mother is dead!
MARIE'S SON: Hop hop! Hop hop! Hop hop!
SECOND CHILD: What is she?
FIRST CHILD: Out there, on the path by the water.
THIRD CHILD: Let's go and look!
MARIE'S SON: *Riding.* Hop hop! Hop hop! Hop hop!
                                    (Berg, A, Nicholas, J. ed., pp. 109–110)

In relation to the concluding passage, and the final scene of the orphaned child, I think it may be relevant to also consider that among Berg's effects, after his death, a photograph of his daughter Albine as a child was found.

III. Postlude

To this point I have taken up Berg's powerful moment with Büchner's play in connection with Gauguin's first two questions, where did he come from, and what is he now? I have suggested that Berg's particular experience of that play may have formed the kernel of the creative impulse that led to his composition of *Wozzeck*. How, then, do these conjectures about Berg and possible unconscious links between his inner life and his first opera relate to my remarks about applied analysis? This might usefully be considered in relation to the epistemic status of my hypotheses. I do not know in an important way whether there was a connection in Berg's mind between his illegitimate child and Wozzeck's and Marie's orphaned child. To know this was the case would require a convincingly authentic expression from Berg to that effect. Skeptics could, of course, argue that the intervention of one variety or another of self-deception is undermining even this sort of corroboration. But this is the process of verification that the clinical psychoanalytic method makes available. The truths derived from the use of this clinical method have often been shown to be corroborated from multiple directions, and to be related to lasting changes in the lives of analysands. The practitioner of applied analysis is left with less than this. Without some direct corroboration, his hypotheses are neither verified nor falsified, as may occur in the schema of the three-step clinical process I have mentioned above. Their epistemic status is something more akin to Winnicott's experience of the late Beethoven quartet; while the experience may have been quite meaningful for him and while its existence depended on his response to the presentation of Beethoven's work, we cannot claim that this establishes any convincingly verified link between Winnicott's compelling experience of meaning and Beethoven's conscious or unconscious intentions.

The best the applied analyst may be able to offer in his or her search for an expanded epistemic status for his or her conjectures is to turn to the argument for the element of continuity. I have made this argument in alluding to the presence of a photograph of Albine, Berg's illegitimate daughter, among his posthumous possessions as evidence supporting her vivid presence in his inner life when he experienced a powerful emotional response to Büchner's play, with its portrayal of Wozzeck's illegitimate child. This might be seen as considering not only Gauguin's first two questions but also his third: where am I going? In other words, what kinds of corroborative information might be found from the artist in his subsequent creative work, or in the unfolding of his inner life in his biography? At times the applied analyst may find some reinforcement for his or her speculations in pursuing such questions, and perhaps in this way a partial substitute for the analysand's missing response in the three-step clinical method. Consideration of the epistemic value of what future developments may offer may not in fact differ so much for the applied analyst and the clinical analyst. Those who analyze living analysands, after all, sometimes weigh the effectiveness of the analytic work on the basis of post-termination follow-up information about their analysands. Indeed research on the effectiveness of psychoanalysis has emphasized the enduring beneficial effects that have been found in analysands long after their treatments have been terminated.

Apropos these reflections, I will conclude with an answer to Gauguin's third question which I think may have some bearing on my hypothesis about a connection between Berg's ambivalent representation of his Marie, and that of Wozzeck and his Marie. On May 20, 1925, anticipating the first public performance of the opera, some orchestral excerpts had their first public performance, under the title of *Wozzeck Fragments*. This occurred in Prague, and Berg stayed for a week with the Fuchs family. In the words of a biographer, "Berg regarded his meeting with Hanna Fuchs in May, 1925 as the fateful turning point of his life" (Floros, 2008, p. 65). Notwithstanding his letter to his wife Helena quoted earlier in which he disavows feelings for others, his love for Hanna Fuchs preoccupied him for the rest of his life. This rather unambiguous manifestation in Berg of a split in his inner representation of women occurred just as *Wozzeck* was being introduced to the public, and just before the premiere of the opera made him famous. Berg's subsequent Lyric Suite has been shown to have been organized around a secret program about his love affair with Fuchs, as I have mentioned. These elements of Berg's biography seem to me to offer substantial support for my hypothesis about a resonance between Berg and his inner processing of his relationships with women in a bifurcated mode, and Wozzeck and his split attitudes toward his Marie. Not until Berg composed his second opera, *Lulu*, which was not quite complete at his death in 1935, would the complexities of his highly conflicted, erotically and aggressively charged, and often split internal representations of women receive their fullest expression. These are the representations, I would suggest, that emerged into Berg's conscious awareness at least in part following his attendance of Büchner's *Woyzeck*. There they appeared as Marie, an intimate of Berg and of Wozzeck.

Notes

1 I am referring here to the case of Daniel Paul Schreber, an account of the paranoid psychotic illness of the author described in *Memoir of My Nervous Illness* in 1903. This work was later used by Freud as the basis for *Psychoanalytic Notes on an Autobiographical Account of a Case of Paranoia* (1911), in which Freud conducted an extensive applied analytic investigation into Schreber's illness, and in the process of doing so articulated his theories of paranoia and narcissism.
2 Splitting is commonly considered in psychoanalytic thinking as a defensive process, which involves an active unconscious division of mental representations of a person into dynamically separated unintegrated fragments in order to avoid anxiety and other painful feelings. For example, an anxious ambivalent representation of a mother may be divided into a "good mother" representation and a "bad mother" representation.

References

Arlow, J.A., Brenner, C. (1990). The psychoanalytic process. *Psychoanalytic Quarterly*, 59: 618–692.
Berg, A., Nicholas, J. ed. (2011). *Wozzeck* (English National Opera Guides). London: Oneworld Classics.

Büchner, G. (1993). *The Complete Plays: Danton's Death; Leonce and Lena; Woyzeck; Lenz; the Hessian Messenger; on Cranial Nerves; Selected Letters* (trans. John Reddick). New York: Penguin Classics.

Busch, F. (2013). *Creating a Psychoanalytic Mind: A Psychoanalytic Method and Theory*. New York: Routledge.

Carner, M. (1983). *Alban Berg*. New York: Holms & Meier.

Floros, C. (2008). *Alban Berg and Hanna Fuchs, The Story of a Love in Letters* (E. Beinhardt-Kabisch, Trans.). Bloomington, IN: Indiana University Press.

Freud, S. (1900). The interpretation of dreams. In J. Strachey (Ed. and Trans.), *The Standard Edition of the Complete Psychological Works of Sigmund Freud* (Vol. IV, pp. ix–627). London: Hogarth Press, 1953.

Freud, S. (1905). Fragment of an analysis of a case of hysteria. In J. Strachey (Ed. and Trans.), *The Standard Edition of the Complete Psychological Works of Sigmund Freud* (Vol. VII, pp. 1–122). London: Hogarth Press.

Freud, S. (1911). Psycho-analytic notes on an autobiographical account of a case of *paranoia (Demetiia Paranoides)*. In J. Strachey (Ed. and Trans.), *The Standard Edition of the Complete Psychological Works of Sigmund Freud* (Vol. XII, pp. 1–82). London: Hogarth Press.

Freud, S. (1928). Dostoevsky and parricide. In J. Strachey (Ed. and Trans.), *The Standard Edition of the Complete Psychological Works of Sigmund Freud* (Vol. 28, pp. 175–198). London: Hogarth Press.

Gay, P. (1988). *Freud, a Life for Our Time*. New York: W. W. Norton.

Jarman, D. (1989). *Wozzeck*. Cambridge: Cambridge University Press.

Jarman, D. (1997). Secret programmes. In A. Pople (Ed.), *The Cambridge companion to Berg*. Cambridge: Cambridge University Press.

Jones, E. (1923). Letter to S. Freud, July 2, 1923. In R. A. Paskauskas (Ed. 1993) *The Complete Correspondence of Sigmund Freud and Ernest Jones 1908–1939*. Cambridge, MA: Harvard University Press, pp. 524–525.

Lear, J. (2014). *A Case for Irony*. Cambridge, MA: Harvard University Press.

Paul, R. (1996). *Moses and Civilization: The Meaning behind Freud's Myth*. New Haven, CT: Yale University Press.

Perle, G. (1980). *The Operas of Alban Berg, Volume one, Wozzeck*. Berkeley, CA: University of California Press.

Reich, W. (1974). *Alban Berg* (C. Cardew, Trans). New York: Vienna House.

Ross, A. (2007). *The Rest Is Noise: Listening to the Twentieth Century*. New York: Farrar, Straus and Giroux.

Winnicott, D. W. (1953). Transitional objects and transitional phenomena – A study in the first not-me possession. *International Journal of Psycho-Analysis*, 34: 89–97.

Winnicott, D. W. (1959). The fate of the transitional object. In C. Winnicott, R. Shepherd, M. Davis (Eds., 1989) *Psycho-Analytic Explorations*. Cambridge, MA: Harvard University Press, pp. 53–58.

Wittgenstein, L. (1953). *Philosophical Investigations* (Trans. G. E. M. Anscombe). London: Blackwell.

13 Janáček's Eternal Feminine

The Makropulos Affair[1,2]

Adele Tutter

The Czech composer Leoš Janáček (1854–1928) drew on two great sources of inspiration. The first was his homeland: he was a child of the Czech National Revival that peaked during his lifetime, and many of his works reflect his rather savage patriotism. The second was the love of his life, Kamila Stösslová, on whom he modeled most of the female protagonists of his later operas and choral works. In this effort, I will argue that for Janáček, Stösslová embodied the "eternal feminine," an archetypal cultural ideal of considerable fascination in nineteenth-century Europe, and a construct that links the composer's infatuation with Stösslová to the cultural matrix that incubated his ardent pan-Slavism.

Janáček spent his childhood in the remote Moravian hamlet of Hukvaldy. His father was the village cantor, responsible for teaching and musical education, and the entire family was enlisted to provide music for church services; music became young Leoš' overriding passion, enriching his otherwise impoverished family life. But Janáček lost both family and home when, at the age of 11, increasing financial pressures drove his family's decision to accept the scholarship granted to the talented youth by the monastery conservatory in Brno. He might as well have moved to the moon: Janáček, who spoke only Czech, was out of place in the largely German-speaking metropolis; as a provincial charity student, he was shunned by the other students. There was no relief from the demanding curriculum and ascetic lifestyle of the monastery, as the prohibitive cost of travel prevented him from returning to Hukvaldy, a two-day carriage ride away, until he graduated. Adding to Janáček's childhood traumas was the death of his father and beloved older sister Rosa while he was away at school – losses that would be compounded by the death of his son Vladimir at age 2 and his daughter Olga at age 21.

As an adolescent, Janáček found an outlet for his rage and frustration in the Czech National Revival, which crested during his lifetime. He trained his rage onto the Austro-Hungarian empire that had dominated the Czech lands for three centuries: defying the Habsburg politics of cultural erasure, he determinedly valorized his culture by immortalizing the prosody and rhythm of Czech speech and folk music into such profoundly patriotic works as his *Lachian Dances* (1888–1925) and *Glagolitic Mass* (1927).

DOI: 10.4324/9781032271408-13

In 1918, at the end of the First World War, the decimated Austro-Hungarian Empire had no choice but to yield to demands for Czech independence. With the birth of the first Czech Republic, the aging Janáček, forever concerned about the preservation of Czech culture and language, now worried about his own posterity. Alongside nationalism, Janáček's other preeminent preoccupying theme – that of longing and loss – fueled his perennial search for love and nurture, and informed the choice of material that he would set to exquisitely expressive music. Thus while the creation of the Czecho-Slovak state in 1918 was something of a dream come true for Czechs like Janáček, this gratification may have paradoxically allowed him to divert more energy to the darkly beautiful woman who a year earlier had caught his eye while taking the waters at Luhačovice, a fashionable Moravian spa town. Janáček needed a new muse to elude him.

The 62-year-old Janáček was short, fat, and white-haired when he first met the dark, voluptuous, doe-eyed Kamila Stösslová, all of 25 years old. Both were married; Stösslová had two small children, and Janáček's two children were dead. Strolling through Luhačovice, Janáček lent an attentive ear to the young bride's tearful complaints about her businessman husband's frequent absences. Little did they know that his subsequent infatuation with her would last until he died, and would prove a major source of creative inspiration – arguably one as critical as his patriotic nationalism.

Janáček was perpetually unfaithful to his wife, but no other woman, no other affair would ever matter nearly as much as Stösslová. His surviving letters to her fill a hefty volume (Janáček, 1994) suggest the source of the title of his second string quartet (*Intimate Letters*, 1928), and tell the story of an unrequited love. Although he was chronically and utterly besotted, it appears that, for a long time, the recipient of his affection merely tolerated him. Janáček's unconsummated, unconsummatable love for Stösslová fueled the astonishing outpouring of musical composition that marks the last decade of his life. Ironically, for this love to be as inspiring as it was, it might have been important, even essential that it be unrequited. Janáček's biographer, John Tyrrell (2006, 2007), describes the central role of fantasy in the composition of his two string quartets, as well as the four major operas that bear her stamp:

> The big advantage of Kamila Stösslová was that she was so passive . . . Making no demands and seeming quite uninterested in Janáček's compositions, she turns out to have been his ideal muse: Janáček needed an empty canvas for his fantasies.
>
> (Tyrrell, 2007, p. 849)

While it is true that Janáček's love for Stösslová was not exactly grounded in reality, her canvas was by no means empty, and his passion for her only partly fabricated. Nonetheless, Stösslová provided a perfectly accommodating, perfectly frustrating container, a ready-made sketch that Janáček could fill in, fleshing out the contours of the ideal object with which he could recapitulate his inevitably thwarted desires. This plastic muse also afforded him a form for the tragic female protagonists to whom he was drawn: he used Stösslová as a substrate and scaffold for these fictional characters the way a tailor builds various garments on one dressmaker's form. The 1921 *Kat'a Kabanova*, the first opera he wrote after meeting Stösslová, is dedicated to her, and in his will, he left her all its future royalties.

The opera concerns the eponymous Kat'a: a married woman with an inattentive husband who is often away, she yearns to fall in love with a man who returns her affection. As Janáček told Kamila, when they first met he

> saw for the first time how a woman can love her husband . . . that was the reason why I took up *Kát'a Kabanová* and composed it.
>
> (29 October 1921, p. 34).[3]

Later, he reflected,

> During the writing of [*Kát'a Kabanová*] I needed to know a great measureless love. Tears ran down your cheeks when you remembered your husband in those beautiful days in Luhačovice. It touched me. And I always placed your image on Kát'a Kabanová when I was writing the opera.
>
> (25 February 1922, p. 38)

The fictional Kat'a's convenient, straightforward parallels to the real life Kamila would not prove to be characteristic. As we shall see, Janáček more often assigned to Stösslová the qualities of the characters that inhabit the literary works that he set to music, to such an extent when preoccupied with a particular text, its female protagonist materially shaped his current object representation of Stösslová – his attitudes toward her, his feelings for her, his very *idea* of her. During the final decade of his life, Janáček feverishly constructed an entire fantasy world around his imagined relationship with Stösslová; its foundation was comprised of the literary texts that he transformed into masterpieces of modern operatic music that were true to their literary source, while infused with his inner fantasy life. Janáček thus illustrates the cyclic evolution of culture, whereby cultural products are filtered through the individual psyche, impacting fantasy life and object representations, which in turn add shape to new cultural products. Here, we will consider three operatic works that are intimately associated with Stösslová – *The Diary of One Who Disappeared, The Cunning Little Vixen*, and especially *The Makropulos Case*. All three are distinguished by an intense engagement with the eternal feminine.

The Diary of One Who Disappeared

Stösslová's impact on Janáček's musical life was momentous and instantaneous, predating even *Kat'a Kabanova*. After their first meeting in Luhačovice, and shortly after Stösslová left for her home in Písek, he turned to a new project, *Zápisník zmizelého (The Diary of One Who Disappeared)*. This haunting song cycle for tenor voice and piano was set to the excerpts from a newly discovered "diary" that had caused quite a stir when published a few months before in a popular daily paper. Kept by an anonymous farm boy, the "diary" tells of his seduction by Zefka, the Gypsy girl who he impregnates and runs away with; years later, it was revealed to be a literary hoax, in actuality the work of the respected Moravian poet Ozef Kalda. For Janáček, however, the story was no joke, but a tantalizing subject that he had played around with but not seriously developed – until he met Stösslová, who in her dark Jewish looks and curly hair was in his mind the very personification of the exotic Gypsy girl. And he would make it plain that when he began to set the "diary" to music, it was *she* who he kept in mind. In a letter he wrote her a few months after meeting, he exclaims,

> Those postcards of yours! They're like speech without speaking, like a song without words . . . In the morning I potter around in the garden; regularly in the afternoon a few motifs come to me for those beautiful little poems about that Gypsy love. Perhaps a nice musical romance will come out of it – and a tiny bit of the Luhačovice mood would be in it.
>
> (10 August 1917, p. 10)

The appellation of the "Gypsy" girl stuck. Coyly, he wrote,

> It's too bad my Gypsy girl can't be called something like Kamilka.
>
> (2 September 1918, p. 23)

Indeed, he often explicitly referred to her as his "Gypsy":

> Wherever I am sad I think to myself: you can't want anything else in life if you've got this dear, cheerful, little 'Gypsy girl' of yours.
>
> (30 April 1927, p. 105)

Janáček did more than call Kamila his little "Gypsy"; his words demonstrate how *The Diary* infiltrated his perception of her, as well as the manner in which he addressed her. Here are the first lines from the poem:

> *I startled this young gypsy girl*
> *Lightfooted as a deer*
> *Black ringlets on her mushroom breast*
> *Her eyes like the night air,*
> *Two eyes that cut deep into me*[4]

Consider a letter to Stösslová in which Janáček joyfully relives his first visit to her and her husband in Písek:

> do you know what else makes me glad? That once again I saw your raven-black hair, all loose, your bare foot: and you are beautiful, wonderfully beautiful . . . your eye has a strange depth, it's so deep that it doesn't shine.
>
> (1 July 1924, p. 48)

In the *Diary*, Zefka appeals to Johnny, the farm boy she seduces:

"Now Johnny, I'll show you
How sunburnt gypsies sleep."
With that she broke a branch
And laid it on a stone:
"There now, my bed is made."

Compare these lines with Janáček's appeal to Stösslová:

if only I could be that rock on which you lie, that water which washes you, that sun which dries you and burns you black.

(8–9 May 1927, p. 113)

In what he correctly felt were the last years of his life, Janáček's overriding wish was that he and Stösslová could somehow leave their respective spouses and raise a family together, restoring the guarantee of a surviving lineage that he lost with the death of his children. One cannot discount illusion of immortality such a lineage may afford. *The Diary*, the first work inspired by Stösslová, who for Janáček would always be the epitome of fecundity – anticipates and realizes this fantasy:

To find my life, I lose it
Destiny directs me.
Life's doorway stands open.
Žefka waits and calls me,
Nursing our firstborn son.

Echoing this narrative in a letter to Stösslová, Janáček prays to fate, enlisting the same metaphors:

Bring us together, fate, give to us those moments about which we don't talk, in which there's forgetfulness, in which a new world opens – and a new life grows!

(27–28 December 1927, p. 174)

The Cunning Little Vixen

In some of the most stirringly lyrical passages in the 1923 opera *Příhody lišky Bystroušky* (*The Vixen Bystrouška*, usually translated as *The Cunning Little Vixen*), the vixen Bystrouška's fox "husband" serenades her:

You are as lovely as ever . . . Do tell me how many more cubs we will have!

Reprovingly, she admonishes him:

We'll talk about it again in the springtime.

He agrees, enthusiastically:

I'll wait! I'll wait!

(Janáček 2003, pp. 156–157)

Janáček waited too, if not so patiently. *Vixen* tells of a forester who traps Bystrouška and tries but fails to domesticate her and make her his "pet": the animal incarnation of the woman he cannot possess. His choice to adapt the rustic fantasy of the elusive vulpine beauty mirrors his growing struggles with frustration and the painful reality that he could not so easily have the woman with whom he had grown dangerously infatuated. Stösslová knew that Janáček viewed her replies to his letters as proof of their fantasized affair, and that he was desperate for her to play along. During the composition of *Vixen*, in lieu of her presence (let alone her acquiescence to anything more than friendship), her letters gained fetishistic value, bolstering his illusions:

I read your letters frequently: I'm glad I have a girlfriend.

(9 January 1922, p. 36)

Using animal imagery, he imagined that she returned his impatience.

You wait for my letters and I pant for yours.

(30 June 1924, p. 47)

Although Janáček did not credit Stösslová as directly inspiring *Vixen* (1923), the consonance between his letters to Stösslová and the libretto he adapted from the story by Rudolf Těšnohlídek suggests otherwise. Imagining her as another kind of "pet," Janáček draws on *Vixen's* motifs of forcible domination, fantasizing out loud:

Oh, I'll bind you hand and foot! And you won't untie yourself . . . on my last visit it was as if I'd caught the most beautiful little bird in a cage, so it seemed to me. And I'll take care that it won't fly away from me. Only when it's nicely domesticated will I then open the door for it. You dear little bird of mine!

But this "beautiful little bird" would not cooperate, and refused to be caged. Irritated when Stösslová once again turned down an invitation to accompany him to one of his premières, he hints at retaliation:

I now see that you're the sort of domestic cat that one has to take away somewhere in a sack – and still it runs home . . . And if I don't get a letter

from you, I'll set off some day and bang on your door at night so much
that you'll get a fright.

(21 May 1925, p. 69)

Belying the hostility behind his unrequited longing, the "bang on the
door" resonates uncomfortably with the rage of *Vixen's* forester, who tracks
down the escaped Bystrouška and shoots her. Although she dies, her plenti-
ful offspring survive her, and life in the forest goes on in an endless cycle of
renewal. At the close of the opera, the forester mistakes one of the vixen's
daughters for her mother. Consuming and frustrating as she was, for Janáček,
Stösslová was, as Bystrouška was for the forester, an exasperating vessel of ever-
replenishing life.

The Makropulos Case

Spearheaded by Goethe's epic poem (1984), the Faust story was a critical narrative in nineteenth-century European culture, and became a staple
theme in romantic classical music. Charles Gounod's 1859 *Faust* was one of
Janáček's favorite operas; two other composers that he particularly admired
also wrote symphonic music around the legend, Hector Berlioz (*La damnation de Faust*, 1846) and Richard Wagner (*Faust Overture*, 1840). Janáček's
own affinity for the Faust theme was made evident when as a young man
he attended a costume ball dressed as Faust, accompanied by the adolescent piano student that he was courting – his future wife Zdenka – as his
Margarethe.

More contemporaneous with Janáček's composing life, the concluding chorus of Gustav Mahler's 1910 *Symphony No. 8* is taken from Goethe's *Faust Part
II*, in which Doctor Marianus calls on the eternal feminine to grant Faust
salvation, summoning *Mater Gloriosa* (the Virgin Mary) and *Maria Aegyptiaca*
(Mary of Egypt), who appear from on high. Goethe thus specifies a gendered
dichotomy: between man, who must barter his soul for a stab at immortality,
and the venerated generative woman, who grants it. This pantheistic conception of the eternal feminine, articulated so clearly by Goethe, was derived from
Romantic conceptions of the unity of man, god, and nature, and dominated
much of nineteenth-century European thought. It also neatly dovetails the
Russian Symbolist movement of the late nineteenth to early-twentieth centuries, wherein:

> women represented the spirituality that could sublimate sexuality into a
> higher realm . . . the male was . . . because of his sexual materiality and
> egotistic drive, dependent for his ability to produce true art on the ideal-
> ized woman who was the incarnation of the moral selflessness, absolute
> perfection, and fullness that God had infused in her.

(Izenberg, 2003, p. 25)

In the same way that German Mahler looked to Goethe as the archetypal German cultural hero, Janáček's pan-Slavic identification is evident in the many Russian texts he set to music, including that exemplar of Russian Symbolism, his beloved Dostoevsky; the author's *The House of the Dead* (Dostoevsky 2004/1862) would be his operatic adaptation. The Russian Symbolist view of the feminine ideal also found its way into Janáček's views of Kamila: extolling her "moral selflessness" and "absolute perfection," they specify exactly the fantasized oneness and "spiritual corporeality" that Izenberg describes:

> A love which wants to drown spiritually and physically and merge into one. You don't know where you'd begin and where I'd end.
>
> (31 December 1927, pp. 179–180)

Given Janáček's search for an idealized woman with whom he could fuse, thereby undoing his history of maternal loss, Stösslová – with her juxtaposition of womanly warmth and near-total unavailability – was both a perfect personification of the eternal feminine, and a virtually ready-made maternal transference object for a man who had been separated from his mother as a boy.

Another significant operatic work of Janáček's time elaborates man's need to possess and control the eternal feminine. Béla Balázs' libretto for Bartók's adaptation of *Bluebeard's Castle*, first performed in 1918, transforms the serial wife-murderer of a French folk tale *(Barbe bleue)* into a man who keeps his successive wives imprisoned. His new wife, Judith, sacrifices her freedom to become his "wife of the night," joining the captive, forever-youthful wives of dawn, mid-day, and dusk. Completing the cycle of day and night in a circadian metaphor of immortality, these women collectively represent the eternal feminine.

The theme of the eternal feminine was very much in the musical air when in 1922, Janáček saw a performance of Karel Čapek's satirical play, *Věc Makropulos* (literally, *The Makropulos Thing*, typically translated as *The Makropulos Case* or *The Makropulos Affair:* Čapek, 1999). In a clever twist on both themes, its protagonist, Emilia Marty is a celebrated opera singer who unbeknownst to all has partaken of a magical potion that grants 300 years of youthful existence to those who ingest it. She roams from country to country, reinventing herself in order to avoid revealing her secret; and so Elena Makropulos becomes Eugenie Montez, and then Else Müller, Ekaterina Myshkin, Elian MacGregor, and finally Emilia Marty. When we meet her, she is almost 330 years old, and, nearing the end of her magically extended life, has lost the secret recipe that she must find in order to live another three centuries.

In Janáček's world, the pregnant Zefka and the fertile Bystrouška represent the eternal feminine: stand-ins for Stösslová, with whom he hoped against all odds to have a child. In contrast, the childless character of Emilia Marty embodies the eternal feminine in its association with the trope of Faust: as a singer, her immortality gives her a decided advantage, because over the years, her voice remains youthful, while continually gaining in technical proficiency.

However, her immortality exacts a Faustian price: in exchange for achieving artistic perfection, Marty must watch her lovers age and die. To this end, *Makropulos* allowed Janáček to engage with the classical cultural tension between mortal love and immortal art while indulging his preference for the fantastical. He also had the perfect muse for the lead part – young Kamila, whom he dreaded losing to the vagaries of age, yet resented for her stubborn resistance to him. Excitedly, he wrote Stösslová,

> I've begun a new work . . . a three hundred-year beauty.
>
> (11 November 1923, p. 43)

Not six months later, well into his work on the opera, she had become a more literal incarnation of the Elena Makropulos.

> And, sometimes, ah, I fear to say it . . . because it's something not to be uttered . . . They say of me that I'll live forever; that's metaphorical. But it's possible to live forever in other ways. Eternal life springs from you, from my dear Stösslová.
>
> (8 July 1924, p. 49)

Janacek saw his love's features in the singer who premièred the role of Marty; pleased with her performance, during the production he assured Stösslová:

> It will turn out well. Mrs. Kerová, who is playing Emilia Marty, has movements like you . . . that lady seems just like you in her gait and her whole appearance.
>
> (28 February 1928, p. 213)

He was especially taken with the great diva's costumes:

> Those outfits of hers! In Act 1 a sort of greenish fur as a lining. Those pearls and long gold earrings (!) In Act 2, a white fur, a long train, in Act 3 a dress made out of gold . . . What a sight! Everyone falls in love with her.
>
> (28 January 1927, p. 98)

Accordingly, as he began work on *Makropulos*, Janacek for the first time began to take note of Stösslová's clothes. As if visualizing her literally turning into the best-dressed mezzo-soprano (complete with multiple costume changes), he imagines her in her own outfits:

> You're here in wicked red, in twittering blue. Another time your eyes peer out in a ladylike fashion from beneath your wide-spreading hat, here again beside me, a young and tender apparition in a white dress and blue slippers.
>
> (4 July 1924, p. 49)

Simultaneously a virginal "apparition in a white dress" and a worldly woman in "wicked red," Stösslová is both innocent and experienced, all women in one. At times, Janáček's imagination trenches on delusion. In an evident flight of fancy, he reports that Stösslová in her little town of Písek generates as much attention as Emilia on the stage in Prague.

> in Brno they're already saying how smartly and with what good taste you go about in Písek. What if they knew about that dress for the concert, and that blue and white dress . . . You have no idea how you're watched in Písek. I'm glad you arouse attention.
>
> (8 October 1927, pp. 131–132)

For Janáček, Stösslová recalled Marty in less complimentary ways too. In her various identities, Marty takes on successive lovers, but rather than of watching them grow old and losing them to death, she abandons them for a new country, new name, and new admirer, her superficial heartlessness leading Janáček to give her a chilly nickname:

> That "icy one" . . . she sent cold shivers down everyone's spine.
>
> (21 December 1926, p. 97)

Janáček refused to accept that Stösslová's reputation as a virtuous married woman hinged on her refusal to accompany him to the opera without his wife. Thus, when he anticipates, correctly, that Stösslová will not accompany him to the première of *Makropulos*, he does not experience her refusal as prudent or pragmatic (let alone plausible), but as cold and aloof, like Marty:

> I think that for me you'll turn into that "icy one" . . . come and see that "icy one" in Prague; perhaps you'll see your photograph.
>
> (28 January 1927, p. 98)

At other times, Janáček's pity and compassion for the "icy one" allowed him to envision Stösslová as suffering – "you're poor Elena Makropulos," he told her, when she was sad – affording a foil for decidedly less benign feelings:

> I'm finished [composing] *The Makropulos Case*. Poor 300-year-old beauty! People thought she was a thief, a liar, an unfeeling animal . . . they wanted to strangle her . . . I was sorry for her.
>
> (5 December 1925, p. 81)

For his part, Janáček himself identified with Goethe, and hoped to share in the immortality granted the poet. Reporting to Stösslová from Frankfurt, he observed,

I walked around the town this morning just as the spirit moved me . . .
I looked at one house and I read: "here lived Mariana von Willemer,
Goethe's Sulejka." What was it that led me here to this place of Goethe's great love? . . . on your house you'll now put up the sign: "here
lives Mrs. Stösslová 'the hoped-for wife' of Drph. Leoš Janáček." And it
will be said one day when other people come, those two 'hopeful' dear
people, who loved one another, will be no more. Such is life! Be well,
my wife.

(1 July 1927, p. 124)

The Eternal Feminine

If "girlfriend" and "wife" – married during the *Glagolitic Mass*, which, Janáček
tells Kamila, is the music of their nuptials – Stösslová was also mother and
daughter. A barefoot "protectress" in a white cotton shift, she was ready to take
him back into her cottony womb:

I think about [you] so much as if I were wrapped round, like that little caterpillar wrapping and turning itself from a caterpillar into a pretty butterfly.
I've wrapped myself up too and what I'm wrapped up in is my Kamilka. In
her I'm complete, with all the joys of life.

(10 June 1928, p. 306)

In his mind, the child that "my Kamilka" would mother for him was a boy,
undoing the loss of his own son, little Vladimir.

Today I wrote that sweetest desire of mine in music . . . You're having a
child. What fate in life would our little son have?

(p. 200, 8 February 1928)

At the same time, it appeared that Janáček could imagine "*Kamilka*" – "little
Kamila" – as his daughter. Out of propriety, Stösslová usually refused Janáček's
persistent pleas that she accompanied him to his premières. In one of the rare
instances when she did consent – her acquiescence no doubt related to the fact
that his wife Zdeňka also planned to attend, thereby eliminating any possibility
of a public scandal – he told her that he instructed Zdeňka to pretend that she
was Stösslová's mother, hinting at a fantasy in which he, by extension, assumed
the role of her father.

Janáček had been cold to his first child, Olga, who was born weak and
frail, and he refused to pay for a wet nurse to supplement her nutrition. He
grew to love her deeply, however, and suffered considerable guilt over her
death from rheumatic heart disease. This guilt, and corresponding pleas for
redemption, are audible in the staggeringly beautiful opera *Jenůfa* (1923).
Written at Olga's deathbed, it is dedicated to her. Stösslová gave the negligent

father a second chance: this new daughter he could feed and fuss over. He admitted to her,

> I feel so much that you're the beloved child that the good-natured fates have sent me.
>
> (29 May 1928, p. 288)

A heaven-sent replacement for Olga, *this* iteration he could keep from dying:

> you're like warm breath, which should be wrapped up and nursed, worried over, so it doesn't disperse.
>
> (19 October 1927, p. 134)

To ensure her safety and health, Janáček dutifully filled page after page with gratuitous concerns over the rather robust Stösslová. Hearing that she had a minor cold, he writes:

> your illness came to mind continually. I'm troubled. Even you believe firmly in premonitions; and I'm almost fearful. It's because you're left on your own. And one always has to watch over a sick person. My Kamilka, be well for me!
>
> (1 April 1928, p. 239)

He dispenses for her pills prescribed for him, recipes for home remedies, and copious words of advice. In shamelessly explicit self-interest, he lectures her to:

> drink a small glass of fresh water every day before you go to bed . . . it will keep you in freshness and in health . . . if you were to fall ill I'd suffer more than you. No, now you overflow with health, no bad thoughts.
>
> (1 July 1924, p. 48)

Mother, daughter, mistress, bride: Stösslová was for Janáček all women in one. He was convinced that her death would mean his.

Written during the dawn of the First Czech Republic, Čapek's *The Makropulos Case* can be read as a comment on the past 300 years of history – accusing the Czechs, perhaps, of a sort of Faustian prostitution – the "selling of their soul" by accepting the meager concessions of the Hapsburgs. More hopefully, it can be viewed as an allegory of the emancipation of the Czech Republic from the exhausted Austro-Hungarian Empire. Within this conjecture, the Czechs, immortalized by virtue of their culture and language, freed themselves from subjugation simply by outlasting their oppressors. And, just as the Czech language survived the Hapsburg politics of cultural erasure – including, most notably, its imposition of the German language – Marty survives the various name changes that reflect the language of her current place. But although she in all her aliases outlives her lovers, her life hinges on an alchemical dependence that dates from the Habsburg, Rudolf II; she cannot be liberated until it is extinguished. In legend, the Czechs are descended from the princess Libuše, founder and first ruler of Prague, long known as *Praga mater urbium* – "Prague, mother of cities." She is the subject of various nationalistic musical works; *Libuše*, Bedřich Smetana's 1872 opera, is an icon of Czech nationalism, much appreciated by Janáček. Extending the allegorical reading of Čapek's script, for Libuše, mother of Czechs, to live, the Habsburg courtesan must die.

In adapting the play for the opera, Janáček downplays its political and satirical aspects in favor of emphasizing the tragic. In Čapek's script for *Makropulos*, Marty's admiring young competitor, the ingénue Kristina, ousts her by destroying her advantage, snatching and burning the recipe for the elixir of life. But Janáček alters this succession scenario: in his telling, Emilia herself tires of her endless life. Having finally found that which she searched for so desperately, she finds the prospect of another 300 years of love and loss too much to bear, and sets the recipe on fire herself. Like the monk in Janáček's early opera *Amarus* (1897), she could not live without love; sacrificing herself, she passes the mantle of greatness to a new generation. In keeping with Janáček's mystical affinity for nature, his *Makropulos* thereby reframes the eternal feminine within *Vixen's* terms of eternal renewal, the immortality that Bystrouška achieves through her offspring. In his hands, Čapek's immortality gives way to the cycle of life.

In most stagings of *Makropulos*, Emilia Marty is surrounded by men: lovers, lawyers she consults to locate the lost recipe for the elixir, and rivals desperate to find it first. The Moscou Helikon-Opera production brings all the past men in Marty's life together on stage, imaginatively visualizing them as ghosts that encircle her in a vivid representation of the collective male gaze that focuses on the object of desire (Figure 13.1).

In contrast, the Deutsche Oper production of *Makropulos* assembles Emilia Marty's pastpersonas – Elina Makropulos, Eugenie Montez, Else Muller, Ekaterina Myshkin, Elian MacGregor – on stage simultaneously, each of them portrayed by different singers (Figure 13.2). Marked as temporally disparate by their period costumes, they are nevertheless related by theshared color of their hair and attire. This radical theatrical device references the traditional operatic expression of the eternal feminine in Goethe's chorus of *Maters*. One may also detect a distant illusion to Bluebeard's wives. And at least to this writer, their red coloration brings to mind the Vixen Bystrouška and her cubs.

But I propose that the Deutsche Oper production encourages us to see Marty as personifying the eternal feminine in an additional, more cryptic way, for *Makropulos* can be understood as an allegorical meta-narrative of Janáček's

Figure 13.1 Emilia Marty and her past lovers in the 2016 Moscou Helikon-Opera production of *The Makropulos Case*. Stage direction, Dmitrij Bertman; set and costume
design, Igor Nezhny, Tatiana Tulubieva.

Source: Image Courtesy of Bernd Uhlig

greatest love, and her role in his musical life: a symbolic elaboration of Stösslová's serial assumption of the fictional identities that animate some of his greatest works. She is at once the lonely, doomed Kat'a; the seductive, exotic Zefka;
the passionate, untamable Bystrouška; and the eternally elusive Emilia Marty
herself. This last, over-arching role includes and subsumes all the others –
including, for Janáček, at least, Stösslová *herself*, for she is at the same time all
of them and nobody. In contrast to the objectification of women by the male
gaze, Simone de Beauvoir (1949) critiques the concept of the eternal feminine
as establishing the woman as an "other," depriving her of her individual subjectivity. Thus Janáček's "Kamilka" was not an empty canvas, but a *primed* one,
a pre-formed cultural construction that accommodated many variations on a
theme, set in different places and times, but ultimately played on the same stage.
If Emilia possesses the mysterious secret of the life-giving woman, then so,
too, does the Kamila Stösslová's imago, which lives on in what Janáček himself
called his offspring, his musical works. Always elusive, forever unattainable, she
was his *ne pas ultra*, his eternal feminine.

Figure 13.2 Emilia Marty and her past personas in the 2016 Deutsche Oper production of *The Makropulos Case*. Stage direction, David Hermann; set and costume design, Christof Hetzer.

Source: Image Courtesy of Bernd Uhlig

Notes

1 This paper draws from and expands on parts of a previously published paper (Tutter, 2015). Biographical data concerning Leoš Janáček and Kamila Stösslová are drawn primarily from biographies by Tyrrell (2006, 2007), as well as Vogel (1962) and Zemanová (2002).
2 Dedicated to the memory of John Tyrrell (1942–2018), Professor of Music at Cardiff University and leading authority on Janáček. Tyrrell's exhaustive scholarship, which includes the definitive biography of Janáček, translation of his letters, and critical editions of his operas, allowed Janáček to emerge as one of the premiere composers of the twentieth century; his kind generosity fostered further studies of his life and work, including this writer's.
3 Dates and page references are given for all excerpts from Janáček's letters to Stösslová, which are taken from Janáček (1994), translated and edited by John Tyrrell. Permission to quote from these letters is kindly granted by Jim Friedman.
4 All quotations from *Diary of One Who Disappeared* are from Kalda 2000 (unpaginated).

References

Čapek, K. (1999). *Four plays: R. U. R.; The insect play; The Makropolus Case; The white plague* (P. Majer, C. Porter, Trans.). London: Bloomsbury Methuen Drama.

De Beauvoir, S. (1949). *The second sex* (C. Borde and S. Malovany-Chevallier, Trans.). New York: Vintage, 2011.

Dostoevsky, F. (2004/1862). *From the house of the dead* (C. Garnett, Trans.). New York: Courier Dover.

Goethe, J. W. (1984). *Faust I & II*. (S. Atkins, Ed. & Trans.). Princeton: Princeton University Press.

Izenberg, G. N. (2003). Intellectual-cultural history and psychobiography: The case of Kandinsky. *The Annual of Psychoanalysis, 31*, 21–33.

Janáček, L. (1994). *Intimate letters: Leoš Janáček to Kamila Stösslová* (J. Tyrell, Ed. and Trans.). Princeton: Princeton University Press.

Janáček, L. (2003). *The Janáček opera libretti: Translations and pronunciation, volume 1 – Příhody lišky Bystroušky, The cunning little vixen* (T. Cheek, Trans.). New York: Scarecrow Press.

Kalda, O. (2000). *The diary of one who disappeared* (S. Heaney, Trans.). New York: Farrar, Straus and Giroux.

Tyrrell, J. (2006). *Leoš Janáček: Years of a life, volume I (1854–1914): The lonely blackbird*. London: Faber and Faber.

Tyrrell, J. (2007). *Leoš Janáček: Years of a life, volume II (1914–1928): Tsar of the forests*. London: Faber and Faber.

Vogel, J. (1962). *Janáček: A biography* (G. Thomsen-Muchová, Trans.). London: Orbis Publishing, 1981.

Zemanová, M. (2002). *Janáček: A composer's life*. Boston, MA: Northeastern University Press.

14 Billy Budd

A Study in Envy and Repression

Milton Schaefer

Benjamin Britten, E.M. Forster, and Eric Crozier's brilliant adaptation of Herman Melville's novella, *Billy Budd*, is considered among Britten's greatest operatic works because of the complexity and subtlety with which themes of good and evil, freedom and oppression, and desire and repression all play out in a world of men captured and incarcerated aboard the cramped, claustrophobic confines of the HMS Indomitable. While one can make comparisons with Melville's earlier great novel of men at sea, *Moby Dick*, *Billy Budd* is a much starker, almost biblical portrayal of envy, repression, and cruelty that charts a relentless pursuit and destruction of what is good. In this discussion of the opera I will highlight two themes: the destructive qualities of envy and the fate of repression of homoerotic desire.

The chief character, Billy Budd, is a young man of extraordinary good looks and innocent yet charismatic character, who has been "impressed" according to British naval law into military service on a passing vessel, The Rights of Man. Life on the warship is one of strict and cruel authoritarian order. Billy, loved by most of his shipmates, is hated from first sight by the master-at-arms, Claggart, who attempts to frame him for organizing the other men into a mutiny. Captain Vere, believing the accusation is false, has Claggart repeat his accusations to Billy, who is overcome by his life-long stammer and is unable to verbally defend himself. To vent his feelings, Billy strikes Claggart inadvertently killing his accuser. Vere, torn between his love for Billy and his obligation to the rule of law, orders an immediate trial in which Billy is found guilty. Vere orders his execution but, even in the face of his impending death, Billy declares "God Bless Captain Vere," thus forestalling the crew's imminent mutiny.

For the most part, Forster and Crozier's adaptation stays close to Melville's novella, but they added a Prologue and Epilogue by Vere, as an old man looking backwards at the end of his life, placing the opera as both reminiscence and *Nachträglichkeit*, a summation and reworking of the meaning of his life. This has the effect of highlighting the internal, intrapsychic dimensions of the opera. In a BBC interview, Forster once stated that they felt Melville was diminishing and disgracing Vere by not mining the depths of his conflict – between law and fear versus justice and love, and had thus endeavored to make him a character of more spiritual, existential, and psychological complexity.

DOI: 10.4324/9781032271408-14

Billy Budd is an opera of orchestral and choral expansiveness, portraying the power of forces beyond one's control, and by contrast, Vere's prologue is accompanied by plaintive undulating strings that suggest the tragedy of inevitable evil:

> Much good has been shown me and much evil, and the good
> has never been perfect. There is always some flaw in it,
> some defect, some imperfection in the divine image, some
> fault in the angelic song, some stammer in the divine speech.
> So that the Devil still has something to do with every human
> consignment to this planet of earth.
>
> *(Forster & Crozier, 1951, p. 7)*

Billy Budd is most prominently a portrayal of the struggle between good and evil. Freud hypothesized that within all people there are competing life and death instincts that are in constant tension and conflict with each other (Freud, 1930). From a psychoanalytic point of view, the good is related to the binding of the libidinal forces of the life instinct, while evil is viewed in connection with the unbinding power of the death instinct. Freud's concept of the death instinct arose as he tried to understand why some of his patients seemed to actively fight against getting better, leading him to believe that there was an innate regressive urge within all people that is in conflict with progressive life-affirming, libidinal instincts. The concept was further developed by Melanie Klein and her followers, who focused on the aggressive and destructive consequences of the death instinct in impeding development within the very early mother-infant relationship.

> One could formulate the conflict between the life and death instinct in purely psychological terms. Birth confronts us with the experience of needs. In relation to that experience there can be two reactions, and both, I think, are invariably present in all of us, though in varying proportions. One, to seek satisfaction for the needs: that is life-promoting and leads to object seeking, love, and eventually object concern. The other is the drive to annihilate the need, to annihilate the perceiving experiencing self, as well as anything that is perceived.
>
> (Segal, 1993, p. 55)

Most central to the Kleinian conceptualization of destructive hatred in human relations – and a compelling force that animates this story – was the emotion of envy. The central driver of envy is the recognition that one is not omnipotently complete and self-sufficient. Envy springs from, and is a reaction to, the fact that others have something that you need or desire, but cannot necessarily control. Psychoanalytically, the core model is the infant's dependence on the caretaker. The very fact of that dependent position inevitably makes one feel small and vulnerable and in the face of frustration also very angry. "You have something I need and I can't stand that I am not totally self-sufficient." Thus, the more one feels incomplete, as of course we all are, and the more that leads to feelings of depletion, the more intense is the destructive wish to eliminate the other, or at least the goodness possessed by the other. It can then be the other's very existence, his goodness, his being what one is not, and perhaps what one wishes one was, that calls attention to one's insufficiency, and to one's badness for having those needs in the first place. This causes a hatred of the other and a wish to destroy him, which then accentuates one's sense of badness in a tragic destructive cycle where both self and object pay the price. This is perfectly expressed in Claggart's powerful Aria at the end of Act 1, perhaps the most vivid description of envy in the entire operatic canon, even more so than Iago's Credo in Verdi's *Otello*.

> O beauty, o handsomeness, goodness! Would that I never
> encountered you! Would that I lived in my own world
> always, in that depravity to which I was born. There I
> found peace of a sort, there I established an order such as
> reigns in Hell. But alas, alas! the lights shine in the dark
> ness and the darkness comprehends it and suffers. O
> beauty, o handsomeness, goodness! would that I had never
> seen you!
>
> Having seen you, what choice remains to me? None,
> none! I'm doomed to annihilate you, I'm vowed to
> your destruction. I will wipe you off the face of the earth
> With hate and envy I'm stronger than love. . .
> I, John Claggart, Master-at-Arms upon the *Indomitable*, have you in my
> power, and I will destroy you.
>
> *(p. 32–33)*

Claggart hates Billy for who he is rather than anything that he has actually done. This is hate at first sight – it is envy's dark equivalent of love at first sight. This aria is sung in F-minor, a key associated in this opera with depression and longing, which reinforces the dark, depressive, and destructive qualities of Claggart. There was a major disagreement between Forster and Britten about the music for Claggart's aria. Apparently, when he first heard it from Britten on the piano, Forster found it wanting in emotional expressivity. He wrote to Britten,

> It is my most important piece of writing and I did not, at first hearing, feel
> it sufficiently important musically . . . I want *passion* – love constricted,
> perverted, poisoned, but never the less *flowing* down its agonizing channel;
> a sexual discharge gone evil.
>
> *(Lago & Furbank, 1985)*

While the criticism bothered Britten, he nonetheless developed a more dramatic aria. But a question remains as to whether Britten went far enough to satisfy Forster in the final version.

The relationship between Forster and Britten was complex, not least because it involved two creative giants at very different points in their careers. Forster was 70 years old, and was renowned for having published *A Room with a View* (1908), *Howards End* (1910), and *Passage to India* (1924). (*Maurice* was published posthumously in 1970). At the age of 70, he had not published a novel for over 45 years and had never worked on a libretto. Britten was almost half Forster's age and his opera, *Peter Grimes,* had just been performed to great critical success a few years earlier as he was coming into the peak of his creative powers. It may be that Forster needed/wanted to have stronger, more explicit stances in the opera, especially the repressed hatred of Claggart, and that he under-appreciated the ways that Britten creates feelings of discontent, uncertainty, and foreboding within a larger tonal structure. In an opera where Billy's psychological vulnerability is his stammer in the face of intense negative emotions, it seems both fitting and ironic that the creators would disagree over the appropriate musical voice.

Contrasting the seemingly innate evil of Claggart, there is the goodness, and almost the perfection of Billy. Even more in the novella than in the opera, we are made aware of Billy's physical beauty, which Melville compares to Hercules, Adam before the fall, and Aldeberan, outshining all constellations in the sky. From the moment that Claggart sees Billy, he is out to destroy him, and I would posit that what sparks his envy and hate is that Billy is the object of his repressed sexual desire. Claggart's wish to destroy Billy is not only out of envy but also, and quite importantly, a result of his repression and hate of his own homosexual desires. Part of the felt badness that Billy sheds light on is Claggart's attraction to Billy and that only serves to exacerbate Claggart's own sense of badness. In this opera, as in life, destructiveness finds rich sources both in envy and in repressed desire.

Billy's flaw is his stammer. But this is just a symptom and only manifests itself when he experiences intense sad or angry affects, for example, when he talks about himself as a foundling, when he discovers someone has been stealing from him, and when he is falsely accused by Claggart. Billy has no way to think about or express negative emotion or to even consider the other's negative emotions and intent. Fairbairn, in observing how traumatic life circumstances can result in feeling oneself to be bad, wrote: "it is better to be a sinner in a world ruled by God than to live in a world ruled by the Devil" (Fairbairn, 1952, pp. 66–67). Billy seems to have gone even further, living in a world where bad intent just doesn't exist at all. This denial may have served him well in maintaining good internal objects in the face of an impoverished and difficult upbringing. So, in ways that are somewhat symmetrical, Claggart has no tolerance for goodness and Billy has no tolerance for badness. Ambivalence thus has little room to exist for either character, with disastrous consequences.

There are dark figures that have homosexual overtones in three of Britten's most important operas: *Peter Grimes, Billy Budd, and Death in Venice.* Britten was generally "out," as much as one could be in England at that time, and he lived with Peter Pears, the great English tenor, with whom he would have 40 years of musical collaboration, and for whom the role of Vere was written. Moreover, he was part of a group of young gay writers that included Auden and Isherwood.

But this was also a time of great homophobia and the opera premiered only a year before Alan Turing, the originator of artificial intelligence, was to be sentenced to chemical castration for his homosexuality. EM Forster, also homosexual, had written *Maurice*, a novel concerning a gay relationship but felt it could not be published during his lifetime because of British Sodomy Laws.

Phillip Brett (1977) depicts these three artists as choosing different paths in their efforts to resolve the pressures of being gay artists in a homophobic environment. Isherwood decided to live in a somewhat more accepting environment as openly gay in his life and art. Forster largely stopped writing novels in 1942 due to his not being able to express his homosexuality in his writing. Britten, however, took a third, less extreme path, by being cautious of the manner in which he addressed themes of the love between men. I am bringing up this background not because I think that Britten and Forster necessarily set out to make queerness a central theme, but rather because the choice of material reflects both conscious and unconscious influences. The ways that one cannot speak of the love between men and the consequences of that silence, in both its external and intrapsychic dimensions, echoes subtly yet powerfully in the lives of both the protagonists and creators of Billy Budd. Britten's genius lies in the ways that he makes these tensions ever-presently embedded in the claustrophobic world of men.

Melville's story occurs in the same year as an actual mutiny on the HMS Nore, and so there was a tremendous fear of what would happen if a crew were to mutiny. Britain was at war with France, and the Man-O-War's purpose was to seek out and destroy French ships. There was a great fear in Britain that the ideas of freedom for all men, as expressed in Thomas Paine's writing, along with the toppling of the Monarchy in France, would spread across the English Channel. There was anxiety about men giving voice to their desire for freedom and perhaps their abhorrence of violence. Thus, the desires for individual freedom set in opposition to the needs of the state are the explicit setting against which the action of this opera unfolds.

Life aboard the HMS Indomitable is portrayed as one of servitude and unreasonable cruelty, ostensibly far beyond the need for order. This is most dramatically represented in the scene in which "the novice," really just a child, is tortured for slipping, and further physically and psychologically tormented by Claggart until he becomes his agent of deceit. Men are broken with a cruelty far beyond the necessary bounds of war. The novice sings after the beating, "the pain will pass, the shame will never pass." This is a world which crushes people who are weak, heightening one's sense of inadequacy. Witnessing this boy's bloody and crippled body, the crew sings with sad resignation, "lost forever on an endless sea".

There was a need to maintain order and the law; the fact that this was a warship is central to Vere's tragic dilemma and his decision to not save Billy. But it may also be that on a ship of trapped and lonely men far from their homes and families, what also needs to be contained is their frustrated desire. Claggart's plan to destroy Billy is to entrap Billy into a mutinous act. It reminded me of the various ways that gay men have been entrapped, and so the themes of oppression work hand in hand with Claggart's repression of his own desire and resultant envy and self-hatred. Furthermore, in the novella, Claggart is portrayed as someone from a lesser station who suffers from his own sense of inadequacy compared to the more privileged officers. Thus Claggart's own sense of depletion, both of class and masculinity, leads him, in a way akin to projective identification, to induce others to feel as he himself feels.

There are authors who wonder if Vere had his own sexual feelings toward Billy. He is certainly deeply moved by him. But I see him as more of a father figure who must struggle between an external sense of duty and morality and his love of Billy, and this is not so different from the themes of love, duty, and redemption explored in the relationship between Wotan and *Brünnhilde* in Wagner's Ring Cycle (Goldberg, 2011). Under Naval Law, a trial certainly could have waited until the ship reached harbor, which was what was most usual in these circumstances. Why did Vere not wait? It might have been that Vere was so hard on Billy because his wish to be more lenient was intertwined with his feelings of attraction and love, which could not be tolerated, no less expressed. Afraid of what he might reveal to himself and others, his sexual feelings had to be denied, and, in their wake, feelings of compassion and pardon were submerged.

In the epilogue, which I think contains some of the most poignant music in the opera, Vere questions and perhaps regrets his decision to not save Billy. He concludes that "he has saved me and blessed me. And the love that passes understanding has come to me. I was lost on the infinite sea but I sighted a sail in the storm". At the end of Vere's life and of the opera, it is the seemingly unconditional love, even in the face of death, that has the power to soothe and contain loss, including the loss of goodness. However, while Forster's libretto would point to the power of love to heal wounds, Britten's score suggests a more unstable balance, where harp, woodwind, and brass join forces to weaken the finality of closure (Harasemovitch, 2019). In the end, one must endure rather than undo the past and, as is often the case in opera, the music has the last word.

References

Brett, P. (1977). Britten and grimes. *Musical Times*, 117, pp. 995–1000.

Fairbairn, W. D. (1952). *Psychoanalytic Studies of the Personality*. London: Tavistock.

Freud, S. (1930). Civilization and it's discontents. In J. Strachey (Ed. and Trans.), *The Standard Edition of the Complete Psychological Works of Sigmund Freud* (Vol. 21, pp. 64–148). London: Hogarth Press.

Forster, E. M. and Crozier, E. (1951). *Billy Budd: Opera in Two Acts*. London: Hawkes & Sons.

Goldberg, S. (2011). Love, loss, and transformation in Wagner's *Die Walkure*. Fort Da, pp. 53–60.

Harasemovitch, J. (2019). Billy Budd. Unpublished discussion following 2019 performance at San Francisco Opera.

Lago, M. and Furbank, P. N. (eds.). (1985). *Selected Letters of E.M. Forster, vol 2: 1921–1979*, p. 242. Cambridge, MA: Harvard University Press.

Segal, H. (1993). On the clinical usefulness of the concept of death instinct. *International Journal of Psychoanalysis*, 74, pp. 55–61.

15 Sendak and Knussen's *Where the Wild Things Are*

A Developmental Journey

Debbie Hindle

Introduction

Where the Wild Things Are is Maurice Sendak's most well-known book (Sendak, 1963). First published in 1963, it has been translated into almost every language and is noted as being one of Barack Obama's favorite books. In an issue of *The International Journal of Infant Observation and its Applications*, Zuppardi (2016) explored another of Sendak's (1970) books, *In the Night Kitchen*. In his thoughtful and imaginative exposition, Zuppardi considers the text from a psychoanalytic perspective, drawing out themes related to primitive anxieties, pre-verbal experience, and defenses such as Bick's (1968) concept of a 'second skin'.

Both Sendak's stories are picture books, which engage children (and adults) on multiple levels. Zuppardi (2016, p. 152) describes vividly his memory of encountering these books for the first time as a small boy and 'being struck by a visceral sense of familiarity and recognition'. He goes on to describe the way in which picture books 'offer child readers a chance to take ownership of a text in an intensely personal way, relating to their own experiences and preoccupations'.

Both stories begin with a child's hunger and both take place either just before bedtime or at night – two areas of a child's experience that might elicit anxiety and raise issues related to separation. The imaginative drawings and text also are indicative of the language of dreams. But the two stories describe very different responses to similar phenomena. *In the Night Kitchen's* main character Mickey searches for a solution to his hunger and, after mistakenly being incorporated in the bakers' batter, struggles free and finds his way to the milk before peacefully returning to his bed. In *Where the Wild Things Are*, the main character, Max, is consumed with anger and oedipal conflicts before he too has his hunger satisfied, this time by his mother, on returning 'home'. Both embark on a journey, but essentially a journey which, in my view, takes place in the mind – an internal journey.

Where the Wild Things Are is one of the few contemporary children's books that have been made into an opera. In opera, the bringing together of the story, the libretto, the set and costumes and the music is one way in which a literary work, in this case for children, may be enriched, allowing us to revisit a familiar story in new ways. I want to focus on Sendak and Knussen's opera based on the book. I shall give a brief synopsis of the original story and a brief account of the

DOI: 10.4324/9781032271408-15

transition from book to opera, before exploring the opera version of the story in more detail. Finally, I want to consider Max's journey from a psychoanalytic perspective. Rustin (2016, p. 141) raised a question about literary works for children – not just whether they could be understood psychoanalytically, 'but also, what we learn from them about the experience of childhood which might enrich our psychoanalytic understanding'.

Synopsis

We first see Max wearing a 'wolf suit' (probably his 'wolf' pyjamas) creating mischief (driving a nail into the wall to hang up a makeshift 'tent' and chasing the dog with a fork). When his mother (not seen in the book) calls him a 'Wild Thing', Max retaliates saying, 'I'll eat you up!' To this, his mother sends him to his room without anything to eat. When we next see Max, a forest gradually grows to overtake his room, soon followed by an ocean and a boat. Max sails 'night and day and in and out of weeks and almost over a year' to 'where the wild things are'. Although the creatures he encounters roar and gnash their teeth and show their claws, Max commands them to 'be still', tames them with a magic trick and becomes King of all the Wild Things. After joining them in an excited rumpus, he sends them off to bed without their supper. Suddenly, he feels alone and longs to be 'where someone loves him best of all'. In spite of the Wild Things imploring him to stay, he sails back 'over a year and in and out of weeks and through a day' to his own room where his supper is waiting for him and, 'It is still hot'.

From Book to Opera

The opera *Where the Wild Things Are* was commissioned by the Opera National, Brussels, in 1978 to coincide with the International Year of the Child. Sendak wrote the scenario and the libretto in collaboration with Knussen who composed the music. Although a first version of the opera was performed in Brussels in 1980, Knussen continued working on and revising the opera until a complete version was performed by the Glyndebourne Festival Opera in London in January 1984. But developing an opera from what was a picture book with only some 380 words posed considerable problems, as Sendak and Knussen summarize in their notes to the libretto. The problem was how to translate the book based on carefully selected words linked to the illustrations into a libretto with arias, duets and monologues.

> The problem was simple – and awful . . . A picture book . . . depends on few but potent words, whose essential meaning can be expanded and embellished by the pictures accompanying those words . . . My problem – to expand that tight little island of a book into a viable opera libretto – was a daunting one. There had to be arias, duets, monologues even! – and Max, in the book, only says a handful of words.
>
> (1985, p. 35)

Sendak cites his close collaboration and friendship with Knussen as making the whole project possible, as together they created something that enriches Max's adventure in a way that only music can do.

> Together, Oliver Knussen and I fashioned a work that, for me, begins to step beyond the book – that enriches Max's mighty little adventure and adds a further dimension – a crucial emotional color and weight that only music – great music – can provide.
>
> (1985, p. 35)

Sendak's words capture the importance of their creativity and collaborative endeavor and open the door to thinking about this 'further dimension'. What is visually striking in the Glyndebourne production is how closely the costumes and set capture Sendak's graphic illustrations, as if they were literally being brought to life.

Knussen notes his own concerns – not to create a 'children's opera', or to write an opera 'for' children, nor to write an opera 'about' children, but to 'respond to the subjects as immediately and colorfully as I knew how' (Sendak & Knussen, 1999). He openly describes drawing on some of his favorite music – Mussorgsky's *Boris Godunov* and Debussy's *La boite a joujoux*. Both composers wrote music which he thought were eminently accessible to children – for Mussorgsky, *The Nursery* and Act 2 of *Boris Godunov* and for Debussy, his music for his daughter Chouchou. Both of which, he states, 'can make children's music not by "writing down" to them, but by illuminating (their) harmonic language in particularly gentle and subtle ways' (The Earl of Harewood & Peattie, 1997).

In her book, *Inside Picture Books*, Spitz (1999, p. 125) makes a thoughtful observation about the relationship between the text and the illustrations in Sendak's book. Although they begin 'in partnership', gradually 'the printed text shrinks in relation to the size of the pictures until finally, when Max (and the child listening) are fully transported inside their own imaginary world, the pictures expand to fill up all the available space'. She describes the double-spread pages at the center of the book, absent of text, as being the point where 'fantasy completely overtakes reality'. In the opera too, there are three points in which the music takes over from the voice, allowing for long uninterrupted interludes. The first is at the end of Scene 3 when the forest transforms into an ocean and the boat arrives to take Max to the island. The second is during the 'Wild Rumpus', Scene 6, and the third is when Max traverses the ocean to return home at the end of Scene 8, 'The Parting'. Each of these sections mirrors the lack of text in the book and captures something of the magical aspect of imagination, perhaps best depicted in visual and musical imagery, like dreams.

The opera falls into the genre of 'fantasy opera', such as Humperdinck's *Hansel and Gretel*, Stravinsky's *Le Rossignol* (The nightingale), and Ravel's *L'Enfant et les Sortileges* whose main character bears many similarities to Sendak's Max. I shall make links between this opera and *Where the Wild Things Are* in the Discussion.

The Opera from a Psychoanalytic Perspective

The opera in one act is divided into nine scenes, each capturing a dramatic moment in the story. I shall consider each scene, drawing attention to the music and staging and reflecting on the 'material' from a psychoanalytic perspective. The opera performance to which I refer as the basis for this is the Glyndebourne Festival Opera production (1985) with the London Sinfonietta, available on DVD (2009).

Scene 1: Max

The music of the opera begins with one slow tone, added to by the woodwinds, which convey a sense of something potentially ominous happening. We see a makeshift tent heaving erratically as the music becomes more frenzied, until Max finally emerges, dressed in a wolf suit and wielding a toy sword. Assertively, he declares his identity – "I'm Max! M-A-X the wolf! . . . . 'A King!" and, later, a "Wild Wolf King!" Repeatedly, he sings his war cry – "VIL-DA-CHAI-AH-MI-MAH-MEEOH!" – dramatically cuts off the heads of his toy soldiers and admonishes his toys, "See what happens when I get mad? See what happens when you don't listen?" (sung almost in a whisper). Momentarily, he sings, "Nothing to eat!" repeating "Nothing, nothing, nothing . . ." while rhythmically beating his teddy bear dangling precariously from a coat hanger. At the end of this first scene, Max's pretend fight ends with his being 'shot' and falling to the floor, singing, "Catch me, catch me! Hurray please and catch me quick – quick!!" Throughout this frenzy of activity and aggression, it is the orchestra that captures the intensity of Max's play with a flurry of rapid accompaniment by drums, then the brass section, followed by the woodwinds and strings.

In this opening scene, Max seems completely engrossed in imaginative play – flailing his sword as if surrounded by potential enemies or persecutors – here he seems to be dramatizing an internal scenario in which he is inflicting harsh punishment on the toys.[1] We can imagine his being in identification with an exaggerated punitive parent, now infused with his own anger and fueled by his hunger. But something more sadistic seems to be aroused when he beats the teddy while singing "nothing to eat". Only after he is 'shot' and dramatically falls to the ground do we sense a part of him who might feel un-held and in need of someone to catch him, so poignantly captured in words and music.

Scene 2: Mama

In the following scene, after a musical interlude punctuated by high pitched woodwinds and piano, full of anticipation, we see Mama's shadow looming across the stage and then her entry, wielding a vacuum cleaner. Max 'ambushes' her, scaring his mother with his war cry – "VIL-DA-CHAI-AH-MI-MAHMEE-OH!" She admonishes him telling him to stop and starts tidying up, but Max is openly defiant and shouts, "I'm hungry!" She evokes father's disapproval –

"I'll tell Papa you were bad!", which only incites Max's defiance – "And I'll tell Papa you were bad!" Mama ripostes, "He'll spank you!" quickly countered by Max, "Then he'll throw you out!" Max goes on to imitate Papa falling asleep quickly. Mama retaliates by threatening that he will get no supper unless he stops. Her initial concern about his falling or hurting himself if he does not get down from where he is standing – high up – soon gives way to anger as she calls him a 'Wild Thing!' to which he jumps down and declares – "I'll eat you up!" Mama's response is quick and decisive – "That's it!! You're going to bed without eating anything", a phrase which has dramatic impact, heightened by being spoken by Mama, rather than sung. Max retaliates by attacking the vacuum cleaner with his sword. Throughout, the music captures the tension of the moment and its heightened emotionality. The music, like the encounter between Mama and Max, is discordant, fast and furious.

As this scene opens, Max is still in his 'Wild Wolf-King' state of mind, unwilling to accept his mother's authority or to see her as part of a parental couple. Rather, at her mention of father, Max evokes him as a potential ally against her, while also portraying his father's inactivity and lack of interest in her (falling asleep quickly). Any attempts literally to bring Max down to earth are rejected, Mama's anger is piqued and she is pushed into punishing him by withholding the very thing he wants – something to eat. It is as if his hunger has stirred up his most primitive anxieties, fear of deprivation and oral aggression. Here Mama stands as not only a source of all nourishment, but also a reminder of his dependence on her.

Mama's impatience with Max – "I don't have time for this!" – drives her to exercise her parental function and to place clear limits on Max's behavior. Max's attack upon the vacuum cleaner, symbolically representing father is all the more telling – there should be no Mama and Papa working together!

Scene 3: Max's Room

Mama takes Max to his room, symbolically taking his toy sword and closes the door, leaving Max alone. Here Max sings his first aria – *Í want! I want! I want'* But soon his song takes on a more lyrical, melodic tone, conveying a sense of longing while repeatedly singing, "Catch it and cook it and keep it hot . . ." as if remembering and re-evoking what he is missing. Throughout, the woodwinds create a dialogue in which they 'reply' to his song. Soon, the sounds of flutes, woodwinds, harp and celeste herald something strange and magical occurring as the room is transformed into a 'lush forest'. But the music soon changes to match Max's changing mood – now filled with thoughts about how he might wreak revenge on his Mama by scaring and biting her:

> I jump and bump and rumpus in the night
> To scare the Mama Wolf away
> VIL-DA-CHAI-AH-MI-MAH-MEE-OH!
> *(Libretto, p. 43)*

Toward the end of this scene, the ragtime rhythms that accompanied Max's outrage slow as the room is transformed again, this time into an ocean. A haunting horn solo, lightly accompanied by piano, marks the appearance of a boat as Max climbs in and sails away. The length of this dream-like interlude underpins what Max sings about in the next scene – the time and distance traversed.

Here Max is faced with his internal conflict – both longing for his mother and what she can provide – and, in the face of her absence and apparent rejection, now also infused with his hatred – his wish to retaliate. But the reference to jumping and bumping and rumpus in the night has veiled intimations of parental sexuality. Perhaps his exclusion from this private endeavor is also at some level frightening. In this excerpt, it is Mama, turned into a 'Wolf Mama' (a combined parental couple?), who is, in his mind, scared away by Max, thus reversing the situation. The transformation of the room – into a forest and then an ocean – seems one way of distancing himself from a persecuting internal conflict.

Scene 4: The Wild Things

The previous calmer scene is soon disrupted by excited, clashing music, briefly echoing his war cry, as Max encounters turbulence and is tossed about in his boat as if by rough seas before being washed up on the shores of an island. On exiting the boat, he sings a beautiful aria drawn from the words in Sendak's book:

> It must be very far to here
> Through days and nights and in and out of weeks
> And almost over a year
> I sailed to where the. . .
>
> *(Libretto, p. 44)*

Soon he hears strange, almost chanting sounds in the distance. Suddenly the Wild Things appear. They are huge and dwarf Max's diminutive figure as they cavort around the stage 'speaking' in an incomprehensible language. As the cacophony of sounds and confusion mounts, the brass section is 'unleashed' until Max's admonishment – "Be still!!" He fixes them with his magic stare and tames them with his war cry.

The Wild Things seem oddly over-sized and although potentially frightening, with big heads and big eyes, they look more like over-stuffed soft toys – not unlike the chubby pink bakers in the night kitchen which Zuppardi describes as "reminding me of worried babies who are anxious because they do not know how to feed themselves" (Zuppardi, 2016, p. 154). The Wild Things also might represent a more fragmented, hungry baby part of Max, as well as his attempts to master the wilder parts of himself, now personified in the creatures. The idea that he could exercise some control, that a part that might create ruckus and mayhem could be tamed, seems momentarily hopeful. Max commands the Wild Things into obedience – something his mother was not able to achieve with him. At the same time, their miming his every move seems like an empty victory in that they appear to have completely lost their sense of self.

Scene 5: Coronation

In the next scene, there is a goat who dances with a crown, teasing and tempting Max, holding it just out of his reach. The rhythmic musical interlude, with intonations of a chant, captures the hypnotic pull of the crown and the repeated sounding of a gong draws the scene to its climax, paraphrasing the Coronation scene from *Boris Godunov* (The Earl of Harewood & Peattie, 1997, p. 400). In time, Max proceeds along a red carpet for a Coronation. But it is Max who crowns himself, subjugating the Wild Things as he shouts his war cry, "VAL-DA-CHAI-AH-MI-MAH-MEE-OH!" which starts the rumpus, announced by Max – "And now – let the Wild Rumpus start!'", ushering in Scene 6.

The addition of a goat as a character in the opera is a departure from Sendak's original story. Interestingly, the goat is not over-sized as the other Wild Things, but more in keeping with Max's actual size. We are left pondering what the goat symbolizes, and why it is the goat who gives Max the crown and scepter. The goat has many meanings in mythological literature and in stories. In the Bible, there is the story elaborating the symbolic meaning of a scapegoat; in Greek mythology Pan (represented as a goat) is the god of wild shepherds and flocks; goats are also seen as representing fertility, vitality, and ceaseless energy, and, significantly, as a sign of the devil. This apparently many facetted symbol, in my reading of the story, goes hand in hand with the idea of the goat being Max's alter ego, now devilishly tempting him and drawing him even further into a manic state of mind.

Max is once again in 'king' mode. We can hypothesize that both in his previous play as 'Wolf-King', and now, Max gets high on usurping his father's position by 'being father'. This is not in terms of trying out what it might be like to be grown-up (anticipatory identifications), so aptly described by Alvarez (1992, p. 175), but more of an exaggerated, distorted caricature of a king (more like a toddler) who only commands. Here Max's vitality contrasts sharply with what he dramatically portrayed in the second scene – his Papa suddenly falling asleep – emphasizing Father's lack of vitality and interest in Mama (or him) – a rather depleted father. It is, perhaps, not surprising that Max and the Wild Things get high with the excitement that follows.

Scene 6: The Wild Rumpus

The quick, frenzied jazz-like music, which is both playful and rhythmic (described in the libretto as 'Waltz – Mazurka') accompanies Max and the Wild Things in their exaggerated dance, and highlights a sense of manic excitement, only interrupted when the female Wild Thing, TZIPPY, literally loses her head! Like the toy soldiers in Scene 1 and reminiscent of the Queen of Hearts in *Alice in wonderland* who decrees "off with her head", it seems that all thinking is lost when manic defenses take hold. The music builds to a crescendo until Max shouts at them:

Now, stop! And off to bed without your supper.

In this frenzied scene, there is one aspect that warrants consideration – the gang of characters that is being depicted – with Max as the 'leader' Rosenfeld (1971, p. 249) aptly described the way in which a defensive organization can coalesce, "as if one were dealing with a powerful gang dominated by a leader, who controls all the members of the gang to see that they support one another". The purpose of the structure seems to be to maintain the idealized and superior power of destructive narcissism,[2] affecting the person's capacity to receive help or acknowledge weakness and dependency. Although described as a pathological organization by Rosenfeld, here we see it in passing as another expression of a range of defensive maneuvers, not yet fixed. It is interesting that the 'gang' soon dissipates when actual damage is encountered, which also indicates the transitory nature of this state of mind in a young child.

When Max shouts, "Now, stop! And off to bed without your supper!" he is clearly in identification with his mother, saying to the Wild Things the very words she had said to him. However, this also evokes her memory and an awareness of her absence, ushering in feelings of sadness and longing, elaborated in his aria in Scene 7. Perhaps also at this point, we are beginning to see the possibility of Max apprehending things from his mother's point of view.

Scene 7: Max Alone

The musical interlude that links the scenes is subdued with the Wild Things singing descending 'Ahs' and crumbling into sleep. The music then mirrors the magical flutes and trills reminiscent of the room transforming, ushering in the longest sustained aria of the opera, Max's song full of pathos and regret.

> I dreamed that one I flew to where
> I stayed away a while.
> I flew so high it scared me so
> *(Libretto, p. 46)*

He dreams of flying so high it scared him, until Mama said, "I've got you tight." At this point in the opera the goat re-crowns Max, in my reading, in response to his acknowledgment of his omnipotence and need for his Mama. But soon his hunger and longing are projected into the Wild Things. (Again, this is sung with the minimum of accompaniment – rather the oboe particularly replies to his words as if in dialogue.):

> Now Wild Things dream that Max is hungry
> And wants to be where someone cooks

And keeps him company.
I'll climb inside that Wild Things dream
And catch my boat back home
Where if I fly so high .
I'll say, 'Now stop' and she'll catch me.

(*Libretto, pp. 46–47*)

Although Max's hunger and loneliness are still displaced into the Wild Things, and are, perhaps, too frightening to feel directly, there is an idea that through climbing inside the Wild Things dream Max could find a way back home. The thought of home enables him to imagine the possibility of stopping himself from flying so high (on his own omnipotence) and the possibility of having a mother who could 'catch him' (played out in a more manic way in the first scene). Max asks the Wild Things to dream of him being with his mother (and not alone or with them), thus intimating that he has needed their help to find his way back home – to a more secure and dependent position.

Scene 8: Parting

As the Wild Things awake and the boat re-enters, the calm of the previous scene dissipates. When Max gets into his boat to leave, the Wild Things beseech him not to go, at first quite menacingly, "We'll eat you up", then more ambivalently, "We love you so!" They sing together in what Knussen calls a 'Barbershop Quintet' of close-knit harmonies. Now, it is the Wild Things who are loaded with Max's feelings of regret as they lament their punishment (being sent to bed without supper) and their abandonment.

Max leaves his crown and scepter behind and gradually the Wild Things retreat one by one. In the notes to the Libretto, Sendak and Knussen (1985, p. 47) say that at the end 'the little goat darts out of the cave, retrieves the crown and gestures vengefully towards Max'. Clearly, a part of Max is unwilling to give up his 'king' position entirely (one never knows when it might be needed again)! However, now it is the Wild Things that are left behind and abandoned as Max sails away on calmer waters, conveyed by a beautiful musical interlude, which ushers in Max's second sustained lyrical aria:

Through days and nights and even weeks
And surely over a year. . .

The Wild Things' reaction to their abandonment by Max mirrors his own previously expressed oral aggression toward his mother. But here, aggression and love are expressed simultaneously as Spitz so beautifully describes, 'The desire to incorporate the loved object in order to possess it is connected to the desire to incorporate the loved object in order to destroy it' (Spitz, 1999, p. 133).

The great distance between the Wild Things and home also conveys a sense of the distance Max has traveled internally. Time and distance provide space – and represents an internal journey – so necessary to processing emotional experience. The boat as a 'container'[3] brings him back to his room and closer in proximity with his mother. He repeats that he can smell good things to eat. Perhaps it is significant that smell and particularly a baby's capacity to differentiate his mother's smell is one of the most developed senses for a new-born infant.

Scene 9: Max's Room

On Max's arrival, we hear a sound, Mama humming in the distance. But we only see Max standing in his room, looking down at a table with a bowl and utensils. It is as if he can hardly believe what he sees – food on the table – and he uses all his senses to determine that what Mama has provided is still hot.

> But is it hot?
> Did Mama make it hot? . . .
> It smells hot. . .
> It looks hot. . .
> It's hot.

The fact that the opera ends with the same point as the book emphasizes the significance of having a mother who could imagine and provide what Max needs, even in the face of his badness, hatred and aggression. Also significant is Max's realization that his mother cares for him, the hot food resonating with warm feelings that could be resurrected between them.

Discussion

Where the Wild Things Are opens on the same note and word as the final line of *L'Enfant et les Sortileges*, 'Maman'. There are many similarities between the stories of these two operas. In both, a young boy, about the age of 6 or 7 years, is sent to his room with no supper as punishment for his bad behavior. In both, their rooms change, by their imagination and also their projections, as anger and internal conflict are unleashed. In both, the sense of undertaking an 'internal journey' is palpable, encompassing the conflict between hate and love, and a growing awareness of loneliness and need. It is perhaps significant that Klein (1929/1981) used the story of the opera to highlight issues related to the Oedipus complex, the concreteness of the phantasy life of children and the interplay between love and hate' (Hindle, 2000a). However, *L'Enfant et les Sortileges* explores in more detail the child's curiosity and ways of learning about the world and other creatures' points of view, which resonates with recent work on theory of mind[4] (Baron-Cohen, Tager-Flusberg, & Cohen, 2000). That is, in the course of his explorations, the boy (unnamed in the opera) experiences empathy toward the squirrel that he wounded and in binding her leg performs a 'spontaneous act of reparative kindness' (Spitz, 1999, p. 135). The opera also captures in depth the process of reparation as described by Meltzer and Harris Williams (1988,

p. 215), involving *restitution* (the giving back of stolen attributes), *re-introjection* (the taking back of projected parts of the self) and restoration (the more mysterious conjunction of internal objects in a way that is not elaborated on in *Where the Wild Things Are*). Spitz describes Max 'bypassing the slower, more difficult path of true reparation that acknowledges guilt and loss' (1999, p. 131).

What *Where the Wild Things Are* illustrates so clearly, is the range of defenses that any child (or adult) might employ when confronted with the complex emotions arising from rejection. In Max we can see splitting and projection, his identification with the aggressor, omnipotence, manic defenses and the 'gang' formation – all employed to offset depressive anxieties. Klein (1937) considered that central to a child's development is their ability to apprehend their separateness from others and their impact on others which is accompanied by depressive anxieties about the harm they have the potential to do to others and to their own internal objects.

The story also allows us to look at the same situation from different perspectives, perhaps more so in the opera when Mama is seen on stage and in interaction with Max. From Mama's point of view, her patience and authority are challenged to the limit. At this point, she literally closes the door on Max and leaves him hungry. In my reading of the story, Winnicott's (1949) 'Hate in the counter-transference' comes to mind. Winnicott's seminal paper focuses primarily on aspects of the transference and counter-transference as encountered in clinical work. But one section describes 'A mother's love and hate' and goes on to delineate some 18 reasons why a mother might hate her baby, 'even a boy' (1949, p. 72). He describes a mother having 'to tolerate hating her baby without doing anything about it' (1949, p. 73). But living and working with an older child in his care, a different approach was needed. In this situation, Winnicott (not unlike Mama) put the boy outside and closed the door, knowing that there was a bell the boy could ring when he was ready to come inside again. Each time, Winnicott told the boy "what happened had made me hate him" (1949, p. 72). As shocking as this seems, Winnicott was at pains to emphasize the importance of not only a mother or a therapist being aware of their capacity to hate, but also a child knowing that they could elicit hate – that it could be known about and encountered and is an important aspect of their development. Children need to be able to mediate their feelings and behavior, to apprehend their parents' limitations and to begin to fit into family life and the world, so aptly explored by Klein (1937/1981, p. 316):

> It is important to realize that the child's development depends on, and to a large extent is formed by, his capacity to find the way to bear inevitable and necessary frustrations and the conflicts of love and hate which are in part caused by them: that is, to find his way between his hatred which is increased by frustrations, and his love and wish for reparation which bring in their train the sufferings of remorse.

From Max's point of view, venting his feelings of anger, 'vanquishing' his parents and being the 'king-leader of the pack' seems, at first, cathartic. But it is soon apparent that this state of mind is not without its problems. Ron Britton describes, the Oedipal situation in 'Subjectivity, objectivity and triangular space' (1998, p. 41), in which the 'phantasised union of parents unites the understanding object with the malignant misunderstanding object, creating a combined figure that personifies contradiction, meaninglessness and chaos'. Britton uses the term 'chaos monster' – drawn from ancient cosmologies and cultures – to describe the way in which order and meaning are threatened by a counterforce that brings chaos to the world. From an infant's point of view, it would be equivalent to having his or her projections of death and annihilation not received and emotionally transformed by the mother, but as invalidating the infant's experience. In Scene 6 of the opera, we could hypothesize that 'The Wild Rumpus' represents an unleashing of such chaos (enlivened in the opera by the music and dancing). From the child's point of view, there has been a failure of containment – an unwillingness to receive his projections, as evidenced by the shut door (Bion, 1962). But being up against a 'closed door', in light of Winnicott's paper, also provides a developmental challenge and propels Max not only into using his imagination, but also into beginning to consider things from a different point of view. That is, the resolution of the Oedipal situation involves an acceptance of the primacy of the parental relationship and one's position as a child, thus creating the triangular space Britton refers to. As Britton states:

> The closure of the oedipal triangle by the recognition of the link joining the parents provides a limiting boundary for the internal world. It creates what I call a 'triangular space' – i.e., a space bounded by the three persons of the oedipal situation and all their potential relationships. It includes, therefore, the possibility of being a participant in a relationship and observed by a third person as well as being an observer of a relationship between two people.
> (Britton, 1989, p. 86)

At the point Max sends the Wild Things to bed without their supper, however, something begins to change. It is as if this enactment ushers in more depressive feelings of regret and of longing for home. Here I am referring back to Klein's (1937, 1946) thoughts about the depressive position and a child's developing concern for others as well as their fears about the potential harm their anger might inflict. Like children at play, when a previous experience is re-worked imaginatively, here we see something of his earlier encounter with his mother, now generating pause for thought. Suddenly he is reminded that he 'was lonely and wanted to be where someone loved him best of all'. These words stand out simply and powerfully in the book's text but are elaborated in the libretto and Max's final aria where he implores the Wild Things to 'dream that he is hungry and wants to be where someone cooks and keeps him company'.

Writing from a psychoanalytic perspective on the story, Gottlieb (2008) comments on the mother's emotional unavailability and lack of containment of Max's exuberance. But in my reading, it is the nature of the interaction between Max and his mother that sets in train all that follows. For both Mama and Max, during their time apart, something happens internally, which cannot be easily depicted. For Mama, it is as if she has found space in herself to have an internal dialogue, even without Papa's presence – evidence of 'triangular space'. Mama is able to recover from her anger and also to imagine what Max might want and need, similar to what Klein (1937/1981, p. 318) notes – the importance of a mother's capacity of 'putting herself in the child's place and of looking at the situation from his point of view'. For Max (unlike Mickey in *In the Night Kitchen* who procures his own milk and satisfies his own need while the parents remain asleep), it is Mama who provides something for him. Apprehending that the waiting food is hot seems to open the door to a realization that Mama holds him in mind – in spite of his (and her) anger and upset, and that she is able to imagine what he wants and needs, just as he would have liked it. In his journey, Max does indeed transcend time and space ('night and day and in and out of weeks. . .'), making a potential shift in his internal world. He moves from harboring a 'bad object', even a 'chaos monster' to introjecting a 'good object'/Mama who provides good things. Order is restored, chaos is vanquished, something lost is regained.

Conclusion

Most children and adults going to see the opera would, no doubt, be familiar with Sendak's story and as readers would have their own associations, thoughts and feelings in relation to the book. Perhaps they would have shared memories of reading it together. As with any book translated into another medium, such as a film, there may be aspects that 'don't fit' or even 'jar' with our own imaginings, while other aspects are utterly familiar or capture a scene just as we thought it should be. Knussen's music, however, adds another dimension that cannot be easily anticipated. In both the book and the opera, the story is compelling, particularly because it captures such a familiar incident, an encounter that may be repeated many times in ordinary family life. Intimate family relationships are rife with conflict, hatred and love. In both *Where the Wild Things Are* and *In the Night Kitchen*, the taking in of food equates to a good experience and, as Zuppardi (2016, p. 155) describes, the introjection or the taking in of the good breast/mother and the enrichment of the ego. Both books can also be read 'in terms of a dream', putting us in touch with unconscious processes (Zuppardi, 2016, p. 153). Klein (1932, p. 8), however, extends this idea to include the symbolic meaning of children's play when she writes:

> For play is the child's most important medium of expression. If we make use of this play technique we soon find that the child brings as many associations to the separate elements of its play as adults do to the separate elements of their dreams.

I think we could also say that children's literature, reading together or independently is a form of play, allowing children to access elements of dream-life, to work through incidents in their own lives, to imagine, to 'be' aspects of the self which are felt to be alien, and so on. Zuppardi (2016, p. 153) beautifully describes the way in which children use picture books

> as a kind of transitional object (Winnicott, 1971) bridging the gap between the 'me' and the 'not me' through a close identification with a story or a character and thereby allowing them to feel both separateness to and connection with a wider world, further highlights the way in which picture books offer child readers a valuable opportunity to take ownership of the text.

I would like to think that Sendak and Knussen's opera captures peoples' imagination in a similar way. In my view, the opera deepens and broadens the things we as adults might learn from what the original story tells us about childhood (and in identification, about our own childhood experiences), and for children, provides a different dimension through music and drama with which to engage their imagination. Both the book and the opera of *Where the Wild Things Are* capture not only a moment, a period of discord between a mother and a child, but also, alone in his room, the child's private response to this incident. Infant and young child observation, carried out weekly over a year or two-year period as part of research or training for child psychotherapists, provides many opportunities to capture such moments. Psychoanalytic observation not only heightens an awareness of the interconnectedness between an infant, a young child and others, but also enables us imaginatively to construe what is going on internally through understanding and reflecting on our own counter-transference. In clinical work also, children can be defiant, omnipotently flaunt boundaries, and openly express and provoke anger in ways that challenge a therapist's capacity to provide a sense of safety and to carry on thinking. The *Journal of Child Psychotherapy* abounds with papers documenting such struggles, for example, Emanuel (1984), Hindle (2000b), Rustin (2001) and Canham (2004), to note just a few. All these papers describe what is involved in dealing with children who act out in sessions and the technical challenges in undertaking this kind of this work.

This brings us full circle to the quotation from Michael Rustin's paper in the introduction to this article (Rustin, 2016). In my view, this deeper consideration of *Where the Wild Things Are* informs observation and clinical practice in highlighting the developmental challenges and the internal processes so clearly illustrated in the story and the opera. What is evident are the incremental stages, which may need to be re-worked again and again in response to numerous encounters, built up slowly, perhaps as precursors to the depressive positions and to full reparation.

Notes

1   Klein describes the propensity unconsciously to split off unwanted thoughts, feelings, or aspects of the self, projecting them into others. This involves disowning or ridding oneself of unwanted aspects and attributing them to others, while retaining contact with the split off aspects through projective identification.
2   Rosenfeld (1964, 1971) described two aspects of narcissism – one based on the grandiose self idealization of the good aspects of the self and internal objects leading to narcissistic

omnipotence and the other cased on the idealization of the bad parts of the self and internal objects and its attack on the dependent self and good objects, which he referred to as destructive narcissism.

3   Bion (1963) used the metaphor of container/ contained to delineate the mental process in which thoughts, feelings of aspects of the self are projected, as between a baby and a mother, so that they are held, understood and fed back in a digestible form. He saw this as the prototype of the development of thought.

4   Rosenfeld (1964–1971) described two aspects of narcissism. One is based on the grandiose self idealization of the good aspects of the self and internal objects, leading to narcissistic omnipotence. The other is based on the idealization of the bad parts of the self and internal objects, which attack the dependent self and good objects. The latter he referred to as destructive narcissism

References

Alvarez, A. (1992). *Live company: Psychoanalytic psychotherapy with autistic, borderline, deprived and abused children*. London: Routledge.

Baron-Cohen, S., Tager-Flusberg, H., & Cohen, D. J. (Eds.). (2000). *Understanding other minds: Perspectives from developmental cognitive neuroscience* (2nd ed.). Oxford: Oxford University Press.

Bick, E. (1968). The experience of the skin in early object-relations. *The International Journal of Psychoanalysis*, 49(2–3), 484–486.

Bion, W. R. (1962). *Learning from experience*. London: Heinemann.

Bion, W. R. (1963). *Elements of psychoanalysis*. London: Heinemann.

Britton, R. (1989). The missing link: Parental sexuality in the Oedipus complex. In R. Britton, M. Feldman & E. O'Shaughnessy (Eds.), *The Oedipus complex today: Clinical implications*. London: Karnac Books.

Britton, R. (1998). Subjectivity, objectivity and triangular space. In *Belief and imagination* (pp. 41–59). Hove: Routledge.

Canham, H. (2004). Spitting, kicking and stripping: Technical difficulties encountered in the treatment of deprived children. *Journal of Child Psychotherapy*, 30(2), 143–154.

Emanuel, R. (1984). Primary disappointment. *Journal of Child Psychotherapy*, 10(1), 71–87.

Glyndebourne Productions Ltd. (1985). *Where the wild things are and Higglety Pigglety Pop!* Warner Music Group Company DVD (2009) WEA International Inc.

Gottlieb, R. M. (2008). Maurice Sendak's trilogy: Disappointment, fury and their transformation through art. *Psychoanalytic Study of the Child*, 63, 186–217.

Hindle, D. (2000a). "L'enfant et les sortilèges" revisited. *The International Journal of Psycho-Analysis*, 81(6), 1185–1196.

Hindle, D. (2000b). The merman: Recovering from early abuse and loss. *Journal of Child Psychotherapy*, 26(3), 369–391.

Klein, M. (1929/1981). Infantile anxiety-situations reflected in a work of art and in the creative impulse. In M. Masud & R. Khan (Eds.), *Love, guilt and reparation* (pp. 210–218). London: Hogarth.

Klein, M. (1932). The psychological foundations of child analysis. In M. Masud & R. Khan (Eds.), *The psycho-analysis of children* (pp. 1–379). London: The Hogarth Press.

Klein, M. (1937/1981). Love, guilt and reparation. In M. Masud & R. Khan (Eds.), *Love, guilt and reparation* (pp. 306–343). London: Hogarth.

Klein, M. (1946/1975). Notes on some schizoid mechanisms. In M. Masud & R. Khan (Eds.), *Envy and gratitude and other works 1946–1963*. London: Hogarth Press and the Institute of Psycho-Analysis.

Meltzer, D., & Harris Williams, M. (1988). *The apprehension of beauty: The role of aesthetic conflict in development, violence and art*. Strathtay: Clunie Press.

Rosenfeld, H. (1964). On the psychopathology of narcissism: A clinical approach. *International Journal of Psychoanalysis*, 45, 332–337.

Rosenfeld, H. (1971). A clinical approach to the psychoanalytic theory of the life and death instincts: An investigation into the aggressive aspects of narcissism. *International Journal of Psychoanalysis*, 52, 169–178.

Rustin, M. (2001). The therapist with her back against the wall. *Journal of Child Psychotherapy*, 27(3), 273–284.

Rustin, M. (2016). Young children and works of the imagination. *The International Journal of Infant Observation and Its Applications*, 19(2), 139–148.

Sendak, M. (1963). *Where the wild things are*. New York: Bodley Head.

Sendak, M. (1970). *In the night kitchen*. London: Picture Lions.

Sendak, M., & Knussen, O. (1985). Libretto: *Where the wild things are*. In *Higglety Pigglety Pop and where the wild things are: libretti* (pp. 34–48). London: Faber Music.

Sendak, M., & Knussen, O. (1999). *Where the wild things are – programme notes*. London: Queen Elizabeth Hall.

Spitz, E. H. (1999). *Inside picture books*. London: Yale University Press.

The Earl of Harewood, & Peattie, A. (Eds.). (1997). Oliver Knussen. In *The New Kobbe's opera book* (pp. 399–400). London: Ebury Press.

Winnicott, D. W. (1949). Hate in the counter-transference. *International Journal of Psychoanalysis*, 30, 69–74.

Winnicott, D. W. (1971). *Playing and reality*. London: Routledge.

Zuppardi, S. (2016). From night kitchen to wolves in the walls: A brief psychoanalytic look at children's picture books. *The International Journal of Infant Observation and Its Applications*, 19(2), 149–164.

Appendix

Synopses by Contributors

Don Giovanni

Music	Wolfgang Amadeus Mozart
Libretto	Lorenzo Da Ponte
Premiere	1787

As Act I begins, Leporello is keeping watch for his master, Don Giovanni, who is attempting in vain to seduce Donna Anna. Her father defends her and Giovanni kills him in a duel. When Donna Anna and her fiancé Don Ottavio find her father dead, Anna makes Ottavio promise to bring the murderer to justice. After escaping, Leporello tells Giovanni that Giovanni is leading an immoral life. Don Giovanni reacts angrily. They hear a woman (Donna Elvira) singing of having been abandoned by her lover, on whom she is seeking revenge. He is the former lover she is seeking. Elvira vows vengeance, and in the next scene while Don Giovanni tries to seduce the peasant girl Zerlina at her wedding to Masetto, Elvira takes Zerlina away with her. Anna and Ottavio meet Don Giovanni. They know he is the murderer and promise again to bring him to justice. Giovanni persists in his seduction attempts and orders Leporello to prepare a party to which Masetto and Zerlina are invited.

When Masetto expresses doubts that Zerlina loves him, she tells him to beat her, if that will make him feel better, and the two make up. Anna and Ottavio then come across Don Giovanni. Anna does not recognize him from the previous night, and they enlist his help in their search for the unknown murderer. In Don Giovanni's ballroom, Don Giovanni leads Zerlina offstage to a private room and tries to assault her. She screams. The three guests unmask and declare that they know all. Don Giovanni escapes.

As Act II opens, Don Giovanni wants to seduce Elvira's maid. He changes clothes with Leporello. Giovanni sings a serenade to Elvira's maid. Masetto and his friends enter, looking for Don Giovanni. Giovanni beats Masetto and runs off. Zerlina finds Masetto and comforts him. In the next scene, Leporello tries to get rid of Elvira and Anna, Ottavio, Zerlina, and Masetto find Leporello and mistake him for Giovanni. They are about to kill him when he throws off his disguise and runs away. Donna Elvira sings that she is still furious at Don Giovanni for betraying her, but that she also feels sorry for him.

The next scene is set in a graveyard where a voice coming from the statue of the murdered Commendatore threatens that justice is near. Don Giovanni responds by ordering Leporello to invite the statue to dinner. Giovanni himself invites the statue, and the statue nods. Meanwhile, Don Ottavio pressures Donna Anna to marry him, but she thinks it is inappropriate so soon after her father's death.

In the final scene, Don Giovanni is eating dinner. Elvira begs him to repent and change his way of life before it is too late. He laughs at her, and she leaves. Suddenly, the statue of the dead Commendatore comes into the room and orders Don Giovanni to repent. He refuses. Flames rise, and demons scream. The statue invites Giovanni to dine with him. Giovanni accepts and takes the Commendatore's hand. Hell opens, and the two disappear in the flames. The Commendatore again urges Giovanni to repent but he still refuses and they descend into hell. Anna, Ottavio, Elvira, Zerlina and Masetto come into the room with the police. Ottavio again offers marriage to Anna, now that vengeance is complete. She asks for one year in which to mourn. Elvira, freed at last, vows to spend the rest of her life in a convent. Leporello determines to find himself a better master. All sing 'This is the end of those who do wrong'.

The Magic Flute

Music	Wolfgang Amadeus Mozart
Libretto	Emanuel Schikaneder
Premiere	1791

Tamino, a prince alone in the woods, is calling for help as he flees a deadly serpent. Fainting from fear, he is saved by three ladies who fawn over him before going for their mistress, the Queen of the Night. When Tamino awakes, Papageno, a comical bird-catcher, boasts that he slayed the dragon. The three ladies return, punish Papageno for his braggartly lie, and show Tamino a portrait of the Queen's daughter, Pamina. Tamino falls instantly in love. The Queen arrives in much distress that her daughter has been kidnapped by the wicked sorcerer, Sarastro. Tamino vows to rescue Pamina, and the Queen offers him Pamina's hand if he succeeds. To aid in this perilous mission, Papageno is given a set of magic bells and Tamino is given a magic flute which was crafted by the Queen's late husband.

However, a surprising twist occurs when Tamino arrives at Sarastro's temple and discovers that the Queen of the Night is an untrustworthy and wicked one, and that Sarastro is actually the high priest of wisdom. A temple priest promises Tamino that the confusion will be lifted during the initiation rites to the brotherhood. He also promises Papageno a wife at this point.

Papageno scouts on ahead and discovers Monostatos, a Moorish slave, trying to force himself on Pamina. Papageno mesmerizes him with the magic bells and he and Pamina escape. The Queen of the Night appears before Pamina and reveals that her late husband was once the owner of the Circle of the Sun temple. When he died, he willed the Queen all his lands and riches but he willed the temple to Sarastro, leaving the Queen weakened and powerless. She tries in vain to convince Pamina to kill Sarastro with the dagger she has given her and sings her famous aria of revenge, *Der Hölle Rache* (Hellish Revenge). Pamina refuses and begs Sarastro to forgive her mother. He reassures her that revenge has no place in his domain.

Pamina and Tamino, protected by the magic flute, pass unscathed through chambers of fire and water. The priests hail their triumph and invite the couple to enter the temple. Papageno, who was previously teased by a haggard old woman who disturbed him by saying she has a boyfriend named Papageno, now feels that he has failed to find his Papagena, but he is advised to summon her with his magic bells. When she appears, the happy couple stutter in astonishment in sing-song bird-like courting sounds as they dream of the many children they will have together.

The Queen of the Night, furious and envious at everyone's good fortune, plots with Monostatos to regain power by destroying the temple. However, all ends well as they are thwarted and cast into the darkness forever as Sarastro declares the dawn of a new era in which day triumphs over night.

Lucia di Lammermoor

Music	Gaetano Donizetti
Libretto	Salvadore Cammarano
Premiere	1835

The story, which unfolds in Scotland during the late 17th Century, is based on Sir Walter Scott's 1819 novel, *The Bride of Lammermoor*, about an event that occurred in Scotland in 1669.

Shortly after the Prelude, we learn from Normanno, the captain of Lord Enrico Ashton's guard, that Edgardo of Ravenswood has saved Lucia from a wild boar while she was taking a walk, ostensibly mourning her mother's death. We learn subsequently that the fountain is the location of Lucia's secret meetings with her lover, Edgardo, who is the despised enemy of Lucia's brother, Enrico of Lammermoor. Normanno reports Lucia's secret rendezvous to Lucia's brother who swears revenge on Edgardo for stealing the Ashton family property. Enrico plots to arrange for his sister, to marry the powerful Lord Arturo which will guarantee his own political fortune. Having pledged her love to Edwardo, Lucia refuses her brother's demand and declares her love for Edgardo of Ravenswood, sworn enemy of the Ashton family.

While secretly waiting to meet Edgardo at a fountain in the woods, Lucia reveals to her companion, Alicia, that she has seen a ghost in the fountain. In her aria Lucia describes the ghost that haunts her, *Il fantasma,* that bodes ill for her as she maintains that the fountain's water turned to blood.

When Edgardo arrives, he informs Lucia that he must report to France on a mission. He also vows to make peace with Enrico. They exchange rings in a private commitment before he departs. In Edgardo's absence, Enrico intercepts

Edgardo's letters and shows Lucia a forged letter which indicates that Edgardo has been unfaithful to her during his absence. Devastated and unsuspecting of her brother's trick, Lucia reluctantly agrees to marry Arturo.

After this marriage contract is signed by Lucia and Arturo, Edgardo unexpectedly appears in Ravenswood and declares her unfaithful to him when she admits she has signed the marriage contract to Arturo. He challenges Enrico to a duel. The marriage between Lucia and Arturo proceeds.

Shortly after retiring to the wedding chamber following their nuptials, Lucia returns to the reception hall bloodstained, disoriented, and carrying the bloody knife she has used to kill Arturo. Hallucinating, she emerges singing her famous Mad Scene where she fantasizes that she has married Edgardo. Following her aria which has musical reminiscences of her love duet (*Verrano a te*) with Edgardo from Act I in the Opera, she collapses and dies of a broken heart.

When Edgardo learns of Lucia's death, in his grief, he takes his own life believing that he and Lucia will be reunited as he declares in the closing moments of the Opera, "I am joining you, my lovely spirit, Your true love will join you. We were caught in a cruel battle, My beloved, God will unite us in Heaven".

The Flying Dutchman

Music	Richard Wagner
Libretto	Richard Wagner
Premiere	1843

As the opera opens, Senta's father, Captain Daland, is forced by a storm to shelter seven miles from home. Daland sees a ghostly ship appear. This ship carries the Dutchman, cursed to forever sail the seas unless he can find a faithful woman who will marry him. The curse allows him to search for her every seven years and condemns her to death if she is not faithful and the Dutchman to return to the seas. The Dutchman learns that Daland has an unmarried daughter named Senta, and he asks for her hand in marriage, offering a chest of treasure as a gift. Tempted by the gold, Daland agrees to the marriage. The kindly south wind blows and both vessels set sail for Daland's home.

Act II begins with Senta, in a room of women spinning and working at other household tasks, dreamily ignoring the pleas of Dame Mary, the housekeeper, to stop mooning over a portrait and get to work on spinning. Then she begins singing the ballad of the Flying Dutchman. Though her local suitor, Erik, tries to caution her, Senta becomes convinced that she will be the faithful woman sought by the Dutchman. Daland enters the room with the Dutchman and introduces Senta to her betrothed, oblivious to the star struck silence of both Senta and the Dutchman. They fall in love and Senta promises herself to the Dutchman.

In Act III, it is evening and the local girls bring Daland's men food and drink. They invite the crew of the strange vessel to join in their merrymaking, but in vain, as the ghostly crew cannot respond. Senta arrives, followed by Erik, who reproaches her for deserting him, as she had once loved him. When the

Dutchman, who has been listening, hears these words, he is overwhelmed with despair, as he thinks he is now again lost and condemned to continue his hopeless sailing for another seven years. The Dutchman summons his men, tells Senta of the curse, and to the consternation of Daland and his crew, declares that he is the "Flying Dutchman." As *The Dutchman* sets sail, Senta throws herself into the sea, claiming that she will be faithful to him unto death. This is his salvation. The spectral ship disappears, and Senta and the Dutchman are seen ascending to heaven.

Tristan und Isolde

Music	Richard Wagner
Libretto	Richard Wagner
Premiere	1865

The first act takes place on a ship sailing from Ireland to Cornwall. On board is Isolde, an Irish princess whom Tristan is charged to deliver, against her will, as the bride for his uncle, King Marke. Tristan has avoided Isolde during the journey, and the enraged Isolde calls upon the sea to destroy the ship. Brangäne, her maid, can't understand Isolde's animosity towards Tristan, whom she views as a hero. Kurwenal, Tristan's loyal servant, sings a mocking song about Isolde's betrothed Morold, who sought tribute from the Cornish but lost his head in battle with Tristan instead. In a narrative, Isolde explains to Brangäne that sometime earlier, she had tended to a grievously injured knight who had washed ashore in a small boat. She discovered that this man was none other than Tristan, who had slain her Morold. She raised Tristan's sword to kill him, but the gaze of the helpless man into her eyes stopped her. This explains the source of her anger, and of her desire that the ship be lost in a storm. The man she fell in love with has betrayed her. Tristan finally agrees to meet, and Isolde, who learned magical arts from her mother, orders Brangäne to prepare a death potion. Tristan and Isolde toast one another, and believing they will die, rapturously confess their love. Unbeknownst to them, Brangänge had substituted a love potion. At the end of the act, the ship arrives in Cornwall and Isolde is presented to Marke, but she is in a daze, oblivious to what is transpiring around her.

Act II is set in a garden on the grounds of King Marke's castle. Marke and his retinue have ostensibly gone hunting, and horn calls are heard in the distance. Isolde is impatient to extinguish the torch, the signal for their tryst, but Brangäne counsels caution. She believes Tristan's friend Melot has deceived him, and that the sound of the horns is still too close. She is unable to dissuade her mistress; Isolde hears only the rippling waters of a fountain. After an impassioned hymn to Frau Minne, the goddess of love, Isolde puts out the light. The ensuing love between Tristan and Isolde runs the gamut of amorous expressions, as they feel inseparable and long for night and death. From her watchtower, Brangäne warns of the approaching dawn, but the lovers are only aware of one another. At the climax of the duet, they are caught by Marke. The hunt was indeed a ruse. The king cannot understand how Tristan could betray him this way and asks, if there is no honor in Tristan, where can one find it? Tristan has no answer. He explains to Isolde that his mother died in childbirth, and asks if she will join him in his true home, death. When Isolde agrees, Tristan drops his guard and allows Melot to strike a mortal blow.

Act III opens in Kareol, Tristan's home on the coast of Brittany, with the ruins of his ancestral castle in the background. Kurwenal has brought him here, and expresses his anguish as his master lies asleep under a lime tree. They await Isolde. A shepherd plays an old, mournful tune but is told to pipe a cheerful one when Isolde's ship is sighted. As the disoriented and delirious Tristan gradually awakens he describes having been at the threshold of death. He contemplates the nature of his existence, from the recent past and his love for Isolde to his childhood memories and the death of his parents. Hearing the shepherd's happy tune, Tristan tears off his bandages in a frenzy and hurries to greet Isolde. With his last breath he sings her name and dies in her arms. Marke's ship lands shortly thereafter and Kurwenal slays the treacherous Melot, but is then killed in turn by Marke's men. After learning of the love potion from Brangäne, Marke had forgiven Tristan and Isolde and planned to bless their marriage. Unaware of her surroundings, Isolde enters a transfigured state and dies.

Die Meistersinger von Nürnberg

Music	Richard Wagner
Libretto	Richard Wagner
Premiere	1868

The opera opens in 16th Century Nürnberg at St. Katherine's church. Walther, a young impetuous visiting aristocrat, exchanges excited glances with Eva, the daughter of wealthy goldsmith and Meistersinger Pogner. Walter and Eva met the day before at her father's house and fell in love at first sight. Walther discovers that Eva's father has offered her hand in marriage to the winner of a Meistersinger song contest to be held the following day. Eva can reject the winner of the contest, but she must marry a member of the Guild or can marry no one. Walther auditions to become a Meistersinger, singing a renegade song that breaks the Guild's strict rules, and is rejected. Hans Sachs, Meistersinger and poet cobbler, finds himself moved by the raw intuitive power of Walther's song.

Act II is set that evening in a street with Pogner's house on one side and Hans Sachs' workshop on the other. Eva learns from her maid Magdalene that Walther has been rejected and that the town clerk, Meistersinger Beckmesser, is on his way to serenade her. Eva instructs Magdalene to dress in her garments and impersonate her. Across the street, outside his doorway working, Sachs is occupied with the memory of Walther's song. Eva joins Sachs hoping to learn more of Walther's audition. Their conversation unveils the complex feelings they share for one another. A father figure, who has known Eva since she was a baby, Sachs has consciously abandoned wooing her, yet unconsciously, his love lives. After revealing her feelings for Walther, Eva runs off. Eva meets Walther and they decide to elope. Sachs overhears their conversation and decides to help them and prevent their flight.

When Beckmesser arrives to serenade Eva, Sachs gets him to agree that he will mark any broken rules of style in Beckmesser's song with his cobbler's hammer. As Beckmesser serenades Magdalene, who is impersonating Eva, Sachs' hammer strokes sound loudly through the night. Awoken by the cacophony, David, Magdalena's lover dashes onto the street, wildly attacking Beckmesser, whom he believes is wooing Magdalene. Roused from their sleep, the night-shirted neighbors spill onto the street and enter the fray, now a full-blown riot. The night watchman's horn disperses the rioters. Pogner leads Eva inside while Sachs drags Walther and David into his shop.

Act III, takes place at dawn, the following day. Sachs is in his workshop reflecting on the evenings' madness when Walter enters to tell him he had a wondrous dream. Together they transcribe the dream that forms Walther's Prize song. Eva arrives and the affection she and Sachs feel for one another is palpable as is her romantic love for Walther, who sings the completed Prize song for Eva. Magdalene and David arrive and Sachs asks that they join them in baptizing Walter's master song into the world of art. All five sing of their happiness.

The citizens of Nurnberg assemble in a meadow for the song contest. Walther's Prize song entrances the people and wins Eva's hand.

Tosca

Music	Giacomo Puccini
Libretto	Luigi Illica & Giuseppe Giacosa
Premiere	1900

Tosca is set in Rome in 1800, during a time of political unrest in which Rome is dominated by Baron Scarpia, the powerful chief of police who suppresses all dissent, while, Napoleon's invasion threatens his power.

Act one is set in a church where the painter Mario Cavadarossi works on a painting of the Madonna. He dreams of the beautiful Marchesa who is his model, but also of his lover, the singer Floria Tosca. His friend, the escaped political prisoner, Angelotti, enters to hide. Angelotti emerges to ask for help, knowing Mario is also in the resistance, but hides again as Tosca arrives. Mario quickly gives Angelotti his basket of food. Tosca expresses jealousy wondering who Mario's model is. He reassures her, and they sing a love duet. She leaves, promising to meet him that night. Mario retrieves Angelotti and leaves to hide him at his home. Scarpia enters, excited because he hears of Napoleon's defeat. A celebratory concert is planned at his palace. The church Sacristan arrives, surprised that the painter is gone, and disappointed that he took his lunch with him. But when they discover the hidden empty food basket, Scarpia becomes suspicious that Mario is hiding the political prisoner somewhere. Tosca returns, to tell Mario she can't meet him because she has to sing at a concert. But Mario isn't there; instead, Scarpia, who lusts after

Tosca, approaches. He shows her a fan, which she recognizes as belonging to the Marchesa, and sees that Mario's painting also resembles the Marchesa. Scarpia insinuates that the two are lovers, Tosca bursts out with jealous rage, and leaves the church weeping. The chorus comes in, and sings the Te Deum, praising God to celebrate Napoleon's supposed defeat, while Scarpia sings of his desire to manipulate and seduce Tosca. The combination of political and sexual tension expressed by the dominating and sinister Scarpia bring the scene to a stirring climax.

Act two occurs at Scarpia's palace. When Tosca arrives to perform, he excitedly sings of his desire to make her yield sexually to his violent approach. He arrested Mario, who refused to reveal where Angelotti is, and is sent out to be tortured just as Tosca is brought in. They embrace briefly in passing, and he warns her to say nothing. Scarpia insists she tell him where Angelotti is. When she hears Mario's screams she gives in and tells him; Mario is furious with her when he finds out. But just then a messenger arrives with the bad news that Napoleon has triumphed after all, and is marching on the city. Scarpia, enraged, sends Mario out to be executed at dawn. He manipulates Tosca, telling her that if she submits to him she can save Mario's life. Tosca despairingly sings the great aria "Vissi D'arte". She then agrees to his demand, but insists he first write a safe passage letter for her and Mario. Scarpia promises that Mario will have a sham execution, then she and Mario can flee the city. As he writes the letter, Tosca discovers a knife. When he approaches, menacing and attempting rape, Tosca desperately stabs him to death. She sings triumphantly of how she humiliated and defeated him, then softens, placing candles and a crucifix near his body.

The final act takes place at the prison. Tosca runs to the prison for a brief, joyous reunion with Mario. She tells him what Scarpia demanded of her and that she killed him, but that after the sham execution in the morning they will be able to flee. But in the morning, when shot by firing squad, Mario falls so realistically that at first Tosca admires his acting, then realizes Scarpia tricked her. Mario is dead. She is devastated. When she hears the cries of men coming for her, grief-stricken and certain that capture and punishment await her, Tosca leaps to her death off a parapet.

Madama Butterfly

Music	Giacomo Puccini
Libretto	Luigi Illica & Giuseppe Giacosa
Premiere	1904

In Japan in the early 20th century, Lieutenant B.F. Pinkerton of the U.S. Navy arrives in Nagasaki for a tour of duty and rents a typical Japanese style house. Along with the house comes a fifteen year-old geisha wife and her trusted servant, Suzuki. Cio- Cio- San, also known as Butterfly, is from a noble but impoverished family; her father had been ordered by the emperor to commit ritual suicide. Pinkerton is unsure whether his passionate feelings for Butterfly will endure, but he marries her in a Japanese wedding ceremony, knowing that in his mind this "marriage" is temporary and that he will have a "real" marriage to an American woman on his return to the U.S. The American consul to Nagasaki, Sharpless, warns him that the girl's view of the marriage is quite different from that of Pinkerton, but the marriage ritual proceeds, as a result of which Butterfly is denounced and disinherited by her family. A long love duet with considerable passion on both sides leads to consummation of the marriage.

When his tour of duty ends, Pinkerton departs for the United States. Butterfly is convinced that he has not deserted her. Pinkerton, however, has no intention of returning. It is now three years later, and unbeknownst to Butterfly, Pinkerton has married Kate, an American woman, in a "real" marriage. He sends a letter to Sharpless, making clear that, although he will be arriving in Japan for a visit, he has remarried and will not be returning to Butterfly. Sharpless attempts to read the letter to Butterfly, but she remains convinced that Pinkerton will return to her and reveals to Sharpless the existence of a little boy, the product of her marriage to Pinkerton. Sharpless is so moved by the existence of the child and so distraught at Butterfly's pain and denial that he is unable to read the letter to her. He promises, however, to convey to Pinkerton the existence of his son.

At this point, it becomes clear to Butterfly that Pinkerton's ship is entering the harbor, and she, Suzuki, and the boy settle into an overnight watch to await him. The next day, Sharpless and Pinkerton arrive at Butterfly's house, along with Kate. They encounter Suzuki, who agrees to tell Butterfly that Pinkerton has arrived, along with his new wife. Pinkerton becomes overcome with guilt, recalling his time with Butterfly in this house, and he leaves the scene. Butterfly appears, sees Kate, and quickly realizes what has happened. She agrees to give up the child, but only on the condition that Pinkerton himself return for him.

Sending everyone away, Butterfly takes out the very sword with which her father had committed suicide, choosing a death with honor rather than a life diminished by shame. When the boy unexpectedly bursts in, she hides the sword and utters her good-bye. She then blindfolds him and stabs herself, as Pinkerton returns and screams out her name in a moment of abject horror.

Elektra

Music	Richard Strauss
Libretto	Hugo von Hofmannsthal
Premiere	1909

The setting of this one act opera is in Mycenae, Greece, where the action takes place in front of the palace, where Clytemnestra and Aegisthus, the rulers of Mycenae, reside. Clytemnestra took Aegisthus as her lover after Agamemnon left for Troy, and they murdered Agamemnon together upon his return. Chyrsothemis, the daughter of Clytemnestra and Agamemnon lives with them, as does Electra, although she is made to stay outside or with the servants. She is treated badly by her mother and Aegisthus.

The opera opens with the maidservants describing the miserable state of Electra and her harsh treatment of anyone who approaches her. Electra is then left alone on the stage, calling to her murdered father, Agamemnon, describing his death in detail and her promise of vengeance.

Chrysothemis enters the stage warning Electra of a plan to imprison her, and beseeching Electra to free them from their misery, so she can become a mother and live a normal life. She also warns her that Clytemnestra is in a terrible state, having had nightmares and fears the return of Orestes. She leaves the scene.

Clytemnestra approaches Electra to seek her counsel, and Electra wishes to speak with her as well. Clytemnestra wants Electra's help to cure her of her nightly torments, possibly through ritual sacrifices. She is instead met with Electra's anger and the threat of death as a punishment for her affair with Aegisthus and the murder of Agamemnon. Clytemnestra is told the news of Orestes death and reenters the palace. Chrysothemis comes out to tell Electra this news, again beseeching Electra to escape with her. Electra instead tries to convince her to commit the murders with her, which frightens Chrysothemis, who hurriedly leaves the stage.

Orestes then appears, encountering Electra, and at first, neither of them recognize the other. When their identities are revealed, Electra describes her tragic fate. Orestes vows to commit the murders and enters the palace, murdering Clytemnestra behind closed doors as Electra listens on. Aegisthus returns, having heard the news of Orestes death, and Electra pretends to be compliant and encourages him to enter the palace. He is murdered by Orestes.

Chrysothemis comes out and tells Electra with great excitement that they are freed. Electra celebrates with Chrysothemis and in a frenzied dance of madness, falls to the ground dead.

Duke Bluebeard's Castle

Music	Béla Bartók
Libretto	Béla Balázs
Premiere	1918

The no-longer-young Duke Bluebeard brings his new bride, Judit, to his gloomy castle. Despite vague rumors about Bluebeard murdering his previous wives, Judit is determined to lighten the gloom of his castle. As they shut the front door behind them, Judit is overwhelmed by the castle's darkness and then notices seven locked doors. Judit insists on successively unlocking each door, in spite of Bluebeard's attempts to warn her off. One by one, she discovers the torture chamber of the castle, the armory, the treasury, the castle's secret garden, Bluebeard's vast realm and his lake of tears. The last chamber contains his former wives. Bluebeard tries to curb Judit's curiosity which threatens his interiority. He wants them to savor each other's love, while he still maintains the secrets of his dark past. By contrast, young Judit conceives love as complete openness. She presses him about his past, while discovering ominous blood marks throughout the castle. At the opera's end, we learn that Bluebeard's former wives are still alive: the first wife is the woman of his youth, or morning, the second is the wife of the midday of his life, the third, the wife of his evening days. Bluebeard calls Judit the woman of his night, the most beautiful of all. Judit realizes too late that she has been robbed of her separate existence, and that she now lives only in Bluebeard's imagination. She has become a ghostly presence, one of the glittering wives of his tortured imagination. Bluebeard's castle itself is an impersonation of what is in his head. In the end, Bluebeard returns to his sad, lonely existence.

Wozzeck

Music	Alban Berg
Libretto	Alban Berg
Premiere	1925

As the opera opens, Wozzeck, a humble soldier, is shaving his Captain. The Captain begins to taunt him about lacking morality because of his illegitimate child. Wozzeck responds with indignation that virtue is difficult for the poor, and that the gospel verse says, "Suffer the little children to come unto me." In the next scene, Wozzeck and Andres, another soldier, are cutting firewood in a field. As the sun sets, Wozzeck has frightening visions and hears terrifying sounds. The earth seems to him to be on fire.

Meanwhile, Marie, the mother of Wozzeck's illegitimate son, with her friend Margaret, watches the military parade, and admires the Drum Major. As Marie sings her son a lullaby, Wozzeck appears, and describes his visions as evil omens. Marie tries to comfort Wozzeck, who, heedless of the child, runs off to the barracks. Marie rushes out of the room, leaving their child alone.

Wozzeck goes to see the Doctor, who pays him to be a guinea pig. Wozzeck tells the Doctor of his visions, and the Doctor is pleased, diagnosing a fixed idea. Meanwhile, at Marie's door, the Drum Major makes advances, and after brief resistance, Marie gives in.

In Act II, Marie is putting her son to bed, while enjoying the earrings which the Drum Major had given to her. Wozzeck arrives abruptly, and suspects Marie about the earrings. He gives her some money and leaves. Marie feels remorseful.

The Doctor and the Captain encounter one another in the street, and the Doctor talks with the Captain about morbid afflictions. Wozzeck walks by, and they taunt him about Marie's infidelities. Wozzeck protests that she is the one thing that is his, and rushes off.

Still, Wozzeck brings his suspicions to Marie, and demands that she confess. She offers no denial, and as he moves to hit her, she defiantly states that she would prefer a knife in her belly to his hand on her. Wozzeck leaves, but later wanders into a beer garden, where he encounters Andres, and sees Marie and the Drum Major on the dance floor. A drunk approaches Wozzeck and talks of his smell of blood. Wozzeck has a vision of waltzing people covered with blood. That night in the barracks, Wozzeck cannot sleep, and talks with Andres about nightmare visions. The intoxicated Drum Major enters, boasts of his conquest, and knocks Wozzeck down in a fight.

In the final act, Marie is in her room, reading the Bible about the adulteress who is forgiven, and about Mary Magdalene. She asks for forgiveness. In the next scene, Wozzeck and Marie are walking near a pond. Marie wants to leave, but Wozzeck insists that they sit together. As the blood-red moon rises, Wozzeck kisses her, comments on her fidelity, and stabs her to death with a knife. Wozzeck is next seen drinking at a tavern where he dances with Margeret, behaving in a wild insulting manner. While she sings at his command, she notices blood on his hands and arms. People begin to shout at him, and Wozzeck rushes off. Returning to the pond under the blood-red moon, Wozzeck walks into the water to search for the knife and wash away his blood stains. He wades further into the pond, and, as the Captain and the Doctor pass by, they hear him drown. The opera closes the following morning, as children play in the street and tell Marie's son that his mother is dead. He appears oblivious, singing and playing by himself.

The Makropulos Affair

Music	Leoš Janáček
Libretto	Leoš Janáček
Premiere	1926

Attorney Dr. Kolenatý returns from court and arrives at his office in Prague, accompanied by the operatic diva, Emilia Marty. She expresses interest in a century-old estate case, Prus vs. Gregor. Baron Jaroslav Prus expected to inherit the estate of his ancestor, Baron Joseph Ferdinand Prus, who apparently left no will, but the financially strapped Gregor family filed a claim on the estate. As the case finally approaches a decision, Emilia contacted Dr. Kolenatý, who represented Ferdinand Gregor, and asserts that his client is the descendant of the bastard son of Baron Joseph and opera singer Ellian MacGregor. Moreover, she believes that Prus did leave a will, and somehow knows where it is hidden, deep in a dusty cabinet in the Prus chateau.

Unbeknownst to everyone else, Emilia Marty was in fact born Elina Makropolous, daughter of Hieronymus Makropoulos, alchemist and personal physician to Emperor Rudolf II, who invented an elixir to grant the monarch an additional three hundred years of life. Wary to be the first one to try it, Rudolf II had Makropoulos test the potion on his young daughter Elina. It worked; her lover, Baron Joseph Ferdinand Prus, took the formula, which was lost when he died. Elina spent three centuries living in various countries, avoiding discovery by assuming different names – each with the initials "E.M." – all the while becoming an increasingly accomplished singer, conveniently enough for Janáček's purposes.

Now, at three hundred and twenty seven years of life, the potion is finally expiring, and Elina needs another dose to stay alive. In her desperate search for Baron Prus' will – to which she believes the secret recipe may attached – she wrecks havoc on the lives of all those involved: Janek, Baron Jaroslav's son, falls in love with her, and commits suicide when she rejects him. Confronted by the ghosts of her past, Elina finally reveals her identity; while living as "Ellian MacGregor," she was Baron Prus' mistress and mother to his bastard son, from whom Ferdinand Gregor was descended. Although the will and the recipe are found, Elina reverses her position, declaring immortality empty and devoid of love. In a gesture of atonement, she gives the recipe to her admirer, Kristina – Janek's girlfriend and aspiring singer – who burns the recipe. Elina collapses and dies.

Billy Budd

Music	Benjamin Britten
Libretto	E. M. Forster & Eric Crozier
Premiere	1951

In the Prologue, Captain Vere, as an old man, looks back over his life at sea, where he has seen much good and evil and remembers his time as Captain of HMS Indomitable during the 1797 French wars where he was tested and came up short.

The first act opens aboard the HMS Indomitable. The crew is scrubbing the deck when a young Novice accidentally trips and is given 20 lashes. A cutter returns with three men who have been impounded from a passing merchant vessel, the Rights O'Man. John Claggart, the master-of-arms inspects the men and it is the last, Billy Budd, who is seen by Claggart as, "a King's Bargain" and elicits admiration from the crew. This, in spite of Billy's one flaw, that of a stammer which reveals itself when he talks of being a foundling. Billy's heartfelt goodbye to the Rights 'O Man, causes the officers to wonder if Billy will foment discontent on his new ship. Claggart orders his corporal, Squeak, to provoke and harass Billy. The Novice returns from his flogging and the experienced seaman, Dansker, warns Billy to watch out for Claggart.

A week later Captain Vere meets with his officers in his cabin where they discuss the recent mutinies aboard the Nore and the Spithead and the influence of the French Revolution. The officers voice their suspicions of Billy but Vere discounts it as anything but high spirits. The meeting ends as a French ship is sighted.

Next we see the men are in high spirits singing shanties. Billy discovers Squeak meddling with his things and a fight ensues. Claggart is called and when Squeak calls on Claggart's protection he instead commends Billy and has Squeak put in irons. In a soliloquy, Claggart give voice to his hatred of Billy and his determination to destroy him. He then coerces the Novice to entrap Billy into leading a mutiny. Billy, furious at the idea can only react with a stammer and Dansker advices Billy to be cautious of Claggart.

Act II takes place a few days later as Claggart approaches Vere to tell him about a sailor who is dangerous to the ship. They are interrupted by the sighting of an enemy vessel to which they give chase but lose due to mist and dying wind. Claggart again accuses Billy of planning a mutiny and Captain Vere orders both Claggart and Billy to his cabin.

Alone in his own cabin, Vere expresses his belief in the young sailor's innocence. Billy is confronted by his accuser and is asked by Vere to give voice to his defense. Overcome by emotion Billy can only stammer and in frustration strikes a single blow at Claggart, killing him on the spot. Vere summons his officers for an immediate drumhead court martial. The officers look to Vere for guidance but when Vere remains silent, they find Billy guilty and sentence him to death by hanging at dawn of the next day. Waiting below deck, Billy contemplates his fate. Dansker appears with food and news that the crew is preparing to rebel but Billy warns against it, saying he has accepted his fate. The next morning the crew assembles to witness the execution. Billy's last words before being hanged are, "Starry Vere, God Bless you." Anger grows among the crew but it quickly subsides.

In an epilogue set years later, Vere is still plagued by doubts as to the rightness of his actions in failing to save Billy. But he feels Billy's last blessing as a benediction giving him comfort and a sense of redemption.

Where the Wild Things Are

Music	Oliver Knussen
Libretto	Maurice Sendak
Premiere	1984

Based on the children's book written by Maurice Sendak, the opera opens with Max, dressed in wolf-suit pyjamas, wielding a toy sword and loudly declaring his presence. Filled with excitement and aggression, he cuts off the heads of his toy soldiers and beats his teddy. When his mother enters the hall, Max jumps out and scares her, then openly defies her and refuses to stop. Exasperated, Mother calls him a 'Wild Thing' and sends him to bed without eating anything.

Alone in his room, Max longs for his supper – 'Catch it and cook it and eat it hot. . .'. In a dream-like interlude, the room transforms into a 'forest' and then an 'ocean'. When a 'boat' appears, he sails off through 'days and nights' as time as distance are transversed, eventually mooring on a small island inhabited by strange incomprehensible creatures – the Wild Things. As they clammer and become increasingly menacing, Max commands them to 'Be still!' and subdues them into submission with his magic incantation 'VAL-DA-CA+HAI-AH-MAH-MEE-OH!'

At first a goat taunts Max with his desire for power, but when Max crowns himself and is once again in 'Wolf-King' mode, he declares 'Let the Wild Rumpus begin!' Only after one of the Wild Things literally loses her head in the heat of the frenzy does the mood of the party change and Max sings longingly about being hungry and missing his mother. At this point, the goat recrowns Max. When the 'boat' reappears, in spite of their protests and beseeching him to stay, Max says goodnight to the Wild Things. Relinquishing his crown, he sails home – through days and nights and even weeks. Before even arriving, he 'smells good things to eat' and hears his Mama humming in the distance. On arrival, a bowl of food is waiting for him which, to his amazement, 'is still hot!'

Index

Note: Page numbers in *italics* indicate a figure on the corresponding page.